THINKING ABOUT POLITICS

two (political sciences)

Mark E. Kann
University of Southern California

WEST PUBLISHING COMPANY
ST. PAUL ■ NEW YORK ■ LOS ANGELES ■ SAN FRANCISCO

COPYRIGHT© 1980 By WEST PUBLISHING CO.
    50 West Kellogg Boulevard
    P.O. Box 3526
    St. Paul, Minnesota 55165

LIBRARY OF CONGRESS CATALOGING IN PUBLICATION DATA
Kann, Mark E.
    Thinking about politics.

    Bibliography: p.
    Includes index.
    1. Political science. I. Title.
JA71.K26   320   79-24727 ISBN 0-8299-0314-3

for
KATHY
and
SIMON

CONTENTS

This book is my attempt to pull together the diverse strands of political science introduced to me as a graduate student and then promoted by me as a professor. The difficulty of accomplishing this became clear to me in the fall of 1977 when I volunteered to teach "Introduction to Political Science." I included sections on politics, political theory, American government, comparative politics, and political methods and analysis. My final examination challenged the students to integrate these sections. As I graded the exams, I began to wonder how I would have integrated them.

Writing this book has been both joyful and painful. The fictive scenarios which introduce each substantive chapter satisfied my earlier desires to write childrens' books. Yet the deep intellectual divisions I found within the discipline sharpened my self-conscious-ness of how deeply my generation was influenced by the turbulence of the 1960s. This influence was both revealing and cathartic.

The arguments in this book are clearly controversial. I began by seeking a common core which explains why political scientists study politics as they do. I ended by arguing that the study of politics is based on two common, but antagonistic cores. I have learned from "political realists," but have resented their belief in the limits of change; I have learned from those seeking "opportunities" for new horizons, but have felt short-changed by their suggestions. Yet, these are my intellectual forebearers, the ones whose arguments I re-construct, but cannot reconcile. Perhaps these alternative intellec-tual perspectives should not be reconciled. If we can clarify the nature of the intellectual and political opposition today, we may be able to understand better the possibilities of developing a more adequate political science and politics tomorrow. I intend this book **ix** to be a step in that direction.

Intellectual and financial support for this book came from several sources. Under NEH Grant CE-28704-77-723, the University of Southern California Center for the Humanities sponsored the Faculty Research Seminar on Structuralism in 1978. This interdisciplinary seminar motivated my search for the "deep structures" of political science and provided some of the basic tools. I thank the Haynes Foundation and the USC Graduate School for their financial support of the final draft of this book. The critical reading of drafts by Professor Edward J. Williams, of the University of Arizona, and the editorial support of West Publishing Company were invaluable.

I would gladly take full responsibility for the book, but I cannot. Robert Booth Fowler deserves much of the praise for whatever strengths one finds in this book. He, above all others, has been the scholar, teacher, and friend who has most influenced my intellectual thought processes. I would like to believe that the problems discussed in this book reflect the political problems my generation has experienced in America.

Mark E. Kann
Los Angeles, 1979

1

GENERAL INTRODUCTION
POLITICAL PRECONCEPTIONS
AND METHODS

CHAPTER ONE There are at least two political sciences. Both are equally intelligible and equally scientific ways of understanding politics. In this book, I hope to elucidate the basic structures of these political sciences by examining the preconceptions and methods which form their essential elements. While I suggest that neither political science is abstractly superior to the other, I will argue that both are *adequate* means to understanding. Their adequacy depends on one's political perspectives.

POLITICAL PRECONCEPTIONS "Political Science" is often introduced as an abstract set of ideas, standards, or steps for studying politics. Like all intellectual abstractions, these are the products of women and men who grow up under particular circumstances, who develop complex preconceptions, and who only then devote themselves to serious, systematic intellectual labor. People's backgrounds, preconceptions, and present situations tend to influence their modes of understanding. So too do they influence what we call "Political Science."

What is politics? This is a question which most of us have answered by the time we reach maturity. As children, we begin to develop some notions of which issues are political and which are not. If we grow up in the more affluent strata of liberal societies, we are likely to learn very narrow definitions of politics. These narrow definitions will reinforce the liberal idea that political decisions should not encroach upon the private realm of life. Children raised in the less affluent sectors of liberal societies or in socialist societies will develop different preconceptions. They will be more likely to learn broad definitions of politics which nurture the value of social responsibility and community sharing. As we shall see, preconceptions about politics and political values are often reinforced by preconceptions about our own political system and other political systems.

As adults, most people have extremely complex sets of political preconceptions. People may or may not be aware of their own preconceptions. For example, some people may think that the right to private property is so natural that they take it for granted or consider it indisputable. Others may view the right to private property as a conscious value which requires a conscious intellectual defense. Still others may see the right to private property as a rationalization of the wealth of a few people and offer conscientious criticisms or pose alternatives. And many people may have extremely complex feelings about this issue but cannot clearly articulate their positions. Consequently, it is not unusual for us to hear someone say, "I think you are right, but I am not sure why."

Let me illustrate the development of political preconceptions by posing two radically different examples. First, consider Judith, born **2** with the proverbial "silver spoon" in her mouth amidst the wealth and luxury of Beverly Hills, California. As a young girl, she learns that politics is somehow connected with the benevolent policeman who protects her neighborhood from criminals. Later on in school, she enlarges her view of politics to include the Presidency, Congress, and Supreme Court which oversee the laws enforced by police. Slowly, Judith begins to feel that politics concerns regular means for protecting people's private rights and avoiding potentially violent conflict. Meanwhile, her parents, teachers, peers, and the mass media tell her that politics should be limited; it should deal with enforcing the peace but not with infringing on people's private lives. In time, Judith is able to distinguish between "political" issues and "private" issues, even though she may have given little thought to this formal distinction.

Compare Judith's political preconceptions to Marco's. Marco, born into a relatively poor Chicano family, lives a few miles from Beverly Hills in the barrios of East Los Angeles, California. His earliest notions of politics might be connected with the Anglo policeman who arrests his brother, the efforts of family and neighbors to raise bail and legal fees, and with the Anglo judge who sentences his brother. Later on, he might learn to associate politics with the efforts of local community groups to augment neighborhood health care, recreation, or legal aid facilities. Eventually, Marco relates the idea of politics to the collective efforts of people to defend themselves against outsiders and to develop a healthy community atmosphere. Marco may feel that he is a member of the Chicano community and see little distinction between his private and political life; both realms merge in community life. As an adult, Marco is likely to have a broad idea of politics, even though he too may have given little thought to the nature of politics.

Were I to extend these examples, I would illustrate other differences in Judith's and Marco's emerging preconceptions. Judith may develop values which suggest that legal processes are a fair way of resolving conflicts; Marco may be less concerned with legal fairness and may more highly value results which enhance community good. Judith could view the American political system as essentially benign, despite some problems, but Marco could be critical of the American political system because of those same problems. Conceivably, Judith would look at the American political system as an example for other nations to follow, while Marco might look at other political systems as examples for Americans. Even with these examples, I have not begun to tap the richness of Judith's and Marco's alternative sets of preconceptions.

Suppose that both Judith and Marco enroll in political science classes. What aspects or perspectives on politics will each find most interesting, significant, or relevant? It is probable that Judith will focus on notions of politics which protect private rights and emphasize legal norms: those which cast America in a favorable light and other nations in a less favorable light. Perhaps Marco would concentrate his intellectual energies on broader ideas of politics which encompass community good, which are critical of American politics and which consider other political systems as conceivable alternatives. People's political preconceptions may become standards for sorting what is interesting or important to study in the multifaceted worlds of politics.

Most political analysts do not grow up in Beverly Hills or East Los Angeles. And most political analysts do not develop preconceptions which are as clearly definable as those of Judith and Marco. Nevertheless, a great many Americans and American political scientists have political preconceptions which approximate those of Judith. They tend to enter or engage in the study of politics in a way which emphasizes the successes of American politics. However, a significant number of Americans and American political scientists share Marco's preconceptions. They focus on politics in a way which highlights systematic problems in American politics. They have a preconceived interest in justifying and promoting major changes.

Understanding the nature of these preconceptions helps to explain some of the major controversies among political analysts. Many of these controversies are argued on the terrain of logic and evidence, but underlying them are often different preconceived notions of what is interesting, significant, or relevant.

POLITICAL SCIENCE CONTROVERSIES

Modern political science is divided into a number of subfields. Many of the major controversies among political scientist appear within the context of a single subfield. Many of these controversies seem unrelated to one another, but they are logically related according to political preconceptions.

For lack of a better term, one subfield might be labelled "The Nature of Politics". In this subfield, analysts investigate the boundaries of the study of politics:

What distinguishes political science from political history, political sociology, political anthropology, or political economy?

The idea is to limit the scope of the study of politics, to define the political scientist's expertise and to establish the political scientist's precise role in the intellectual division of labor. Implicit in this general question are more specific ones: What kinds of behavior or issues are political and therefore are appropriate objects of political science analysis? Conversely, what kinds of behavior or issues are not political and therefore are appropriate objects of study for other social scientists? A major controversy, already hinted at, is over the narrowness or breadth of what is meant by "politics." As we shall see in Chapter 2, this serious controversy goes beyond academic concerns. A narrow definition of politics implies a narrowing of the realm of political action in society; a broad definition of politics implies a broadening of the realm of political action. The former definition justifies limited possibilities for change, while the latter one suggests extensive possibilities for change.

The second subfield is "Political Theory," which includes the analyses of great political philosophers like Plato, Aristotle, Hobbes, Locke, Rousseau, and Marx. Political theory also encompasses discussions of how to justify political values, which political values to justify, and what is meant and implied when some political values are justified. Furthermore, political theorists sometimes evaluate the moral nature of contemporary issues like abortion, human rights, and racial equality. A major controversy among political theorists concerns the nature of justice. Some suggest that justice is a matter of developing fair laws and procedures for resolving conflicts; as long as laws and procedures are fair, the end results are also fair. Others argue that justice is a matter of achieving the good society in which people share common goals; procedures for achieving those goals are secondary. This controversy is important in terms of how we relate means and ends in politics. I will consider it more fully in Chapter 3.

"American Politics" is the third subfield in political science. Its components include discussions ranging from very particular policy issues in local governments to broad analyses of American foreign policy. A major dispute here relates to the nature of American political processes. Some analysts characterize these processes as pluralistic and competitive. They believe that many different American groups bargain, compromise and exert pressure to achieve their goals; American government is a relatively neutral arbiter among these groups. Others argue that American political processes are essentially elitist. A small and relatively cohesive group of Americans exerts the greatest influence; American governors tend to favor the interests of this small group. This controversy is extremely important to anyone interested in determining how democratic the American political system is and what kinds of changes are necessary to make it more democratic. Chapter 4 will consider the latest developments in this controversy.

The fourth subfield is "Comparative Politics." It essentially deals with the similarities and differences between the political systems of nation-states. A central argument is how one compares American politics to the politics of other nation-states. Does one search for broad generalizations which characterize the similarities and differences across many nations? Or should the researcher base his analysis on the particular similarities and differences among a few political cultures? In Chapter 5, I will compare cross-national and cross-cultural approaches to comparative politics and demonstrate how these approaches affect our understanding of the limits and potentials for political change.

These are not the only subfields in political science nor the only controversies. Subfields such as "Policy Analysis," "International

Relations," or "Political Behavior" have their own share of disputes. The four I have chosen are adequate for my purposes. They illustrate that neither the subfields nor the major controversies are singular, but are bound together by two logical sets of preconceptions.

Numbered transition sections are between each chapter in Part One. In these transition sections, I suggest that there are two logics or sets of preconceptions which underlie most controversies in political science. One is the Logic of Political Realism:

1. There is a logical connection between defining politics narrowly, viewing justice as a matter of procedures, considering the American polity pluralistic, and searching for broad generalizations by which to compare America to other nations.

In a more systematic fashion, this logic reproduces the preconceptions which Judith developed in Beverly Hills. It tends to legitimate the American political system and restrict possibilities for change. It is "realistic" in the sense of accepting the basic structures and ideas of modern American politics as the primary context for understanding and for political action.

The transition sections will also develop a second logic; the Logic of Political Opportunities:

2. There is also a logical connection between defining politics broadly, viewing justice as a matter of the good society, considering the American polity elitist and comparing America to other nations on the basis of cultural characteristics.

This second logic approximates the political preconceptions Marco developed in the East Los Angeles barrios. It tends to be critical of the American political system and to expand the possibilities for political change. It is "opportunistic" in the sense of seeking alternatives to present political arrangements in America.

My point is that political analysts often take sides in intellectual controversies in ways which reaffirm their own political preconceptions. Those who accept the constraints of American politics, either because they have benefited from those constraints, or see no alternative *tend* to commit themselves to the Logic of Political Realism in all subfields; those who perceive themselves or others as being deprived by the American political system and who seek viable alternatives *tend* to affirm the Logic of Political Opportunities in all subfields. I certainly do not consider myself an exception. My preconceptions about the need for change lead me to affirm the second logic.

If political analysts have preconceptions which affect their analyses, how can the study of politics be considered "scientific?" Part Two of this book is devoted to answering this question by considering the two major methods of political analysis and their relationship to scientific norms.

SCIENTIFIC METHODS

Two major methods of study dominate political science today. Both claim the mantle of science and both deny that the alternative method is really scientific. One is "Post-Behavioralism" and the other is the "Interpretive Approach."

Post-behavioralists hope to achieve the successes of natural scientists by emulating their methods. They hope to generate laws of politics in the same way Newton generated laws of gravity. They wish to develop sophisticated ways of testing these laws as rigorous as the tests performed by physicists in their laboratories. Ultimately, they want to develop a body of objective political knowledge which can be used to better the human condition. In Chapter 6, I will discuss this method more fully.

The "Interpretive Approach" is based on the assumption that the human world cannot be understood or studied in the same way as the natural world. On the one hand, atomic particles or chemicals may "behave" according to natural laws because they have no choice. They are merely manipulated chess pieces on the worldwide chess board. But people do more than behave; they "act" on the basis of preconceptions, motives and intentions, and circumstances. While one atom may be similar to the next, people's different histories, cultures, and experiences affect both how they behave and the meanings they attribute to their actions. If we are to understand politics fully, we must interpret people's actions in light of their histories, cultures, and experiences. On the other hand, natural scientific objectivity is impossible to achieve in the study of politics. The natural scientist has few preconceptions which lead her to prefer $E=MC^2$ over $\sqrt{E}=MC$, but the political scientist almost always has preconceptions which lead him to prefer one interpretation of politics over another. Consequently, in the process of interpreting political actions, the analyst must also interpret his own preconceptions. I will discuss the Interpretive Approach more in Chapter 7.

Which method is more scientific? I cannot answer because I have no reason for believing either is more or less scientific. However, I believe it is possible to show that each method is especially appropriate to particular purposes. Analysts with preconceptions approximating Judith's usually find that post-behavioral methods are consistent with their preconceptions, affirm those preconceptions, and provide the type of political knowledge useful for acting on the basis of those preconceptions. Analysts more sympathetic to Marco's preconceptions generally find that the interpretive approach is more consistent with their preconceptions, affirms their preconceptions and provides the kind of political knowledge useful for acting on their preconceptions.

Let me illustrate this with a brief example. Assume that you have a preconceived interest in maintaining the present laws and order. Post-behavioral methods might help you by generating and testing generalities about crowd behavior. One such generality might be: If political leaders appoint blue-ribbon commissions to study the problems which upset protesters, then protesters will likely disperse and await commission reports. This generality may serve as a political tool for alleviating the possibilities of violent protests and lawless challenges to the present order. However, if you had a preconceived interest in changing the laws and altering the political order, you may find such generalities less useful than particular interpretations of the needs and desires of protesters. One such interpretation might be that these protesters will use all means possible to win their demands. You might then develop a number of imaginative interpretations of the kinds of laws or political orders capable of meeting those demands. People tend to adopt the method of analysis which is most useful to them in terms of their different preconceptions and perceived interests.

We now encounter a final paradox: There are at least two systematic political sciences. Political Science I is based on the Logic of Political Realism and post-behavioral methods. It is the political science which Judith would be likely to practice were she to become a political scientist. Political Science II is based on the Logic of Political Opportunities and the interpretive approach. It is the political science which would make most sense to Marco. But is it possible that there are two scientific approaches to the same subject matter?

TWO POLITICAL SCIENCES Our everyday ideas about the natural sciences are more often drawn from fictional accounts of natural scientists' lives, than from the practice of actual natural scientists. For most of us, science is the physicist developing laws of motion, doing controlled laboratory experiments which validate or invalidate his claims, and producing additions to the storehouse of human knowledge. This is the image of science which advocates of Political Science I hope to adapt to the study of politics.

However, this scientific method is one of several employed by natural scientists. Consider the plight of the astronomer who is interested in understanding the evolution of our solar system. Can she generate laws which apply to all solar systems? Probably not, because she knows so little about other solar systems. Instead, she makes a rather limited statement often known as "The Big Bang Theory"; she suggests that the earth is a by-now cooled spin-off of the sun, due to an explosion which took place billions of years ago. Can she observe this explosion, or manipulate the sun and planets in her controlled laboratory? No. Her theory is an interpretation, or an imaginative reconstruction of events which makes sense because of what she does know about other solar systems. The political scientist and our astronomer who cannot test their theories by controlled observation and experiment can only piece together a puzzle which others may find persuasive.

In Chapter 8, I will suggest that two political sciences are conceivable in the same way that two sciences of physics or biology or astronomy are conceivable. Both political sciences have particular advantages and disadvantages; both help illuminate aspects of the political world, only to ignore or distort other aspects of the political world. The political science that you or I find most sensible or scientific is more likely to be a matter of our political preconceptions and interests, than a matter of abstract ideas or standards.

Chapter 9 is a summary and conclusion to this argument. I ask how adequate my "two political sciences" thesis is, consider some criticisms, and conclude that the "political adequacy" of any study of politics is partially a function of our political preferences. However, our preconceptions or political preferences do not necessarily determine what we accept as adequate political knowledge. Preconceptions and preferences change as we participate in new political experiences. To the extent that this book helps you articulate your own preconceptions, preferences, and understanding of political experiences, you will have a new political experience which will allow you a chance to face and possibly change your own ideas on politics and actions in politics.

ONE

PART ONE
Introduction

There are many reasons which explain why friends and neighbors often avoid talking about politics, even though they will discuss sex and sports without hestitation. One reason is that our feelings about politics are often submerged. We like one candidate and dislike another but cannot say why we feel this way. Events in the political world seem so distant from our everyday lives that we have little interest or knowledge about them. A second reason, the flip side of the coin, is that we fear political discussions will breed antagonisms we would just as soon live without. Longtime friendships may dissolve when one discovers one's friend is so irrational that he is a conservative; how one could have been friends for so long is a mystery. Or, arguments over particular issues like busing or abortion lay bare other controversies which make mutual respect difficult. Consequently, we can avoid these threats to our relationships by avoiding discussion of touchy topics like politics. Indeed, as a teacher of political science I sometimes wish I taught biology instead. Whatever I say about politics is bound to alienate some students, although I have difficulty imagining a biologist facing the same controversy.

Part One of this book discusses politics in a way which clarifies many of our feelings about politics and the nature of our political controversies. For some readers, this may serve the purpose of explaining why political communication with friends is so difficult. For other readers, it may serve to identify the basic lines of controversy in many political discussions. Either way, I hope it raises to the level of consciousness common feelings and disagreements in politics. At this level, we can at least recognize our political selves and begin to understand our relation to others.

Part One is also an exploration of many of the common assumptions and controversies that systematic political analysts have. In most cases, these assumptions and controversies are well articulated and sophisticated representations of the preconceptions and disagreements most people have about politics. The major difference is that political analysts are more willing than most people to explore the logic and implications of these varying political viewpoints.

The major thesis of Part One is that some Americans and some American political scientists tend to share a logically related set of preconceptions about politics which allow them to believe that their political views are common sense. However, other Americans and other American political scientists share a different logically related set of preconceptions about politics, which they believe, makes equally common sense. One set, "the realists," basically define and perceive politics in ways consistent with modern American politics; the second set tries to expand political "opportunities" because they define and perceive politics in ways inconsistent with the modern

12 American system.

The differences in preconceptions or assumptions between these two sets of Americans cut across many areas of political studies. In Chapter 2, I will consider the different ways they define politics and the scope of political action. In Chapter 3, I will investigate the different moral criteria of justice they have for evaluating politics. Chapter 4 is a discussion of the distinctive models they build of American politics. And Chapter 5 considers the different means by which they compare American politics to the politics of other political systems.

Ultimately, these controversies in various areas of political studies are related to one another. In the "Transition" sections between each chapter, I discuss the systematic links which connect preconceptions in one field to preconceptions in another, and which connect alternative preconceptions in one field to alternative preconceptions in another. For example, in the First Transition, I suggest reasons why someone who defines politics narrowly is likely to emphasize the value of fairness while someone who defines politics broadly is likely to emphasize the value of goodness. In the Final Transition following Chapter 5, I summarize these linkages.

By the end of Part One, I will have argued that two equally logical and coherent ways of viewing politics exist at present. These alternative modes of political thinking explain why many people avoid political discussions. On the one hand, many people do not articulate their political perspective well enough to use it coherently in discussions. Politics is more complicated than many of us think. On the other hand, because there are at least two different political perspectives, committing ourselves to one is likely to alienate or confuse others committed to the alternative.

Some people suggest that political science can solve this dilemma. Perhaps one of the two political viewpoints is more "scientific." I will investigate this in Part Two. However, be forewarned: I do not believe that "science" will help us reconcile our different preconceptions and eliminate our political controversies.

2

THE NATURE OF POLITICS: CONFLICT AND COMMUNITY

CHAPTER TWO What is politics? Most of us would agree that it has something to do with government or perhaps power over people. But these are rather vague generalities. If we propose more specific definitions, we immediately embroil ourselves in controversy. Narrow definitions of politics imply a narrow field of study for political scientists and a narrow range of alternatives for political activists; broad definitions imply the need for breadth in political studies and broad options for political activists. Consequently, how we define politics is not arbitrary; it constitutes a commitment to percieve and to act in ways which shape the political world.

In this chapter, I will outline and examine two major notions of politics. I will suggest that both perspectives clarify some areas in the political world, only to distort or ignore other areas. While I can find no reason for saying that one perspective on politics is necessarily superior to the other, I do believe that each perspective is most consistent with the particular political values to be discussed in the next chapter.

Let me begin with the following fantasy.* It is probably not obvious to you whether any "political" questions are raised in the fantasy because it does not *directly* involve government or overtly coercive uses of power.

POLITICS AND THE SPA Imagine that you live in a small western village which bases its economic well-being on tourism. Your town is quaint and lovely, but there are many quaint and lovely towns in the area. The main tourist attraction of your community is the health spa, known nationally for its healing and rejuvenating powers. For the past several years, your town's spa has been the "in" place for tourists, despite the fact that nearby towns have built their own spas.

The success of the spa has not only brought great wealth to its developers and owners, it has brought about local business expansion. Homeowners have built additions to their houses to provide room and board for visitors. The local press has installed new printing equipment to meet demands for greater advertising space and increased circulation. And local factories have bought new machines and hired more workers to manufacture souvenirs for the tourists. It is no exaggeration to say that the tourists pay for the bread on virtually all the townspeople's tables.

One day, a local doctor who oversees the health conditions at the spa discovers that the spa's water has been contaminated by a deadly micro-organism. To confirm his findings, he sends a water sample to the modern laboratory at a nearby metropolitan university. The news from the university is bad. University scientists cannot determine the source of the contamination, but they warn that people who come

*This fantasy is based on Henrik Ibsen's play, "An Enemy of the People."

into contact with this water are seriously endangering their lives. The doctor thinks back to the last tourist season when several visitors got sick. Perhaps they were the first victims of the micro-organism.

The doctor brings his scientific findings to the attention of his employers, the spa owners, and to the local residents. All hail him as a hero for uncovering this health menace. Meanwhile, spa engineers trace the source of the contamination to the mislaid pipes which feed water into the spa. They inform the owners that the pipes must be relaid, a process which could take up to two years during which the spa would have to be closed down. However, this would be cata-strophic for the town's economy.

You consider what the closed spa would mean for the owners and other townspeople. First, closing the spa would cut deeply into the owners' profits. They would have to take out long-term loans to finance reconstruction without the expectation of income for several years. They would have to lay off numerous spa workers. And once word got out that the spa was contaminated, would not the tourists patronize other towns in the area? And would this not mean that even once the spa reopens, it would be difficult to lure those tourists back? Surely, reconstruction would be a risky investment.

Second, you consider how closing the spa would affect the town in general. How would local businesses be able to pay their over-head, workers, and loan installments without tourist trade during the next two years? How would homeowners be able to meet their mortgage payments without summer rent income? How would the newpaper survive the loss of advertising and circulation? And what would happen to the workers who would be laid off at the souvenir factories? It is clear to you that reconstructing the spa would spell the economic death of your community. It is also clear to your neighbors.

The doctor considers these contingencies irrelevant. All that is important is that the health of spa patrons be protected. The spa must be shut down. The spa owners try to persuade the doctor to re-consider his findings. He is not to be persuaded. The test results from the university labs, along with his own, are definitive. Trying a new tactic, the spa owners praise the doctor for his findings and offer him a higher paying, higher status position in the company. In turn, the company will hire a new doctor to oversee spa health conditions. The doctor says that he will not accept such a "bribe." Finally, seeing no other alternative, the spa owners label the doctor a quack and fire him.

The doctor then takes his case to the press and the townspeople. Lower echelon reporters are initially willing to give him their support. But those responsible for the economic well-being of the newspaper refuse to print articles favoring the doctor's position. After all, supporting the doctor means alienating powerful busi-nessmen who buy advertising. And the townspeople do not want to hear about the contamination because such publicity threatens the tourist trade upon which they depend. If the press does publish the doctor's findings, it will lose the financial and public support the press requires. The press ignores the doctor's pleas. Moreover, the paper's owners tell the doctor that they will publically raise questions about his "scientific qualifications" if he persists in being such a social nuisance.

Undaunted by threats, the doctor continues to plead his cause, if not in the newspaper, then in the streets. Your fellow townspeople are becoming more than irritated by this malcontent. His old friends stop visiting him, his old patients go elsewhere for medical help, and local businessmen find excuses for not selling to him. At one point, a group of local people stone the doctor's home; he is a threat to their future livelihoods. Amidst such controversies, the doctor and his family leave town.

The issue is seemingly resolved: the contamination is hushed up and hopes for a prosperous tourist season flourish. You, however, are not exactly elated. You are somewhat sympathetic to the doctor and especially to the tourists who may get infected. Then again, how certain can you be about the doctor's "scientific" findings and the huge economic sacrifice the town would have to make, perhaps for no real reason at all?

Is this merely a "private" affair because government is not directly involved? Is it a "political" or "public" affair because government has an essential role to play? Is it a "political" affair because some people are exerting their "power" over others? And if it is a "political" affair, in what sense? Should government intervene in the "private" affairs of the spa owners? Should government play a role in the conflict between the doctor and his neighbors? The answers to these questions are not obvious. However, the answers which you and political scientists ultimately choose reveal a great deal about your preconceptions concerning the nature of politics and what political scientists consider the appropriate subject matter for the study of politics.

I will not abstractly or arbitrarily define politics for you in this chapter. Rather, I will present two models for understanding the nature of politics. I believe these two models best reflect the diverse ways in which people understand politics today.

POLITICS AS CONFLICT-RESOLUTION
A Brief History

The idea of politics as conflict-resolution began to bud and blossom in the seventeenth century. During this time, people experienced two major and related changes. First, they lived through a period of tremendous political transition. Monarchical and aristocratic forms of government were weakened by the demands of entrepreneurs for more representative and more limited forms of government. Both the American and French Revolutions converted these demands into realities in the ensuing years.

Second, seventeenth century people experienced the transition from a relatively stable social order known as Feudalism, to a new and dynamic social order, later known as Capitalism. Old social relationships broke down as wage labor, factory life, and production for the marketplace began to dominate the time of more and more people.

Those who supported the newly emerging political and social orders were interested in developing an understanding of politics which would (1) resolve the conflict between the old power relations and the new ones and (2) resolve the conflicts among individuals struggling to gain a foothold in the new marketplace. Great political thinkers like Thomas Hobbes and John Locke developed an idea of politics based on the notion of "conflict-resolution." As the old political and social orders gave way to the new, the notion of conflict-resolution became predominant in the Western world. It continues to be predominant in America today.

The Logic of Politics as Conflict-Resolution

Politics as conflict-resolution is a model of the political world initially developed to help explain and justify the modern Western world. Its logic can be outlined as follows:

1. People have different interests and goals in life.

2. Often, the interests and goals of some people come into conflict with those of others.

3. Such conflicts can be settled peacefully or violently.

4. When people cannot resolve their conflicts peacefully, they turn to violence, but violence threatens the interests and goals of everyone.

5. In these circumstances, an authoritative means of conflict-resolution is necessary to minimize violence.

6. Politics is the authoritative means of conflict-resolution in all societies. Government is the organizational mechanism by which conflicts are resolved peacefully.

7. A political issue involves any conflict among people which threatens to begin or end in violence.

Let us examine this logic of politics more closely.

Adherents of this logic begin with the assumption that people are naturally different from one another. Some people prefer work to play and others prefer play to work. The human world can be characterized by a plurality of individual needs, wants, and desires. Unfortunately, the resources for fulfilling these diverse needs, wants, and desires are finite; everyone cannot have their own way. Your need for peace and quiet may conflict with my desire to practice my trumpet lessons, if we happen to live in the same apartment building. Or your desire to park your auto in the last remaining space on the block may conflict with a similar desire on my part, if we happen to notice the space at the same time. People are constantly in conflict with one another.

In many cases, we peacefully settle our conflicts among ourselves. You might persuade me to practice my trumpet during times you are not at home. I might offer you five dollars to let me have the parking space, if it is that important to me. Or we might just shout at one another until one of us gets tired enough to search elsewhere. Much of our daily life is spent finding peaceful solutions to these mundane disagreements. Occasionally, however, our disagreements begin or end in violence. You call me a dirty "@#&*#&" and I hit you over the head. Those who believe we are above such uncivilized behavior ought to consider this situation: We are waiting in a long line when someone casually steps to the front of the line without waiting. How many of us have not fantasized about violently removing the intruder? Often the line between fantasy and reality becomes blurred.

Situations of violent conflict are likely to develop whenever more than a few people live together in societies. They are especially likely to develop when traditional means of conflict-resolution begin to break down. When children lose faith in parental authority, they will not likely "go tell Daddy or Momma" for help in solving their conflicts. However, they may try to persuade, bribe or fight their antagonist. Without general respect for traditional authority, violence becomes one alternative for settling disputes.

When violence becomes the primary means of resolving conflicts, paralyzing fears become pervasive. Everyone else must be considered a potential threat to our well-being for they may employ violence to get what we have or to stop us from doing what they resent. Even the strongest person lives with fears that a group of weaker people will effectively use violence against him or her. With the advent of sophisticated technologies of violence and with the relative accessibility of guns, a weak individual need only be strong enough to pull a trigger to shatter all of our needs, wants, and desires. Fearful of everyone, we remain on constant guard against others; we lock ourselves into our personal fortresses. We dare not make grand future plans or hope to achieve many goals because we must spend so much time protecting ourselves from others. According to the notion of politics as conflict-resolution, politics is a process people develop to minimize the paralyzing threat of constant violence.

Politics is a systematic process through which people maximize peaceful resolutions of conflict and minimize violent solutions. It has three aspects. First, politics is the means by which people establish an authority or a popularly recognized judge for ruling in cases of conflict. Traditionally, authority figures based their right of decision on religion or heredity. More recently, legitimate authority is often based on consent of the governed through popular elections. Second, politics consists of the processes by which authorities make their decisions. Every potentially violent conflict may be referred to the King for an arbitrary decision, or only manifestly violent conflicts are referred to the judiciary for constitutionally-based rulings. Third, politics concerns the means of enforcing authoritative rulings to minimize violent conflict. In some societies, this aspect of politics is characterized by officials' efforts to persuade people to comply with rulings; elsewhere, large numbers of soldiers or police may be the main source of winning public compliance.

While the function of politics is peaceful resolution of conflict, one should note that politics may or may not include the use of violence to fulfill this function. Often political authorities are established through very violent means: wars, revolutions, and assassinations. However, the aim of this violence is to establish a new order in which more conflicts can be settled peacefully. And to secure the new order or even an aging order, authorities often monopolize the means of violence as a threat to would-be dissidents who might use private violence. Authorities may decide to use police violence against selected individuals or groups to assure that they will not use violence on their own. Included here are violent activities to prevent disobedience (e.g., forcible entry into the homes of alleged dissidents) or to punish and deter manifest violence (e.g., forcible arrests, imprisonment, torture, or even capital punishment). From this perspective, politics concerns the authoritative use of minimal violence to prevent people from maximal use of private violence in settling their conflicts.

The political process is generally most efficient when political authorities need employ little actual coercion. If most people believe the authority of their king, assembly, or judges is legitimate (or justifiable), they will likely abide by political decisions, even when they feel those decisions are personally disadvantageous. For example, even though legislatures pass tax laws which many believe are unfair, people nevertheless pay their taxes because they believe legislatures have the legitimate authority to pass tax laws. And those of us who consider a tax rebellion, must also consider the likelihood that we will be fined or imprisoned if we carry the rebellion forward. In a society where most people respect political authorities and simultaneously fear being punished for noncompliance, violent conflict-resolution is dramatically minimized. To the extent that political authorities can make decisions without fear of noncompliance, we can also say that their political "power" is maximal.

Consequently, if my trumpet playing is enough of a nuisance to you, today in America you could institute a law suit against me with the expectation that both of us will abide by the court's decision. Or, if we cannot solve our argument over the disputed parking place, we can call in a "peace" officer to arbitrate. And as long as both of us fear imprisonment, we will be less likely to employ personal violence to have our ways. On the other hand, conflicts settled peacefully are less likely to be political. Thus, despite the fact that married couples argue over where a tube of toothpaste should be squeezed, most societies do not have to make political decisions here. Usually, married couples can resolve such disputes peacefully.

Of course, some political authorities may do more than attempt to minimize violent conflict-resolution. They may strive for "national greatness" or they may try to regulate the "peaceful morals" of citizens. Whenever authorities make decisions on some basis other than minimizing violent conflict, they go beyond politics. They are usurpers of power and they are often overthrown by revolutionary movements. The political realm is strictly limited; the private realm may be quite large if people can generally settle disputes without violence.

Politics as Conflict-Resolution: A Political Lens

If someone asked you to describe your room, you could spend the rest of your life answering. You could describe the room's dimensions, air quality, color scheme, history, location, and uses. You could then describe the shapes, textures, and chemical composition of the objects in the room. And you might want to include your parent's or friends' ideas on the social atmosphere of the room, or perhaps some statement of interpretation regarding how it became your room. Similarly, if someone asked you to describe the politics of your town, there is no end to the possibilities for answering. Nevertheless, we do answer such questions without devoting our whole lives to our answers. How?

We develop models of what is or is not significant in particular situations. These models allow us to communicate with one another and to narrow down multiple possibilities. If you are asked about your room, you can be fairly certain that the questioner is not interested in the chemical composition of your wallpaper; she is more likely to be concerned with its size or the objects inside it. You can make this assumption because you and she share a model concerning what is significant in the category "rooms" in this context. The idea of politics as conflict-resolution is basically a model of what is significant in the category "politics."

As a model of significance, politics as conflict-resolution is a lens through which people observe the political world. Like all lenses, it focuses our vision on some aspects of reality but blurs our vision of other aspects. These other aspects we take for granted as insignificant, irrelevant, or perhaps unchanging. We have already seen how politics as conflict-resolution focuses our political vision on potentially violent conflicts, the limited nature of politics, and the behavior of individuals pursuing their personal goals. To understand the other aspects let us now consider how this lens blurs our political vision.

Politics as conflict-resolution blurs our vision of three factors which we may want to treat as significant. They are:

1. The potentially positive aspects of conflict.

2. Functions of politics other that conflict-resolution.

3. The "social" nature of politics.

By either rendering these factors insignificant or by blurring them, advocates of politics as conflict-resolution tend to ignore the private uses of power which do not lead to violent conflict, but which may have a major effect on how most people live their daily lives.

Those who view the world through the lens of conflict-resolution are likely to be sensitive to major conflicts, which are systematically manifest in people's behavior. Persistent crime problems, continual group conflicts, and political dissidence will be important foci for them. As analysts, they are likely to concentrate on the ways in which political authorities minimize the potential violence inherent in these disputes. They might concern themselves with "socialization" processes which nurture moderate viewpoints. Or they might consider the governmental institutions which deal with conflicts: executive orders, laws, judicial injunctions, etc. Or they could look at informal processes for resolving conflicts: bargaining, arbitration, compromise, persuasion, bribery, etc. From their perspectives, these would be the most significant aspects of the political world.

Were we to accept their perspective, we would be unlikely to consider the possibility that politics includes the promotion of conflict and violence to attain goals other than maximal peace. Conceivably, political authorities or citizens may consider potentially violent conflict useful for clarifying their commitments and attaining goals like racial equality. From the Supreme Court's 1954 decision to end school desegregation, to more recent decisions to enforce busing of children, political officials have stimulated greater conflict as a means to increase people's commitment to an integrated society. In this instance, peaceful relations are secondary, though not insignificant. While some of these decisions may have been efforts to resolve racial conflicts, others clearly were not, though this would be difficult to see wearing the lens of conflict-resolution.

Politics as conflict-resolution sensitizes its adherents to the limits of political life, but blurs their vision of the potential of politics beyond conflict-resolution. This model leads us to believe that political issues do not exist where conflict is clearly not threatened or already manifest. Implied here, for example, is the idea that major ecological damage is not a political issue or an appropriate object of political decision-making unless people show a willingness to fight over it. By narrowing the world of politics in this way, the lens of politics as conflict-resolution allows us to differentiate politics from economics, ecological sciences, sociology, and even history. This differentiation makes possible a division of labor: political scientists study potentially violent conflicts, economists study the production and distribution of material goods, and ecologists study people's relation to the environment. Through our various understandings of political man, economic man, and ecological man, we get the fullest possible understanding of human life.

While we reap the intellectual benefits of this division of labor, we tend to ignore the fact that politics may concern economic or ecological issues, though violence is not threatened. For example, private industries have been filling our airways and waterways with unhealthy pollutants for many years. Because there was little conflict over pollution, it was left to ecologists, not political scientists, to study the matter. It is only recently that people have been willing to engage in serious conflict over pollution; it is only recently that most political scientists have treated pollution as a serious political issue. And very often it is considered in a very narrow way: How do we eliminate the conflict over pollution? This is the first question the adherent of politics as conflict-resolution is likely to ask. Actually figuring out how to eliminate the pollution problem itself is a serious consideration only if it is instrumental to eliminating the conflict.

The implication here is that problems are not political problems until people are willing to fight over them. Slavery is not a political problem until people are willing to fight over it. Cruel working conditions are not a political problem until people are willing to fight over it. Sexual and racial discrimination are not problems until people exhibit a willingness to engage in dangerous conflicts. This is also the case with urban decay, economic depression, and potential ecological or nuclear disasters. According to politics as conflict-resolution, a political issue does not exist unless people show by their actions that they will devote the time, resources, and take the risks involved in major political disputes. Until then, political issues do not exist, major problems are ignored and possibly simple solutions lead to greater difficulties.

And even when people demonstrate a willingness to engage in conflict, the object of policymakers or political analysts will be to suggest ways to alleviate conflict and not necessarily to solve problems. Often this means that advocates of politics as conflict-resolution will suggest small or incremental changes which will temporarily satisfy disputants, but which will not necessarily begin to solve problems. For example, when the American public gets upset about high crime levels, politicians and analysts often suggest "beefing up" police technology and manpower. While this may satisfy the public, it does little to solve crime problems; a solution here would require a major inquiry into the sociological basis of criminal activity and reforms which might drastically alter the socio-economic structure of American life. Had we another model of politics concerned with a "public or community interest," we might be more sensitive to such problems and possible solutions before they reach gigantic proportions.

Finally, politics as conflict-resolution sensitizes us to individual conflicts and individual issues, but it blurs our visions of the "social" nature of political life. On the one hand, this model focuses our attention on the concrete behavior patterns of individuals or groups of individuals. Do some patterns of behavior tend to result in greater or lesser conflict? Do particular patterns of political responses tend to minimize or maximize potentials for conflict? Moreover, the model concentrates our attention on specifiable individual issues.

How can the plight of the urban poor be alleviated? How can America's supply of oil be increased? This focus on concrete behavior and issues helps us eliminate the tendency to speak in abstractions such as "the masses" or "the people" or "society" when we do political analysis. In short, politics as conflict resolution forces us to realize that real, individual human beings are the basis of all politics.

On the other hand, there may be instances when we wish to treat something as political despite the fact that particular individuals do not play a central role. For example, it is conceivable that many Americans today believe that the major oil companies have acted irresponsibly in terms of engineering shortages, withholding information, and reaping superprofits. However, while they might gripe about all this, they may not be willing, at present, to engage in overt conflict over this issue. A number of reasons would explain this. First, like city hall, people might feel that the oil companies are so entrenched that they cannot be challenged. Second, people might regret oil company actions but see no practical alternative, in the present context, to oil company power. Or third, Americans may simply be ambivalent, and feel that oil companies should have the right to pursue profits but not in ways detrimental to public needs. Whatever the reasons, politics as conflict-resolution leads us to ignore these feelings because they are not openly expressed or manifest in terms of conflict. They are literally "non-feelings" from a political perspective. However, we may still wish to consider these feelings as significant aspects of politics, on the basis that society as a whole has something to gain from translating these nonconflictual perspectives into political issues.

Also, our focus on concrete individual issues might distort our understanding of the causes and solutions to political problems. For example, some people argue that the energy shortage in America cannot be fully understood or remedied unless analysts consider three things: the economic system which gives oil companies such great freedom, the political system which seems unable to regulate oil companies, and the social relations which nurture citizen acquiescence to this whole process. To understand a single issue requires an ability to relate politics to broader social concerns, and not to narrow politics to a limited realm.

In summary, politics as conflict-resolution is a lens which focuses our attention on the day to day conflicts of individuals over specific problems. Through its lens, we can study the ways in which peaceful co-existence among different individuals is possible. However, our vision of the uses of conflict to achieve society-wide goals is likely to be blurred. We will likely ignore the ways in which some people dominate, indeed tyrannize, others, generate major social problems, and render limited solutions ineffective in our complex social worlds. In a sense, politics as conflict-resolution focuses our attention on the political trees but blurs our vision of the health of the political forest.

Politics as Conflict-Resolution and the Spa

Let us apply this model of politics to the contaminated spa to illustrate the ways it affects our vision of politics. Immediately after the doctor leaves town, an old friend visits you. In the course of the evening, he asks you to describe the politics in your community. If you view politics through the lens of conflict-resolution, you would probably consider the following questions significant.

Should you bring up the issue of the contamination of the spa? On one level you answer, "No." The health of the spa patrons and of the town's economy is not a political issue because it does not threaten to stimulate violent conflict in the foreseeable future. Moreover, the conflict between the doctor and the spa owners, the press, and the townspeople is not a political issue. The fact that the doctor was fired from his job, threatened by the press, and isolated by patients and friends, merely illustrates that there are many nonviolent ways by which people resolve their own differences. However, you remember the stoning of the doctor's house; here is an obvious political issue.

You begin to tell your friend about town politics with the story of the stoning. Describing the events leading up to the stoning with minimal detail, you relate the alternatives considered by the authorities. One possibility had been to arrest the stoners for disturbing the peace and damaging private property. However, this was considered a doubly-dangerous solution. Since most of the townpeople felt justified in stoning the doctor's home, arresting them would mean turning their resentments against the political authorities. This move would undermine the legitimacy of the authorities and make it more difficult to get people to comply with other decisions. In addition, arresting the stoners would probably lead to potentially violent protests by friends and relatives. Nevertheless, the authorities knew that they could not allow the stoners to go unpunished. Without punishment, what would stop other townspeople from engaging in further stoning or further acts of violence? Neither arrest nor avoidance seemed like a good way of maintaining public peace.

In fact, you continue, the authorities actually rebuked the stoners for having broken the law, took down the names of the offenders, and threatened to arrest them if they did it again. You explain this grant of "amnesty" to your friend in the following way. The doctor has left town so there is little chance that the stoning will recur. By reprimanding the stoners, the authorities affirm their right to manage conflict; by freeing the stoners, the authorities secure the continued compliance of the townspeople. As such, the authorities maximized their political power to resolve conflicts peacefully in the future. This decision, you comment, is analogous to the worldwide practice of granting amnesty to draft evaders once the war is over; it is the best way to assure peace.

Feeling somewhat uncomfortable, your friend asks what will happen if the doctor returns to town or decides to spread the word of the contamination to potential tourists. You respond first by considering how violence can be avoided if the doctor returns. If he cannot be persuaded to desist by nonpolitical means and is likely to provoke further stonings, political authorities might give the doctor a warning. If he continues his harangues about the spa being contaminated, they will have to arrest him for inciting a riot. Then if the doctor persists, he will be locked in jail.

If the doctor does not return, it is not clear that any significant political questions remain. If he succeeds in turning away a few tourists, violent conflict is not likely to ensue. However, if he succeeds in destroying the reputation of the town's spa, it is likely that people will be economically frustrated and potentially violent. A volatile political situation will then exist. Under these circumstances, political authorities have a number of options. They can provide townspeople with information about jobs elsewhere; they can beef up the police force; or they can perhaps float a loan to see people through the hard times ahead. You predict that political authorities will do as little as possible as long as public order is maintained. You add that all of this is unlikely. The owners of the spa have allocated a huge sum of money to enhance the spa's public image and, covertly, to destroy the doctor's reputation. The doctor will not likely turn away many tourists.

Your friend, generally a polite listener, can no longer contain himself. In rapid succession, he asks, "What about the health of the tourists? What about all the power used to get the doctor out of town? What happens to the town's economy when tourists eventually learn the reality of the contamination?" And so on. With a genuine look of surprise, you ask your own question, "Didn't you want me to talk about town politics? However, I would also be glad to talk about town medical practices, sociology and economics *as well!*"

Politics as Community-Building
A Brief History

During the eighteenth and especially the nineteenth century, a number of political thinkers including John Stuart Mill and Karl Marx, argued that politics as conflict-resolution constituted a perverse understanding of politics. It was perverse in two ways. First, it helped politicians who refused to confront the major social problems which emerged with capitalism. For many politicians, poor working conditions and wages, urbanization and decay, and the general disruption of social life were not appropriate political issues. Consequently, they could be ignored. However, when people mobilized to demand greater democracy, more political responsiveness and solutions to social problems, and when it became clear that they were willing to back up their demands with violence, the issues were politicized in a particular way. Politicians, viewing the world through the lens of conflict-resolution, sought reforms aimed at minimizing violence but not necessarily solving social problems.

For example, if workers organized to protest brutal working conditions in factories, politicians might respond by passing a law limiting the normal sixteen hour workday to twelve hours. The more moderate workers, seeing that gains could be won, would likely cease their protest, praise their victory, and hope to win further change through more typical political means. The more radical workers, isolated by the desertion of moderates, might demand "real" changes: not a trade of sixteen hours of brutality for twelve hours, but a change in the economic system which generated such brutality. However, because the radicals are now isolated, the politicians could use minimal force to quiet or imprison them. The message would be clear: moderate reforms could be won through peaceful means, but radical demands backed up by violence would be treated severely. The historical result of such confrontations was often the temporary restoration of civil order, but the brutal working conditions remained. Politics as conflict-resolution directs the adherent to treat symptoms, not causes. In this sense, it is perverse.

Second, critics of politics as conflict-resolution pointed out that the model ignored the most important aspects of political life. The critics looked back to a more classical understanding of politics developed in ancient Athens and Rome. For classical thinkers like Plato and Aristotle, politics concerned the pursuit of common public goals. Politics was a matter of building a community on the basis of common public interests and common public feelings. This understanding of politics was especially attractive to critics who felt that life in modern capitalist societies tended to fragment people's lives, separate them from one another, and set them into social opposition.

The critics began to develop a model of politics which made community-building its central focus. And sometimes conflict, even violent conflict, was necessary for pursuing communal interests. Let us now examine this model more closely.

The Logic of Politics as Community-Building

Politics as community-building is a model which was developed to allow analysts to focus on political solutions to major social problems which were seen as more significant than violent conflict. Its logic is based on the following points:

1. As members of a common species, people share basic similarities. In this sense, people are "social" animals.

2. Despite their conflicts, people have the potential to work together to achieve common human goals.

3. To realize this potential, they must coordinate their diverse actions in the interest of community goals.

4. Coordination requires an authoritative means by which community members can understand and act to achieve community goals.

5. Politics is the authoritative process of coordinating community understanding and activity to fulfill community goals.

6. A political issue involves any question related to the means and ends of community life. It may or may not be related to questions of potentially violent conflict.

As we examine this logic, note how very different it is from our first model.

Adherents of politics as community-building usually assume that people are significantly similar. While their particular needs, wants, and desires often differ, they all share an interest in living together harmoniously and in achieving many common goals. Above all else, politics is concerned with nurturing cooperation among people.

On the one hand, all humans are members of the same species. They share a number of needs and goals. For example, for me to develop my trumpet playing capacities requires that someone must mine the raw materials which go into a trumpet, make the trumpet, teach me to play it, and develop the language and processes necessary for coordinating all this activity. The day I perform my first solo is the day I recognize the contributions of many other people to my own development. Whenever anyone develops their human capacities, they do so with the aid of others. Moreover, my musical capacities remain immature until I play with other musicians, in an orchestra in order to produce fuller, richer sounds. While animals may also develop their natural capacities in harmony with others of their species (e.g., a wolf in a wolfpack), humans are unique. Humans can consciously plan to create a community in which natural human capacities can be nurtured and developed.

On the other hand, this planning capacity can be severely limited under particular historical circumstances. Where resources are scarce, people may conflict over who gets what. Where populations are large and impersonal, some members of society may dominate in order to secure the lion's share of scarce resources. Despite the fact that everyone might believe the earth's resources are humankind's common inheritance, conditions of scarcity make such plans difficult. Why should I rely on a common plan which may somehow neglect me when I know that I have the power today to get what I want from others? Human history is filled with such conflicts. Unfortunately, politics as conflict-resolution stops here and assumes that the best that can be done is to minimize the violence.

However, human history is also filled with growing cooperation and conscious planning. Once upon a time, the world was divided up into small tribes which were internally cooperative but externally conflictual. Today, the world is divided into large nations where an incredibly high degree of cooperation among vast numbers of people exists. Without an historical perspective, the analyst will focus on today's conflicts; with an historical perspective, he is more likely to focus on the growing trends toward and opportunities for greater human cooperation. Indeed, modern industrialization and technology make it conceivable that people need no longer compete over scarce goods. The major problem of the future may be avoided with conscious planning of priorities for producing and distributing scarce and abundant goods.

Conscious planning requires coordinating the activities of different people in the interests of the group as a whole. This is no less true under conditions of scarcity than under conditions of abundance. Assume we have three hundred would-be trumpeters competing for the twenty trumpets a society is able to produce. Should we resolve the conflict by letting those who can pay the market price purchase the few trumpets? Should we resolve it by putting all would-be trumpeters' names into a hat and then pull out twenty? Either way, society as a whole might lose out. It may turn out that we have wasted society's limited resources on the twenty poorest risks, thereby denying other community members the opportunity to hear beautiful trumpet music. Moreover, trumpet teachers, frustrated by such poor students, may lose their desire to teach and future generations of music lovers may lose access to beautiful trumpet music. An how will our orchestras sound without trumpets? Resolution of conflicts may be peaceful, but if they are unplanned, society as a whole may suffer a great loss.

The community-building model of politics proposes an alternative understanding. It assumes that politics is the planned coordination of the activities of diverse individuals and groups in the interests of the community as a whole. All societies motivate their members, especially the young, to develop ideas and talents beneficial to the community. All societies have processes for determining community priorities under conditions of scarcity. And virtually all societies have planning mechanisms for motivating people and setting priorities. In many cases, these processes occur within government circles. But in many cases, they occur throughout society. And often times, violence is not an issue here.

Consider the following example. Assume that after living with slavery for one hundred years, citizens of Country X peacefully decide that slavery should be abolished. Emancipation is proclaimed by government officials. The slaves are now "free." How are they to earn a living? Some look for new jobs only to discover that their lack of skills (a product of slavery) means that they are the last hired and first fired. Some apply for jobs with their old slaveowners. But because so many ex-slaves are looking for jobs, the old slaveowners offer them wages so low that their standard of living would be worse than under slavery. Under these conditions, the ex-slaves naturally become a very alienated segment of the community and are locked into a vicious cycle of poverty. How are we to understand this communal disharmony?

Government is clearly one factor. It proclaimed emancipation without providing the ex-slaves the means of supporting themselves. Moreover, leaders of the economic system must be taken into account. They are the ones who have shaped the economic system in such a way that unskilled laborers can find no new jobs and that they can be paid subhuman wages at their old jobs. And of course, let us not forget the citizens who tacitly accepted government and economic priorities; also, let us not forget the educational institutions which motivated citizens to accept these priorities. According to the model of politics as community-building, government is one factor among many in political explanations. No aspect of society is immune from either political analysis or political action.

From this perspective, there are at least two major types of political organizations. First is the formal institutions which overtly function to coordinate human activities. Included here are government and its various agencies, political parties, and quasi-governmental units. Their ability to motivate people, set priorities, and plan is central, but not unique. Second, one must also focus on informal political institutions which play a role in these processes. Private as well as public schools are "political" to the extent that they nurture or retard the growth of communal attitudes. Corporations are "political" to the extent that they set priorities and make plans which affect the abilities of workers and consumers to live cooperatively and achieve common goals. Indeed, virtually any institution or issue is "political" according to politics as community-building if it affects the ability of members to build harmonious relations among themselves.

How does this notion of politics relate to the question of violence? Violence is generally treated as a symptom of communal disharmony; it is seen as a manifestation of dissatisfaction by some part of the community. Consequently, manifestations of violence or threats of violence often function as indicators of social problems which must be solved in the name of communal harmony. However, nonviolent situations are just as important. The alienation or unhappiness of a group of citizens may cause no immediate social conflict; these citizens may temporarily alleviate their frustrations by turning to cultist religions or television fanaticism rather than political protest. Nevertheless, the alienation of these citizens poses a serious political problem if it affects their motivation or ability to function as community members.

Politics as conflict-resolution narrows the political realm to the relatively clear but limited world of potential violence. Politics as community-building broadens the political realm to encompass all social factors which contribute to or retard community development. And implicitly, politics as community-building also broadens the realm of action appropriately considered political.

Politics as Community-Building: An Alternative Lens

Like our first model, politics as community-building is a lens which sharpens our vision in some ways, only to distort our vision in other ways. In particular, it blurs our vision in precisely the same areas which the first model highlights. These are:

1. The centrality of avoiding potentially violent conflict.

2. The distortions involved in broadening the idea of politics.

3. The dangers of ignoring individual behavior by focusing on social interdependence.

In short, politics as community-building heightens our awareness of the political forest but desensitizes us to the political trees. Let us see why.

Advocates of politics as community-building tend to focus on major conflicts as potential instruments for establishing community harmony. Such conflicts may indicate ruptures or threats to community cohesiveness; or they may be necessary for defeating groups which benefit from a lack of community. Where conflicts are non-existent or not apparent, advocates must consider the possibility that conflicts should exist if community goals are to be realized. Social peace may be dysfunctional. As political analysts, we must look at potentially violent behavior, nonviolent behavior, and even the absence of particular behavior in terms of overall community health. We must be willing to consider conflict as a vaccination which functions to protect the body politic; and we must be willing to consider peace and stability as potential diseases threatening the community. How does this affect our political studies?

Assume that we are interested in studying the politics of a government agency. Looking at this agency through the lens of conflict-resolution, we are likely to ask the following type of questions: How do agency heads detect conflict among their personnel or clients? What processes exist for personnel or clients to win demands peacefully? However, if we view this agency through the lens of politics as community-building, our questions would be quite different: Do agency heads effectively respond to public needs? Do agency decisions and actions effectively meet those needs? The point here is that advocates of different models of politics are interested in, or treat as significant, different factors in politics.

What distortions are involved in the second model? Politics as community-building tends to underplay the significance of conflict in the political world. Conflict, and especially violent conflict, may indeed be necessary to achieving community goals; but as analysts, we too often ignore the fact that most people see conflict as extremely costly and would rather avoid it. Conflict is costly in terms of time, resources, and risks; conflict tends to be painful to those involved. And the outcome of conflict is always uncertain: it may or may not result in positive benefits to the community. This may explain why so many people are willing to live with today's inconveniences rather than upset present modes of conflict-resolution. For example, many of us prefer to live with our neighbors' noise rather than risk their enmity in a confrontation. Politics as community-building often ignores the very real possibility that individuals may desire to live geographically near one another without incurring the risks involved in establishing close, communitarian relations.

A related implication of this model is that it sensitizes us to the possible extent, rather than limits of politics, but here too, a price is exacted. On the one hand, there is a very real sense in which politics encompasses all aspects of social life. Political scientists must be concerned with the ways in which child-raising methods, psychology, economics, culture, technology and medicine affect the health of the body politic, provide new means or alternatives for political relationships, or limit the possibilities for community. Therefore, it is certainly appropriate for political scientists and/or political participants to investigate industrial pollution, water fluoridation, the impact of television and the need for public daycare centers, prior to particular conflicts. All these issues affect community health, if not today, then possibly tomorrow.

On the other hand, there are two major dangers to extending our notion of politics to this degree. One is that almost every social issue becomes a political issue. And rather than relying on accepted means of peaceful conflict-resolution, people who use this model are prone to flood the political system with their every concern. To accommodate such extensive citizen demands, government must expand to the point that it becomes coextensive with society. In America, we can see this trend manifest in the rising numbers of law suits; the major result has been the enrichment of lawyers with few community benefits. A second danger here relates to the study of politics. Political scientists who view the world through this lens must become experts in child-raising methods, psychology, economics, etc., to demonstrate how a multitude of social issues affect community good. However, given the proliferation of theories, facts, and information in general, we cannot really expect any individual to understand adequately these areas. Without a division of labor, which requires a relatively narrow definition of politics, we can expect much poor, ill-informed analysis under the guise of political science.

Finally, politics as community-building focuses our attention more on collectivities than on individuals. It justifies consideration of broad issues which individuals have not yet raised through conflict; it forces us to deal with broad, almost undefinable generalities like community good. For example, with this model we may examine how a major overhaul of the economy would be in the longterm interest of the public despite the fact that few citizens desire or will fight for such an overhaul. In one sense, this endeavor can be seen as a basis for understanding future political potentials.

In another sense, it can be seen as unscientific, utopian thought which disregards how individuals exist today. Were politicians or political scientists to develop studies and plans for such grandiose projects, two implications would follow. First, in a longterm perspective, individuals would represent a threat to the political scientists' understandings and plans. It is only a short step from here to suggesting that people must be re-educated (e.g., reprogrammed) or constrained (e.g., physically coerced) in the name of future good. Second, from the vantage point of those of us who see the world through this expansive lens, it is relatively easy to oversimplify the vast complexities of individual lives. A broad analysis of necessary ecological changes often neglects the impact of those changes on particular individuals. Implementing these changes may indeed expand the number of overall jobs in our society, as some believe, but we must not forget that the worker who is laid off because of pollution controls might not have access to one of the new jobs; rather than nurturing a greater sense of community, greater individual alienation may result. Indeed, the ramifications of broad explanations and recommendations are so extensive and complex, we can only hope to develop a sophisticated understanding by focusing on individual behavior itself. Otherwise we base understanding on myths, rather than realities.

In summary, politics as community-building sensitizes us to community-wide issues, to the interconnections linking all spheres of social life, and to the broad collective issues of the past, present, and future. With it, we can gain a general understanding of the nature of and possible solutions to broad problems like poverty, racism and the urban crisis. However, our vision of the centrality of conflict, of the particular nature of politics, and of individual behavior is likely to be blurred. We are especially likely to ignore the impact of political institutions and processes on individuals.

Politics as Community-Building and the Spa

Assume that your friend disagrees with your last statement that you are *also* willing to discuss *nonpolitical* issues. "In fact," he responds, "you have not begun to describe the political situation in your town." As an adherent of politics as community-building, he presents an alternative understanding.

He argues that the political issues in your town go far beyond the stoning of the doctor's home. The doctor's revelations, even without the conflict, are political in the sense that they directly affect the community good. They reveal negligence on the part of spa owners resulting in a danger to the community's guests and the community's economy. Moreover, the response of townspeople, protecting their immediate self-interests, indicates a lack of public concern for the overall good of the community. Finally, the conflict itself signifies that political authorities have been remiss in coordinating the actions of various community sectors. It may be important to let this conflict continue in order to better understand the kind of re-coordination necessary to promote collective ends. In each of these instances, the contamination of the spa highlights a number of political questions which should not be ignored.

Even if people peacefully persuaded the doctor to leave or to be silent, townspeople would have a responsibility to raise the issue.

Local political analysts would appropriately consider the issue despite efforts to make it disappear; indeed, the causes and implications of those efforts would be crucial to understanding community politics. It may be argued, for example, that tourists are likely to discover the contamination as water quality deteriorates further. Unless action were taken now, tourists would be fatally sick and the town's economic status would be substantially weakened in the long run. Obviously, your friend concludes, strong political action is called for.

You ask, "And what political actions do you believe are appropriate?" Your friend continues. In the long-term interests of the community, the government might consider regulating or directly controlling spa ownership to assure responsible management. Government might support educational and culture efforts aimed at getting your neighbors to consider the importance of community goals. Furthermore, government might consider enacting harsh penalties against those who endanger public good. Or they could commission scientists to do a more extensive study of spa water quality. In short, government may appropriately act in as many ways as are possible for strengthening the community. Had it done so sooner, it would be less likely that your town would be faced with the present crisis.

In terms of the short-run, government might take responsibility for refinancing and rebuilding the spa, guaranteeing full employment during this period, or declaring a moratorium on all loans. It might put together a public relations campaign to encourage future patrons to recognize the community's concern for their health and enjoyment. And do not forget, your friend adds, appropriate political acts need not be centered in government. The younger staff members of the local press could go on strike on the basis of ownership's unwillingness to print *all* significant news. There are many possibilities and they all deserve serious analysis.

You are feeling quite uncomfortable at this point. You ask, "Precisely what is this 'community good' which you abstractly refer to time and again?" Your friend hesitates a moment. Then he says that there are a number of ways to understand the nature of "community good." But that gets you into a discussion about political justice. And while this topic is certainly related to the one you have been discussing, your friend would rather discuss it tomorrow.

SUMMARY AND CONCLUSION To study politics, we must understand the nature of our subject matter. We must be able to specify what is or is not politics or appropriate political actions. In this chapter, I have presented two basic models of politics: (1) Politics as Conflict-Resolution and (2) Politics as Community-Building. These models represent basic lenses through which many people and political analysts view the political world. I do not believe that they are the only models or that they are employed without variation. Rather, they are general models around which many people interested in politics cluster.

Depending on the particular lens people use they are likely to see the political world in a way quite different from others using an alternative lens. Adherents of the first model see politics wherever potentially violent conflict exists; they see governments as mechanisms for settling those conflicts peacefully; and they see the realm of politics as relatively narrow. Adherents of the second model will likely see politics wherever community good is affected; they see government as a mechanism for coordinating social groups to achieve community good; and they see government as only one of many such mechanisms and consequently broaden their realm of politics. To a large extent, the model people use will also affect the political alternatives they will consider. Politics as conflict-resolution people will likely see politics as a limited realm of activity concerned with economical ways of minimizing conflict; adherents of the second model will likely see politics as an extensive realm in which non-governmental actions play a significant role. The former will take a narrow perspective when dealing with political problems, while the latter will take an expansive view of the possibilities for political action.

It is important to point out that neither model implies a preference for a specified form of government. In theory, a monarchy or a democracy can be equally effective in minimizing conflict; in theory, both forms of government can be equally effective in promoting community goals. Furthermore, neither model necessarily implies support for a particular kind of economy. Both capitalism and socialism are logically consistent with the models.

Is choosing a model of politics then an arbitrary process of replacing one lens with another, just as we sometimes replace our blue-tinted sunglasses with amber-tinted ones? After all, each model provides a systematic way of viewing the political world; each model highlights particular aspects of the political world only to blur other aspects. Why employ one rather than the other? While I cannot suggest any basis for saying that one model is theoretically superior to the other, I do believe I can explain why some people and some political analysts employ one model rather than the other.

SELECTED REFERENCES Bay, Christian. *The Structure of Freedom*. Stanford, California: Stanford University Press, 1970.

Boorstin, Daniel J. *The Genius of American Politics*. Chicago: University of Chicago Press, 1953.

Dahl, Robert. *Modern Political Analysis.* Third Edition. Englewood Cliffs, New Jersey: Prentice-Hall, 1976.

Edelman, Murray. *Political Language: Words that Succeed and Policies that Fail.* New York: Academic Press, 1977.

Hobbes, Thomas. *Leviathan.* Ed. Michael Oakeshott. New York: Collier, 1962.

Lakoff, Sanford A., ed. *Private Government.* Glenview, Illinois: Scott Foresman, 1973.

Locke, John. *Two Treatises of Government.* Ed. Thomas Cook. New York: Hafner, 1965.

Marx, Karl and Engels, Frederick. *The German Ideology.* Moscow: Progress Publishers, 1968.

Mill, John Stuart. *Principles of Political Economy.* Ed. D. Winch. Baltimore: Penguin Books, 1970.

Wolin, Sheldon. *Politics and Vision.* Boston: Little, Brown, 1960.

Perceiving the political world is doing two things simultaneously. One is a physiological act. We record perceptions of the outside world through sensory mechanisms of vision, sound, smell, feel or taste. The second is a cognitive act. We categorize those perceptions in ways which make them intelligible to us. In the case of political perceptions, we ignore some as nonpolitical or not significantly related to politics. Other perceptions we categorize as political and then go on to place them in subcategories such as "democratic politics" or "totalitarian politics." Once we *really* perceive what goes on, we utter statements like "Oh, now I see how politics works." Everything fits into place and we can now describe what we have observed.

The simplicity of these two processes is deceptive. The human act of categorization is extremely complex. Why do we ignore some perceptions or relegate them to categories of insignificance? Consider this story. You live in an apartment overlooking a major city expressway. At first, you are bothered by the constant noise of traffic and cannot understand how others can tolerate it. But after a month or so, you get used to the noise; it has become a part of your daily life which you take for granted. A few months later, a new friend comes to your apartment and asks, "How can you stand *it*?" You have no idea of what *it* is so you ask for clarification. Your friend says, "It? The traffic noise,

of course!" Like a building veteran, you respond, "Noise? Oh yes. You eventually get so used to it that you don't even hear it."

As children, we are acutely sensitive to all aspects of the environment around us. Babies, for example, will test all sorts of objects for taste. Does a plastic airplane taste good? Does a wooden block taste good? In time, babies learn to categorize objects into those which are not tasty and those which are. When those babies become adults searching for a midnight snack, they will not even consider plastic airplanes or blocks as possible objects; they have long taken for granted the fact that plastic airplanes and wooden blocks are not tasty. Throughout our lives, we categorize our worlds into things not worth considering and things worthy of consideration. We do this so regularly that we are often unconscious of our own classification schemes.

This same maturation process occurs in people's perceptions of the political world. Many of us learn to take for granted the notion that people are basically selfish. When we observe political events, we look for the clash of selfish interests without even considering the possibility of altruism; we have relegated altruism to the category of insignificant or nonpolitical. Or examine a national party convention in America. Every four years, responsible, relatively reasonable adults

38

congregate before television cameras and behave like children. Most Americans take such behavior for granted and do not consciously perceive it as a basic aspect of political conventions. However, to an outsider witnessing his first convention, the child-like behavior of delegates may strike him as the most significant aspect of the convention. Only when he mentions this are Americans likely to perceive consciously such behavior.

On the one hand, to take things for granted is necessary if we are to focus on and describe the political perceptions we deem most important. We do not have to waste our time on details. On the other hand, by taking these details for granted or simply ignoring them, we tend to forget them. This is dangerous. We may not notice small changes in these details which make them very important; we may not be able to communicate with people who believe they are politically significant. We may even go so far as to consider people who dwell on these details as ignorant or unnatural.

Those perceptions we do not ignore or take for granted are categorized. Our categories allow us to distinguish perceptions from one another. And as we become familiar with our standard set of categories, objects and events make "sense" to us once we discover their appropriate categories. Suppose someone describes to you a very large duck with an extraordinarily long neck. This description may make no sense to you because you know ducks are relatively small with short necks. On further questioning, you figure out that the animal is not an "ugly duckling" but a lovely swan. Now everything makes sense; you have successfully categorized a strange object into a familiar class of animals.

Now consider the importance of categorizing the political world in order to describe it. Someone asks you to *describe* your political system. You proudly announce that it is a "democracy" based on "popular sovereignty," "consent of the governed" and "political equality." At some point, your questioner interrupts and says, "You are not describing your political system, you are giving it your *praise*." Categories like democracy, popular sovereignty, consent, and equality are not neutral descriptive terms; each contains an element of praise or value preference within it. We generally assume that something "democratic" is morally good until someone demonstrates otherwise. Consequently, when we categorize the political world to describe it, we often do not realize that our categories are impregnated with value assumptions.

Our two models of politics are no exceptions. Both models ignore or render insignificant some aspects of the political world, to focus on other aspects. Both models employ categorizations as a basis for description but their categorizations are also infused with value assumptions. While there may be no absolute reason for preferring one model to the other, there are good reasons why some people and some political scientists actually do prefer one model to the other. One model's implicit notions of significance and values may be more attuned to a person's political preferences than the other model. In other words, people are likely to adopt the model of politics which focuses on the perceptions and categories consistent with their political values.

Politics as Conflict-Resolution and Values

We have already seen that politics as conflict-resolution is a model which assumes the significance of the following perceptions: individual diversity, violent conflict, and peaceful conflict-resolution. Simultaneously, this model treats as insignificant or ignores human similarities, non-governmental forms of power, and community. What values are implied in these categories?

First, the model assumes that the most significant relations in politics are those between individuals and government; harmonious relations among individuals are considered politically insignificant. Consequently, this model focuses our attention on conflicts and political *processes* for resolving conflict. It is process-oriented. Second, the particular categories employed in the model are value impregnated. "Individualism" and "peace" are not only descriptive terms; like "democracy", they are implicitly desired goals unless otherwise specified. Consequently, politics as conflict-resolution is a model impregnated with preferences for individual rights (i.e., individualism) and political stability (i.e., peace).

As we shall see in the next chapter, this system of significance and values is quite consistent with a particular notion of justice: Justice as Fairness. This notion of justice is particularly concerned with processes for resolving conflict; politics as conflict-resolution is a useful lens because it focuses one's vision on these processes. Justice as Fairness is also concerned with processes of conflict-resolution which treat individuals fairly (equally) and which result in peaceful relations. As such, the categories of politics as conflict-resolution are likely to make sense to adherents of this version of justice.

Politics as conflict-resolution is a set of categories for *describing* the political world; Justice as Fairness is a set of categories for *evaluating* the political world. Despite this difference, the two are logically related. Both share a system of significance and categories with explicit moral implications. Consequently, people who believe that justice is fairness have good reasons for preferring to view the political world through the lens of politics as conflict-resolution. According to their values, our first model is most useful and sensible.

Politics as Community-Building and Values

What does politics as community-building treat as especially significant or insignificant? It highlights harmonious relations between people, viewing government as one possible barrier or aid to these relations. Consequently, this model is less concerned with processes of conflict-resolution and more concerned with the state or *results* of human relations. It is result-oriented. Furthermore, its categories are infused with values quite different from the first model. Human "sociality" and "harmony" are assumed to be descriptive terms, but are also implicitly desired goals—again, unless otherwise stated. Consequently, politics as community-building is a model containing a moral preference for cooperation (i.e., human sociality) and community (i.e., human harmony).

In the next chapter we shall also consider a second notion of justice: Justice as Goodness. This set of moral ideas is quite consistent with the system of significance and values implicit in politics as community-building. Justice as Goodness is particularly concerned with ways to nurture and to develop the "good society." Like our second model of politics, this notion of justice is result-oriented. Justice as Goodness is also concerned with creating a cooperative community wherein people will be equal in all aspects of their lives. As such, it is consistent with the categories of our second model of politics. In other words, adherents of Justice as Goodness are likely to find politics as community-building, a more useful and sensible model than the other one.

Again, the function of politics as community-building is to provide categories for political description; the function of Justice as Goodness is to provide a number of moral norms for evaluating politics. Despite this difference, their descriptive and evaluative categories are logically connected. Both share a system of significance and categories for approaching political studies. People who believe that justice is goodness are likely to prefer using politics as community-building as their lens on the political world.

Political Description and Political Theory

Why do people and political scientists choose one definition or model of politics over another? We can summarize our answer in the diagram above.

	Logic I	Logic II
Definition of Politics	Conflict-Resolution	Community-Building
	↑	↑
Political Values	Justice as Fairness	Justice as Goodness

The arrows in this diagram indicate logical relationships. People who believe in "Justice as Fairness" have good reasons for using "Politics as Conflict-Resolution" as their vehicle of description. I label this relationship Logic I. Similarly, people who believe in "Justice as Goodness" have good reasons for adopting "politics as Community-Building" as their preferred model. I label this linkage Logic II.

These logics should not be considered as absolutes, but tendencies. People who prefer one set of political values tend to choose the appropriate model of politics for the reasons mentioned. Exceptions and variations are always possible and are usually probable. In addition, these tendential links are usually experienced by people at a preconceptual or subconscious level. Many people may not be able to articulate the models of politics or values or their connections, but nevertheless adopt the model of politics which somehow "makes" sense to them given their values. However, many political scientists may develop very sophisticated arguments defending the superiority of one model of politics over the other. But often, underlying these arguments is the logic developed here: one model makes more sense because it is more consistent with the political scientist's value preferences.

The validity of this analysis depends on the distinction I have made between Justice as Fairness and Justice as Goodness. Some would argue that such a distinction is unwarranted. In one sense, they are right. Most people believe that justice is a matter of both fair procedures for resolving conflicts and good results which harmonize human relationships. For example, we can conceive of a *fair* trial which has *bad* results: despite due process of the law, an innocent woman may be convicted and executed for a murder she did not commit. We can also conceive of an *unfair* trial with *good* results: a vicious rapist is convicted on the basis of an illegal wiretap. Regardless if we think fair procedures are more important than good results, or the opposite, we can all deplore the plight of the woman and applaud the man's imprisonment.

"Deploring" and "applauding" are important aspects of normative political theory; a subfield of political science. But another aspect of political theory is the use of moral norms as guides for political action. With this in mind, the distinction between fairness and goodness seems justified. Those who value fairness above all else are likely to re-examine courtroom procedures to minimize the chance of convicting the innocent and freeing the guilty. In the meantime, they will likely conclude that the innocent woman's execution is sad but just, and the rapist's conviction is fortunate but unjust. Conversely, people who value good results above all else are likely to examine the ways in which society can be restructured to minimize murders and rapes. If this can be done, then courtroom procedures for freeing the innocent and convicting the guilty will be secondary. In the meantime, the woman's execution must be considered unjust and the rapist's conviction just; the procedures are secondary to the results. Let us now examine more closely these alternative models of political values.

Selected References

Connolly, William E. *The Terms of Political Discourse.* Lexington, Massachusetts: D.C. Heath, 1974.

De Crespigny, Anthony and Wertheimer, Alan, eds. *Contemporary Political Theory.* New York: Atherton Press, 1970.

Fowler, Robert Booth and Orenstein, Jeffrey, *Contemporary Issues in Political Theory.* New York: John Wiley and Sons, 1977.

Pitkin, Hanna F. *Wittgenstein and Justice.* Berkeley: University of California Press, 1972.

Taylor, Charles. "Neutrality in Political Science," in *Philosophy, Politics and Society: Third Series.* Eds. Peter Laslett and W.G. Runciman. Oxford: Basil Blackwell, 1969. pp. 25-57.

Toulmin, Stephen. *Foresight and Understanding.* New York: Harper, 1961.

CHAPTER

3

POLITICAL VALUES:
FAIRNESS AND GOODNESS

CHAPTER THREE   What does it mean to give higher priority to procedural values than to end results? Consider the following story. It poses the problem of fair procedures and good results so that you must give one priority over the other. How you or political scientists would choose in these circumstances reveals a great deal about your political values. And as we shall see near the end of this chapter, your choice is likely to be a good indicator of your ideological preferences.

DORMITORY JUSTICE?*   You live in a relatively small dormitory on the campus of a midwestern university. According to university bylaws, all dormitory residents must pay a small fee to be spent to improve dorm life in general. Payment is a mandatory condition of dorm residence; however the use of the money is determined by a majority vote of dormitory residents.

Once each month, dorm residents gather in the lounge to discuss and decide issues of common concern, such as food service in the cafeteria, noise in the hallways, dorm-wide parties, etc. Occasionally, you find yourself voting with the majority and are happy with the results. Other times, when you are a part of the losing minority, you are still not dissatisified. After all, the majority process of arriving at decisions is fair, win or lose.

The major item on today's agenda is the purchase of a newspaper subscription. Upon entering the lounge, you notice that a number of dorm residents who rarely attend meetings are present. The meeting gets started and the issue of the newspaper subscription is raised. In the discussion, virtually all those present support the idea of subscribing to a newspaper out of dorm funds. By a unanimous vote, the group decides to allocate up to eight dollars a month for a newspaper. The only remaining question is "which newspaper?"

There is one local newspaper and four metropolitan newspapers from nearby cities. Discussing the virtues and deficiencies of each takes quite a while. A number of students are bored and leave the meeting; they are not particularly concerned with which newspaper is selected. Any will do. The choice is eventually narrowed to two newspapers, the local *Gazette* or the metropolitan *Sun*.

So far, supporters of the *Gazette* have argued that it is the superior paper for its local news reports, especially university news, and entertainment section. Supporters of the *Sun* stress the paper's broader news coverage, superior sports section, and syndicated columns. As the discussion ends, one of the dorm's few black students stands up to speak for the first time.

Pat Baker says, "Look, you people have ignored the most important difference between the two newspapers. The *Gazette* is

*The idea upon which this story is based is taken from Peter Singer, *Democracy & Disobedience* (New York: Oxford University Press, 1974).

44

so obviously racist that I can't believe you are actually considering it." Pat explains that the *Gazette* has no black pressmen, reporters, or administrators. "The only blacks they hire are newsboys to deliver the paper!" Furthermore, the *Gazette* consistently reflects the prejudices of the conservative white people who fear racial equality will simultaneously endanger their jobs, the virginity of their daughters, and the whole American way of life. In its editorial pages, it has repeatedly opposed minority demands for racial equality and justified apartheid in South Africa—a most vicious form of racism. "If we subscribe to the *Gazette*," she concludes, "we are subscribing to racist oppression." She sits down.

A number of those residents who rarely attend dorm meetings immediately stand up to be recognized. In an almost orchestrated fashion, they systematically challenge the black woman's statements with comments ranging from, "Who reads the news section anyway?" to "Oh, you people see racism everywhere." Another adds, "If black people would work as hard as everyone else, there would be no racial problems." Finally, one student says, "It's getting awfully late. We're not going to solve the racism issue here. Let's vote so we can all get back to our homework." A vote is called for.

Assume that you are persuaded by Pat Baker's arguments; a subscription to the *Gazette* is indeed a subscription to racism that you deplore. The vote is taken and tallied. Pat, the two other black students, a few white students, and you vote in favor of the *Sun*. But, the rare-attenders plus a scattering of other students have enough votes to constitute a comfortable majority in favor of the *Gazette*. On the basis of the majority vote, the dormitory treasurer is instructed to buy a subscription to the *Gazette* tomorrow. You express to a number of friends your unhappiness with this decision. But as the meeting adjourns, you think to yourself, "It was a fair procedure. The majority did prevail. There really is no other fair way of making decisions. Only the result is unfortunate."

You receive a telephone call from Pat Baker the following morning. She asks you about your feelings on the meeting. You tell her that you agreed with her, voted with her, and that you believe the majority made a bad decision. She then tells you that those who opposed her last night, and rarely come to meetings, are a new chapter of the local Ku Klux Klan. They are organizing campus-wide, hoping to deny equal rights to blacks, then Jews, then Catholics. Although they are few in number, they are so well organized that they usually prevail. "It is time," she says, "that they be stopped!" You ask for further explanations.

Pat unravels a plan that she and a few others have spun. "With the cooperation of a few students, the *Gazette* can be intercepted and trashed before it ever gets into the dorm. This will have two consequences. First, it will demonstrate to others the seriousness of our commitment to racial equality. Apathetic students will be forced to commit themselves on this issue. Second, we will publicize the reasons for trashing the *Gazette*. We hope that this will win supporters. At the very least, students will learn that they cannot support racism without expecting some costs", Pat explains.

"Are you with us?" she asks.

You are quite ambivalent. Even if the Ku Klux Klan stacked the meeting with their members, do they not have a right to their opinions and votes? And what right does a minority have to overturn a majority decision? Nevertheless, is racism and support of it ever justifiable? Can one condone majority rule even when a white majority can use it to deny racial minorities their rights? These questions race through your mind but not the answers. You suddenly come up with an alternative that would be fair and have good results simultaneously. "Why not launch a campaign to educate and organize dorm residents so that we will be a majority in the next meeting? Then we could fairly overturn last night's bad decision," you say to Pat.

Pat says that she wishes that it were possible but it is not. "Most of the students in the dorm are white, come from white communities where questions of racism are rarely faced, and are acculturated to believe that whites are somehow superior to minorities. Not only would it be difficult to educate them in such a short period, but it would be difficult getting them to listen. Most like to believe that racism is an issue that died with the Emancipation Proclamation. And," she adds, "how long must we patiently wait to challenge racism?" To some extent, you agree with her: there is little chance of winning majority support in the near future, but the issue of racism cannot be relegated to the distant future either. Racism is an injustice.

You must now make a choice. Do you follow the fair procedure of majority rule and accept the racist results in the meantime? Or do you subvert a fair procedure like majority rule in order to oppose racism? If you believe that Justice is Fairness, you will be likely to support fair procedures and sadly accept bad outcomes. But if you believe that Justice is Goodness, you will probably take decisive action today even if it temporarily circumvents fair procedures. Certainly most people would like to live in a polity where fair procedures always result in good decisions; unfortunately, this is not often the case. The choice here is common in today's political world.

Again, I will not suggest that you choose one way or the other. Instead, I will present two models of political values that partially explain how some people justify one choice or the other.

JUSTICE AS FAIRNESS
Political Legitimacy

Political systems rarely survive for very long unless most citizens consider them to be legitimate, justifiable ways of regulating human interactions. Most people will settle their conflicts in peaceful, prescribed ways to the extent that they actively support a system of rules and conventions. Most people will be law-abiding citizens insofar as they take for granted the rules and conventions. Consequently, authorities could make decisions with good reason to believe that most citizens will comply. The authorities need maintain only a small police force to deal with those who refuse to comply. These isolated few are labeled criminals.

Now consider an illegitimate political system—one in which few people actively support or take for granted the rules and conventions. Under these circumstances, most people believe that the governors do not have the right to make or to enforce authoritative decisions. What could governors do to win compliance with their decisions? Each time governors made a ruling, they would have to send out the army or police force to make sure the dissatisfied obeyed. And since all citizens are likely to be dissatisfied with at least some rulings, governors would have to create armed forces large enough to watch everyone. Such a political system is rightly labeled a police state; it is likely to be highly unstable.

After all, who are the police but a special category of citizens who are also likely to disagree with some rulings? Who will watch them? Will they not be tempted by offers of higher rank or salary among dissident forces? Will they not consider using their coercive skills to support more legitimate alternatives? And is it not likely that at least some citizens, resenting the constant threat of force, will oppose governors with counterforce: assasinations, bombings, civil war, revolution? And will these counterforces not be able to win much popular support among people who consider them legitimate alternatives to present governors? Although the answers to these questions are not obvious, they do generate a fairly clear implication: A political system that wins the general support of the population is more likely to be stable than is one which is considered illegitimate.

The problem of political legitimacy was particularly striking near the beginning of the nineteenth century. A great many people argued that the traditional political systems based on kingship and aristocratic privilege were illegitimate. Throughout the Western world, tremendous political discord reigned. From revolutionary movements to small-scaled protests, people demanded that traditional political systems be abolished or altered, which they eventually were. In country after country, the power of "divine" monarchs and aristrocratic families was drastically diminished. In turn, new political orders evolved, stressing the right of the "sovereign people" to control public decision making through their elected representatives.

In many cases, the new political orders were challenged at the very moment of their conception or soon thereafter. In order to survive, they needed the approval of most citizens. A set of ideas developed to persuade citizens that the new political order was just. It emerged and continues to be widespread in many Western nations today. The set of ideas can be characterized as Justice as Fairness. Let us explore this set of ideas.

The Logic of Justice as Fairness

Justice as Fairness can be considered as a set of political values that justify a particular system of conflict-resolution. Its logic can be outlined as follows:

1. Individuals naturally compete for scarce values such as wealth, power or status.

2. Individuals often assume unfair advantages over their competitors to enhance their chances for success.

3. To assure everyone of a fair chance of success, everyone ought to follow an impersonal (neutral) set of rules.

4. Once individuals consent to such rules, they are morally obligated to accept the outcome of competition regardless of whether they personally win or lose.

5. A master set of rules (a consitution) is necessary to ensure that the rules are fair and to outline procedures for changing unfair rules peacefully.

6. Justice is playing fairly and abiding by the results. Justice is fairness.

Let us now add substance to this outline.

In all historical periods, human existence has meant competition for scarce values. Most people devote a major part of their lives to competing for the tools and resources necessary for sustaining life. Even in our present era of relative economic abundance, people's material desires continue to outgrow their ability to satisfy them. Consequently, the race for wealth continues with no end in sight. Whether we like it or not, economic competition is perhaps the most certain fact of human existence.

People also compete for power and status, which are also scarce resources. If power is the ability to control the behavior of others, then one can become more powerful only by another becoming less powerful. Similarly, if status is the ability to win deference from others, then the growth in one person's status implies shrinkage in another's status. Consequently, there is never enough power or status to satisfy everyone and the competition for them never stops.

There is no perfectly just distribution of wealth, power, and status because every distribution plan gives an unfair advantage to at least one group. If these scarce values were allocated according to skill level, those born with natural talents would be rich and powerful while those born with few talents would be poor and weak. But is it fair that a fact of birth, one for which the particular individual bears no responsibility, should determine these outcomes? Or if these scarce values were allocated evenly, is it fair that hardworking, skilled people receive the same as lazy loafers? Whatever the criterion is, there are good reasons for arguing that it is unfair to some people.

Even if we could agree to a just distribution, could we possibly apply it fairly? Suppose we agree that skillful performances should be highly rewarded. How do we decide *which* skillful performances should be highly rewarded? Surely we do not want to reward equally the very skillful construction worker and the very skillful gangland murderer. Applying our criterion of justice becomes more complicated when we consider that many people believe their own particular skills are the ones which most certainly merit rewards. As a writer, I believe good books merit greater rewards than Chris Evert's minor accomplishment of hitting a ball over a tennis net. Of course, I assume that Chris Evert and her supporters would disagree.

Finally, even if we can agree on which skill should be rewarded highly, how do we judge skill levels and appropriate rewards? Some people believe that the drawings of five-year-olds are as skillful as many famous abstract paintings are. Despite the disagreement of many art critics, there is no certain method of comparatively evaluating the works of five-year-olds and the masters. We find these disagreements throughout society on a vast array of issues.

One of the reasons it is so difficult to get people to agree to a criterion of justice or an appropriate application of justice is that people are poor judges in their own cases. They are already involved in the competition for scarce resources and dearly hope to win. They generally select a criterion of justice or advance an application which improves their competitive edge. Consequently, poor and weak people are likely to support a relatively equal distribution of wealth to improve their own position; wealthy and powerful people are likely to support a distribution based on skills they have already mastered to protect their position. The only way to fairly reconcile these differences is to discover procedures that arbitrate conflicting demands without particular advantage to any group.

Justice as Fairness adherents believe that all individuals deserve a "fair" chance of winning. This is possible only if individuals may not make judgments in their own cases. A neutral set of processes is needed for developing a neutral set of rules that are administered by neutral institutions. In a more concrete and modern sense, a fair system of elections, a fair system of legislation, and a fair system for administering the laws are needed.

First, an electoral system based on one person-one vote provides an equal opportunity to choose representatives as prospective decision-makers. Some people may elect representatives who will strive for an equal distribution of wealth, power, and status; others may elect representatives who will strive for a distribution according to effort or skill or some other criterion.

Second, an ideal legislative system would develop rules to assure each representative an equal chance to convert his or her criterion into law. The conflict of differing viewpoints would be worked out according to majority rule. Depending on what kinds of representatives are elected and the various chances for coalitions, it is reasonable to expect that any one representative will win sometimes and lose other times. The laws which emerge from this process are fair in the sense that all representatives and the people who elected them have an equal chance of being influential.

Third, the application of these laws must be neutral. A fair set of judicial procedures is needed to guarantee that all people are given the same rights in the courtroom and are subject to the same penalties. In theory, you and John D. Rockefeller should have to obey the same rules and suffer the same consequences for infractions.

Note that the idea of justice is applied to procedures and not to results. As long as everyone has a fair chance of influencing elections, the outcome is morally secondary—though not irrelevant. That some despicable people may become representatives is unfortunate; but as long as the election process is fair, these people merit their positions. As long as every representative has a fair chance to influence legislation, the resulting laws are morally secondary. Again, bad laws may be enacted but with fairness behind them, these laws deserve to be obeyed and enforced. Finally, as long as everyone has the same courtroom rights, judicial decisions must be considered just. Justice as Fairness primarily concerns procedures which provide potential influence to all; the only alternative is to force one group's particular notion of a just distribution of power on everyone else.

Advocates of Justice as Fairness usually apply the same moral criteria to the economic marketplace. They hope to ensure fair processes of competition by assuring everyone an equal opportunity to compete, by limiting monopolization, and by penalizing those employing unfair means (e.g., industrial sabotage) to win the competition. They hope that fair political processes result in a set of laws which establish rules of fair economic competition so that everyone has a chance to attain his private political and economic goals.

To the extent that their hopes are realized, no individual or group need answer the question regarding the just distribution of wealth. Skill, effort, and need may or may not be rewarded according to the neutral or impersonal dynamics of the economic marketplace. Some employers may prefer to hire highly skilled workers; others may be more interested in hiring those who show the greatest enthusiasm and effort in their work; still others may wish to reward worker loyalty by awarding seniority. Moreover, some employers may make a practice of hiring the needy (e.g., the handicapped) for any number of reasons. And in the case of deciding which skills (or efforts or needs) are to be rewarded, the marketplace is again the determinant. If there is a high demand for skilled construction engineers, they will receive high salaries; if there is no demand for extremely talented artists, they will receive little or no economic rewards. Depending on what people will pay for at any particular moment, authors, or tennis players may be rich or poor. Finally, no particular individual or group decides what constitutes a skilled performance, great effort, or great need. If people wish to view a five-year-old's art as skillful, they will pay for it; if people think Picasso's art is amateurish, Picasso must decide if artistic poverty is preferable to another line of work. In the ideal marketplace, as in the ideal political system, justice is a matter of fair processes of competition rather than specific outcomes.

Of course, competition necessarily implies that these outcomes will include both winners and losers. A five-year-old's art may not sell, but Picasso may become exceedingly rich. Or there may be a high demand for Democratic candidates in some districts but not for Republican ones. What is expected of the losers in fair competition? At the very least, compliance with the results is expected. Five-year-olds may not go out and steal Picasso's rewards and losing Republican candidates may not usurp political office. At best, losers will reconsider their options. Five-year-olds might decide to go to art school to hone their skills or to enter a new line of work; losing Republicans might consider how to win greater support in the next election or even jump across party lines. Winners and losers alike may always enter and exit the competition for scarce wealth, power, and status at many points; if they are wise, they will enter where their chances of success are greatest.

Now it may be argued that the competition described above is not really fair. Assume that our five-year-old artists were naive enough to believe that people would buy their work on the basis of merit alone, whereas Picasso invested a great deal of money in getting his name known and in advertising his work. Or assume that our Republican loser spent only $5000 in her campaign while the Democratic winner spent hundreds of thousands of dollars for advertisements, campaign workers, and leaflets. May our five-year-olds or Republican loser claim the competition was unfair? Of course. But who determines whether their claims are justified or not?

Justice as Fairness advocates understand that rules of competition may be unfair. Consequently, they usually support establishing a set of master rules which provide (1) a standard of fairness and (2) a procedure for altering unfair laws or rules. In some political systems, this set of master rules is called a constitution and the procedure for altering unfair laws is called judicial review. Assume that our losing Republican contests the election. She argues that, according to the national constitution, all political candidates must have an equal chance to be heard by the voters. She has been denied this equal chance because of the vast inequality of campaign funds between her and her opponent. The judges must then interpret the constitution. Assume they argue that the discrepancy in campaign funding did put her at a disadvantage but it was a disadvantage of her own making. She had just as much right to win financial support as had her opponent. She loses the court battle. In her case, fair procedures worked to the advantage of her opponent. In other cases and capacities, she can hope to benefit from them.

But suppose she is outraged by the court decision. She can continue along the fair procedure route and appeal the court decision at higher levels. She can vent her rage by going home and chopping wood. But according to Justice as Fairness advocates, she may not "take the law into her own hands." To do so is to declare that one stands outside society and is at war with society; to do so is to declare oneself a common criminal.

One important qualification should be added here. The most sophisticated presentations of Justice as Fairness focus on fair procedures without ignoring the results. John Rawls' recent *A Theory of Justice* offers two principles of justice. The first essentially advocates fair procedures. The second principle includes the importance of equal results. In Rawls' scheme, fair processes should be combined with equal results wherever practical. But when the two conflict, as is often the case in politics, the first principle must prevail. Ultimately, fair procedures with highly inequal results must be considered just.

Justice As Fairness And The Dorm Newspaper

Imagine that your own values are consistent with the Justice as Fairness model. You would most likely comply with the majority's decision to subscribe to the *Gazette* even though you disagreed with it. Moreover, you would probably refuse to assist Pat Baker in her "criminal" plan. Your telephone conversation with Pat might continue along these lines.

"Look here," you say, "if we followed your plan we would be no better than those Ku Klux Klan guys. They use the vote whenever they can win. And when they lose, they use unfair methods like scare tactics, cross-burnings, and even bombings. On a less violent level, we'd be doing the same thing, using the vote when we can win and resorting to theft when we lose. No one wins when sheer force opposes sheer force."

Pat disagrees. She says it's not the same thing. The Klan uses unfair tactics to achieve unjust ends like racial oppression and white domination. And if they ever get their way, we would be back to slavery, a slavery which would include blacks and Catholics, Jews, Chicanos, Native Americans, and others. She says that her goals include equal treatment for everyone and an egalitarian society: "That is why we are different from them. We are justified in using these tactics because racists must be stopped by whatever means possible!"

You agree that the goals of the Klan are immoral and your goals are not. But you add that Klan members have the opposite view, believing their goals are moral and your goals are immoral. Who is right? You tell Pat, "I think you are right, but I am not an ultimate moral authority willing to force my moral views on others. Everyone would force their views unless we abide by fair procedures."

Pat now examines your notion of fair procedures. She makes two points. First, she establishes that racists have rarely, if ever, granted blacks a chance to compete fairly. If blacks were not legally excluded from voting or holding office, they were indirectly excluded through devices like literacy tests, poll taxes, and gerrymandering. "But," you interrupt, "these have been declared unconstitutional and are being eliminated through fair procedures. Anyway, it's not relevant to the dorm. All blacks may vote in our meetings."

"Second," she says harshly, "even when blacks win the right to vote, they are both a racial and a political minority. Consequently, in the name of majority rule, whites can continue to pass laws or make decisions which oppress black people. This is precisely the condition which exists in this dorm."

You come up with your final suggestion. "Why not go to the Board of Trustees? Show them that this decision is opposed to University bylaws banning racial discrimination on campus facilities. Meanwhile, we could try to get the support of more dormies. It will take time but we still have some chance of winning."

With the obvious intention of ending the conversation, Pat Baker comments, "Sure, appeal to the lily-white Board of Trustees and appeal to the lily-white majority of students. You have been living in a white world!" She hangs up. You feel that you understand her anger but still disagree with her decision. Without fair procedures and general compliance with their results, people would be unable to live together.

JUSTICE AS GOODNESS
Challenging Legitimacy

By the middle of the nineteenth century, the idea of Justice as Fairness was well entrenched in a number of Western cultures. It was developed further and employed to legitimize various representative governments and capitalist marketplaces. A number of critics were extremely dissatisfied with these political systems. They believed that the capitalist marketplace resulted in a highly unequal society marked by fabulously wealthy owners and extremely impoverished workers. Many of the critics believed formal institutions such as electoral processes, legislative systems, and judiciaries functioned to protect the privileges of the wealthy and powerful. As they saw it, Justice as Fairness was an ideology used to legitimize this system.

Briefly, the critics argued as follows. Even in the fairest economic marketplace, there are winners and losers. Today's winners can reinvest their profits to expand, take advantage of economies of scale and technological improvements, engage in research and development, and ultimately capture a larger share of the marketplace. The rich have broad opportunities for becoming richer. But today's losers lack investment capital. They must work for someone else to secure their subsistence and to save for investment. This is extremely difficult, for employers pay the lowest wages possible. And, in time, it becomes more expensive to invest in a new enterprise because one must be able to purchase machines and skilled labor. Even if today's loser can save and reinvest tomorrow, the first recession is likely to wipe him out, but the richer, more powerful firms can afford to ride out the storm. According to the critics, there is a natural tendency for the free marketplace to become dominated by a few, monopolistic firms.

These firms can then use their vast economic resources to win favors from political officials. They can use their wealth to support the election of "trusted" candidates or to persuade citizens that their interests are the nation's interests. Or, they can use their tremendous economic power to put pressure on politicians already in office. For example, if you lodge a complaint about a local official, you can be ignored. But if the director of Chase Manhatten Bank lodges a complaint, he cannot be ignored. His investment decisions have a tremendous effect on the overall health of the economy and on many people's everyday lives. He can offer sympathetic politicians tremendous benefits in and out of office; and he can bring them much pain through his connections in various government agencies, the media, educational institutions, and other economic institutions. It is clearly in the interest of most politicians to cooperate with this man.

In summary, the critics argued that the fairest economic procedures were advantageous to those with an early edge in the competition. In time, monopolization replaces competition. The existence of a few economic giants then reverberates in the political system. Regardless of how fair the electoral, legislative, and judicial processes are, economic power and wealth will be converted into political privilege for the very few.

Responding to the critics, Justice as Fairness advocates occasionally admitted that many procedures were imperfect and that decisions were sometimes deplorable. But they maintained that their ideas were most practical. Imperfect procedures could be made fairer through reforms and fair procedures would spawn less deplorable decisions. Nevertheless, they challenged the critics to suggest a superior alternative. The critics obliged with Justice as Goodness; a system of values aimed at contesting the legitimacy of capitalist republics and at legitimizing a more communally oriented alternative.

The Logic of Justice as Goodness

The logic of this alternative set of political values can be summarized as follows:

1. To be truly human is to think and act with concern for other humans.

2. Social and political systems based on competition compel people to think and to act with concern for themselves; such people are "alienated" from their own humanity.

3. Material abundance in the modern era renders economic competition unnecessary; people can cooperate to fulfill their basic material needs.

4. Planned economic cooperation is a primary basis for allowing people to develop their concerns for other people. It is a basis for political cooperation.

5. The good society is the one in which economic cooperation and political cooperation are the characteristic modes of human interaction.

6. Justice concerns the steps necessary for creating the good society; Justice is Goodness.

Let us examine more closely this logic and consider the kind of political system it legitimizes.

Animals behave according to instincts. They neither think about other animals as potential fellows do nor act toward other animals as potential comrades do. Rather, animals follow their instincts to maximize their chances for survival. Human beings are similar to animals in that they too must be concerned with self survival. But, the human species is unique in two ways. First, people have the capacity to think abstractly and therefore to plan methods of maximizing survival chances for themselves and others. Second, people have the capacity to act in accord with their plans; they can live their lives in ways that allow them to develop their many capacities in harmony with others. In brief, to be *truly* human is to take other people as the object of one's thoughts and actions; to live in a truly human society is to live in a community where everyone takes everyone else as the object of his thought and action.

However social systems based on competition compel people to put their personal survival and gratification first. Assume that two good friends find themselves competing for the same job during a depression. The situation is structured so that each must view the other as an obstacle to personal survival, to family survival, and to minor gratifications. Friendships very often dissolve. Assume that many people are competing for a few jobs. There is little likelihood that many friendships will be formed in the process. At best, human relationships will be instrumental rather than affectionate. People will cooperate with one another to the extent that they see one another as useful in providing a competitive edge. And when they see the aid of others as obsolete or counterproductive, they will discard these relationships. The reason has little to do with any natural selfishness or greed in human nature. Rather, the economic or political marketplaces are structured so that one person's gain is another's loss. Here we act out the animal aspect of our lives but are separated or alienated from our essential humanity.

A competitive social structure is sometimes a product of scarcity. Without an adequate food supply, we fight for each morsel lest we succumb to starvation; without adequate consumer demand, businessmen must compete with one another to keep their particular companies solvent. Think of your own classroom situation. Your professor might announce that she grades according to a bell-shaped curve: 5 percent of the class will receive A's, 20 percent B's, 50 percent C's and so on. You know that everytime another student does better than you on an exam or paper, your chance for a high grade diminishes. It is in your interest not only to turn in your best performance but also to see that others turn in relatively poor performances. You will cooperate with classmates, in a study group perhaps, only to the extent that you believe cooperation is more beneficial to you than to them. As they are likely to follow the same strategy, most modes of cooperation will be avoided.

Your professor, however, might announce that it is possible for everyone in the class to receive A's if everyone turns in superior performances. All modes of cooperation now become conceivable. You have no reason for not helping others and they have no reason for not helping you. And through a cooperative study group, all of you may raise your grades and, not incidently, develop new friendships. Similarly, a noncompetitive economic system would allow producers to work out common plans for maximizing their common material values and developing community relationships.

Economic abundance in advanced Western nations considerably simplifies the problem of nurturing human cooperation. Within these nations, it is now possible to fulfill virtually everyone's basic needs: food, clothing, shelter, and health care. If we can cooperate to use our vast economic resources to the benefit of everyone, within and across national boundaries, competition for scarce jobs, for resources, or for government aid would diminish dramatically. And possibly, we could begin to develop our multifaceted capacities in harmony with others; we would have little need to fear that the help we give others today will be used against us tomorrow.

If such cooperation is possible, why does it not become a reality? Although many of us would love to opt out of the competitive rat race or "modern times," a few economic giants have a very strong interest in promoting an economic system based on competition and private profit rather than on public or collective needs. Their interest is an effective one to the extent that (1) they can use their wealth to persuade citizens to support an economic system in which individuals must compete with one another and (2) they can use their political influence to assure that legislators will pass laws protecting that system. In short, because of the extraordinary benefits a few people derive from competition, most people remain alienated from their true humanity.

The only real answer to human alienation is to recognize and act upon the need to restructure the economic system. People must use whatever means are available to dislodge economic elites and their political representatives from power. And then they must reorganize the economic system in such a way that cooperation rather than competition will be nurtured and rewarded. For some thinkers, such an economic system would mean a return to small-scaled artisanries and businesses wherever possible; other thinkers believe that the public must collectively plan the use of society's material resources. Despite their differences, both groups agree that a considerably higher level of economic equality is a prerequisite to nurturing greater coooperation and to minimizing alienation.

When greater economic equality exists, there will be no great economic giants effectively blocking political cooperation. People could collectively decide on measures necessary for eliminating industrial pollution without fearing that a major corporation, profiting from pollution, will block their plans. Or people could collectively decide what part of society's resources should be allocated to national defense without fearing that a major defense industry will blow an international crises out of proportion for profit. Political decisions could be made on the basis of the human community's needs and not on the corporate community's profits.

Justice means two things here. First, justice implies an effort to restructure the economic system, to redistribute wealth more equally, and to plan resource allocation in the interest of the whole community. Second, justice means the establishment of the good society—the society in which people can overcome their separation and develop their unique capacities in harmony with others. Political justice is one aspect of both definitions. It involves restructuring the economic system and nurturing the truly human in all people. Justice then is taking whatever steps are necessary to create this good society.

What does Justice as Goodness mean in terms of fair procedures? At the very least, it means that fair procedures are secondary. Fair procedures are certainly a civilized way of resolving conflicts, but conflict-resolution is never satisfactory in itself. Some resolutions are just and others are not. A conflict that is fairly resolved with competition rather than cooperation as the end product is an unjust resolution. At the very most, Justice as Goodness implies that procedural fairness is not possible in a society where there are winners and losers in economic competition. Regardless of the fairness of the procedures themselves, the winners tend to be best able to take advantage of the procedures while the losers are less able. We may all be equal before the bar of justice, but somehow the rich man who can afford the best attorneys and years of litigation is a little more equal. Procedural fairness cannot be gauged without taking into account the unequal ability of various groups to employ fair procedures.

Finally, insofar as people succeed in pressing toward the good society, issues of procedural fairness are likely to become less pressing. When people are generally cooperative and equal, they are more likely to work out a consensus or compromise among themselves than vote on every issue, seek out Robert's Rules of Order, or call in a neutral third party. Since this may sound quite utopian to many of you, consider the following mundane occurence: Five friends get together on Saturday night to go to a movie but have difficulty agreeing on which movie. After some discussion, they agree to compromise; perhaps they follow Brook's advice this week and Tom's next time. Suddenly Billy discovers that he is short of money. The others chip in to pay his way. Billy promises to pay them back, but they tell him to forget it. Billy will help them out when they need it. The quintet go off to their movie; no votes, no parliamentary maneuvers, no arbitrary neutrality. The bond of friendship makes it all possible. Now imagine a society composed of groups like this quintet. Perhaps Justice as Goodness becomes more conceivable. And if you are still having difficulty, consider Justice as Goodness as a set of values that legitimize a society and a polity worth striving for. Decisions which move us in that direction would then be considered just.

Justice as Goodness and the Dorm Newspaper

Were your values consistent with Justice as Goodness, you would be more likely to go along with Pat Baker's plan; but you would not necessarily go along with it. However, the nature of your telephone conversation with her now would be radically different than before, something like this:

"Let's look at your plan more closely," you suggest. "Will trashing the *Gazette* every morning accomplish our ends?" On the one hand, people who might not otherwise take you seriously will and they will therefore examine the feelings on racism more fully. And in the process, they might discover that racism is a separation among people that dehumanizes both the racist and the victim." So far, Pat agrees with your analysis. But now you pose a question, "On the other hand, isn't it also conceivable that many students will be angry with us? They will resent our actions. They will either consider us no better than the Klan people or they will examine their feelings and discover that they believe racism is justifiable; our "criminal" actions will be further evidence.

Pat suggests that even this likihood is not necessarily bad. It brings people's racism out into the open where it can be directly challenged. You can then begin to show them why racism is dehumanizing to all involved.

"But," you interrupt, "you are ignoring the causes underlying racism. Black slaves were brought to this country to serve as instruments for plantation owners' profits. Even after emancipation, blacks have served as a source of cheap labor and as a psychological standard against which poor whites can feel superior. This makes it very difficult for whites and blacks to cooperate with one another. And it certainly benefits economic elites who would rather have workers fighting with one another than united against elites. Our trashing the newspaper will have no effect here."

"Oh yes it will," Pat contends. "During the Civil Rights Movement economic boycotts were proven effective. They give business people a self-interest in supporting racial equality. Boycotts ensure that profits will diminish if businesses do not support racial equality. If we can get the dorm to boycott the *Gazette*, we can then begin to work with other dorms and other student units. With the campus as a conceivable base, a campus-wide boycott of the *Gazette* may be very effective. Meanwhile, the more students we can involve in the boycott, the more we can give them a real experience of interracial cooperation. Actions," Pat concludes, "often speak louder than words."

"You may be right," you tell Pat, "but then why waste our time with this dorm subscription? Perhaps we should use our time to organize a general boycott. Then we could raise the issue all over campus." Pat disagrees. She suggests that you need an example of success before you go university-wide.

At this point, one of you suggests a meeting with other sympathizers. The whole group could discuss possible strategies and develop some consensus. Surely something can be worked out because you all agree that the racial separation of people is an injustice; you all agree that racial equality is a good cause worth fighting for today.

POLITICAL VALUES AND POLITICAL IDEOLOGIES A set of political values consists of moral standards for evaluating the political world. A political ideology contains an additional element: a prescription for how these moral standards should direct political actions. In other words, political ideologies are action-oriented. If we add an action-orientation to Justice as Fairness, we are likely to arrive at liberalism; if we add an action-orientation to Justice as Goodness, we are more likely to arrive at socialism. There are, however, important exceptions.

Liberalism Great liberal thinkers have always shared the belief that individual rights ought to be the moral basis for all politics. Famous liberal documents like the Declaration of Independence are filled with statements about individual rights to life and liberty. But the problem with supporting the primacy of individual rights is that some individuals are willing to pursue their rights by trampling on the rights of others. For example, it is not unusual for a controversial person, exercising his right to free speech, to be shouted down by hecklers in the audience exerting their right to free speech. Furthermore, we all recognize circumstances in which free speech should be abridged, e.g., shouting "fire!" in a crowded auditorium. How are individual rights to be reconciled or limited in practice?

On the whole, liberals have suggested that reconciliation and limits are justifiable only if individuals consent to them through fair procedures. In theory, people may consent to elect a representative government that passes laws and enforces laws specifying modes of reconciliation and limits. And if people consent to such a government, they essentially promise to obey the decisions of that government; their consent entails an obligation to obey. Traditionally, this argument has been called the social contract theory.

Were individual rights and consent of the governed the only basic values of liberalism, we would have to say that Justice as Fairness and liberalism are perfectly consistent: justice concerns the fair procedure of consent as a means of resolving conflicts among individual rights. Liberals might disagree about what acts constitute consent, but they agree that once consent is given, it is only fair that individuals obey authoritative outcomes, win or lose. But liberalism has a third basic element.

Liberals have always held dear the right to private property. Individuals have the right to own, to use, and to dispose of their property in whatsoever way pleases them. They may use their property to grow wheat or to lie fallow; they may sell their property or give it away in a lottery, if that pleases them. Like other rights, conflicts of property rights or essential limitations are established through fair procedures like consent of the governed. In the past, governments' main economic function in liberal societies has been to arbitrate property disputes and set some limits on individual property rights (e.g., a man who owns property with a stream running through it may not dam that stream and deny his neighbor access to its water).

In advanced industrial societies, conflicts over property rights become extremely complex. Individuals have rights to own property, but do corporations? Do property rights include the right to tear up hillsides to mine for coal? Do condominium builders have the right to buy and to build on limited coastal lands? Does the right of a factory owner to dispose of his property freely include the right to exclude workers (fire them) because workers unionize, talk back, or vote for the opposing political party? These questions could continue indefinitely. The conceivable and actual conflicts between property rights and individual rights to life (to earn a livelihood?) and liberty (to live decently?) are infinite.

How do liberals respond to these conflicts? Most liberals respond in the traditional way of referring all conflicts to arbitration by fair procedures. Whenever new conflicts arise, individuals vote for representatives who will pass laws settling the disputes, and the laws are applied in the courts. Conflict-resolution through fair procedures is the preferred response of liberals. The increase in the number of conflicts and the growing complexity of the conflicts only mean that government will have to become larger and more active in order to deal with them. This has been the case in most industrial societies.

Nevertheless, at least some liberals feel uncomfortable with this piecemeal approach. They believe that some conflicts are so pervasive and have such a negative impact on most people that the public interest must be considered. For example, consider consumer safety. It is in the interest of most individuals in a society to be offered goods for sale that are not detrimental to their health. Yet, some companies manufacture goods containing dangerous chemicals, defective parts, or perhaps hidden sharp objects. Imagine how difficult and time-consuming it would be for each potential consumer to analyze every purchase; imagine how difficult and time-comsuming it would be for each consumer to sue each manufacturer each time a conflict arose over a purchase. Would not individual rights to purchase safe goods be better protected if all marketable goods had to pass government inspection, if all manufacturers had consumer representatives on their boards, and if all suits against manufacturers covered all cases rather than one individual case? Now extend this logic to the rights of workers to decent employment, decent working conditions, and decent salaries; extend it to the rights of residents to healthy air and water, or to the rights of poor people to decent food, clothing, and shelter.

These quantitative extensions sometimes result in a qualitative change in the way liberals apply their values to politics. Traditional individualism is replaced by the public interest of all individuals. The importance of individual conflict is now secondary to the general welfare of citizens. Politics becomes less of a set of fair processes for resolving conflict and more of an organizational means for nurturing the public good. Government may legitimately regulate the economic realm insofar as the public good requires severe restrictions on individuals' property rights. Taking one more step, some liberals seem to cross socialist ideological boundaries when they argue that the public good requires government ownership of some of the means of production.

Public interest liberals (sometimes called radical liberals, progressive liberals, populist liberals), given their action-orientation toward the interests individuals share in common; toward extensive overlap between politics and the economy; and toward public good; are more likely to view Justice as Goodness. For this reason, I believe that the following statement is accurate:

On the whole, the value set I have called Justice as Fairness is consistent with the ideology of liberalism. For some liberals, however, individual rights are better understood and protected when the good of the entire society is the basis of political action. These latter liberals are likely to see Justice as Goodness.

For this reason I have avoided calling Justice as Fairness the basis for liberal ideology, even though it usually is.

Socialism Great socialist thinkers, though interested in individual liberty, generally agree that human equality ought to be the moral basis of politics. Although the precise meaning of human equality varies among socialist thinkers, it generally includes the following statement: All people should have an equal right to develop their capacities in harmony with others. This is possible only when all people are guaranteed the ability to fulfill their material needs. Such a guarantee is conceivable only when all people exert equal control over the production and distribution of society's material resources. Consequently, people's equal right to develop their capacities is possible only when people collectively control economic decisions.

Socialists often disagree among themselves about the most appropriate means of collectively controlling economic decisions. Some socialists believe that the workers in a factory should control decisions regarding the processes of production, the goods to be produced, the investments to be made, and the disposal of the goods. Other socialists believe that the community, through elected representatives, should plan production in ways consistent with members' needs and abilities to develop their capacities. Still other socialists believe that a centralized state apparatus is necessary for planning and executing such production plans. Whatever the means, socialists agree on the ends: a harmonious society in which alienation gives way to egalitarian relationships.

This understanding of the ideology of socialism is perfectly consistent with the political value set of Justice as Goodness: justice is concerned with constructing a society where individual conflict and competition give way to social harmony and consensus. This consistency is somewhat questionable, however, when one takes into account the action-orientations of socialists.

Most socialists believe that the good society cannot be achieved through fair procedures in liberal societies. Too many citizens are fooled into believing that competition is natural, that liberal political institutions are neutral, or that no alternative system is possible. Too many powerful politicians and captains of industry will use "fair" procedures to protect themselves and their narrow interests. For example, although it is possible for citizens to win piecemeal reforms in legislatures or courtrooms, those reforms rarely are basic steps toward the good society. Antitrust laws have been won in many industrial societies; but instead of protecting workers or consumers against monopoly with any consistency, they are more often used to outlaw workers' or consumers' organizations, strikes, boycotts, and so on. Positive steps toward the good society require that people, even a minority of people, take decisive actions to raise public consciousness and to challenge elite power. In some cases, these positive steps include revolutionary upheaval.

When socialists are challenged to defend their willingness to use illegal and sometimes violent tactics, they generally have two responses. One response is that the illegality or violence of their tactics must be viewed against the illegality and violence that regularly occurs in liberal societies. Illegal practices like price-fixing are common among companies who can count on friendly political figures not to enforce appropriate laws. And consider the psychological and material violence suffered by workers when they accept poor pay, boring jobs, and unhealthy working conditions because they have no other choice but starvation (or dehumanizing welfare).

A second response is that major historical changes always involve illegality and violence. Consider the American Revolution or the Civil War as only two examples among many. Socialists generally hope to minimize illegal and violent means, but they argue such means are justified to the extent that they are necessary for attaining a just end: an egalitarian community.

Some socialists, however, are much more hesitant to adopt this position. They are very sensitive to the fact that all means are not justified by good ends; they are sensitive to the experience of Stalinism where, in the name of good ends, tremendous repression took place. These socialists, or social democrats, have a very different action-orientation.

Very much as liberals do, these socialists believe that individual rights and the consent of the governed must be protected under all circumstances. On the one hand, this will provide socialists with the freedom of assembly and speech needed to win general support. On the other hand, once general support is won, people can use legitimate consent processes like voting to legislate socialism into existence. The more that people accept socialist values, the more they will vote for socialist parties. The more socialists in office, the better the chance that government will effectively regulate or control major economic institutions. In time, this control can be used to eliminate competition and introduce an economic cooperation that will be the ultimate basis for achieving communal harmony.

Social democrats such as these are more likely to view Justice as Fairness. They will look at individual conflicts in the hope that they can be resolved in ways consistent with establishing greater equality. They will support fair procedures with the hope that a majority of people will support socialism and vote socialists into power. Conversely, they will look askance on either liberals or socialists willing to adopt any means in the name of the public good or the socialist community. Stalinism is an extreme that reveals one possible implication of the Justice as Goodness approach: forcing people to conform to a vision of goodness they may, at the moment, oppose. This will certainly not end alienation; it is more likely to increase it.

Given the disagreement in action-orientations among socialists, I have not labeled Justice as Goodness as the necessary value system of socialists. But the following statement is generally accurate:

On the whole, the value set I have called Justice as Goodness is consistent with the ideology of socialism. For some socialists, however, the good society is better achieved when fair procedures are supported. These latter socialists are more likely to see Justice as Fairness.

One important qualification must be added. When I say that liberals tend to support Justice as Fairness, I do not mean to imply that they are not concerned with the goodness of ends because generally they are. Rather, I am saying that their *primary* moral view concerns the fairness of procedures. This also applies to social democrats who disagree with many liberal ends. Similarly, when I say that socialists generally support Justice as Goodness, I do not mean to imply that they consider the fairness of the procedures irrelevant. Rather, their first priority concerns achieving good ends. So too with many public interest liberals who practice civil disobedience in the name of rather different ends.

SUMMARY AND CONCLUSION

I have previously argued that people are likely to see the political world through a lens consistent with their political values. In this chapter, I have considered two clusters of political values: (1) Justice as Fairness and (2) Justice as Goodness. These two clusters represent two basic sets of political values that many people use when judging what is significant in politics and what is preferable or undesirable in politics. I do not believe that these two value clusters are the only systematic sets on political values or that they are employed only in the ways outlined. Rather, they are meant to be theoretical center-points around which many variations radiate.

People will evaluate politics very differently depending on which cluster they find more attractive. Adherents of Justice as Fairness are likely to be concerned if individual rights are equally protected, if processes of conflict-resolution favor no particular party, and if decisions are administered without discrimination. Advocates of Justice as Fairness are likely to be liberals though they may be social democrats.

Adherents of Justice as Goodness are likely to have other concerns. Does a particular decision constitute a step toward greater cooperation? In what ways can greater public control of the economy help promote economic equality? What kinds of economic equality are necessary for providing people a foundation upon which they can make consensual political decisions? People who ask these questions are likely to be socialists, though they may be public interest liberals.

We again come to the point of considering which set of alternatives is preferable. Most liberals will tell you that justice *really is* fairness; most socialists will tell you that justice *really is* goodness. Who are we to believe? Can we step outside this ideological debate and examine it objectively? Some people suggest we can. Since most of us agree that democracy is a goal worth striving for, we could examine democracy to see which cluster of values is most appropriate to democracy; Justice as Fairness or Justice as Goodness. But beware: adherents of both clusters usually believe that they are also advocates of democracy.

SELECTED REFERENCES

Crozier, Michel J., Huntington, Samuel P. and Watanuki, Joji. *The Crisis of Democracy*. New York: New York University Press, 1975.

Dahl, Robert. *A Preface to Democratic Theory*. Chicago: University of Chicago Press, 1956.

Gewirth, Alan. "Political Justice" in *Social Justice*, edited by R.B. Brandt. Englewood Cliffs, N. J.: Prentice-Hall, 1962.

Kann, Mark E. "The Dialectic of Consent Theory" in *Journal of Politics* 40 (1978), pp. 386-408.

Macpherson, C.B. *The Life and Times of Liberal Democracy*. Oxford: Oxford University Press, 1977.

Miliband, Ralph. *Marxism and Politics*. Oxford: Oxford University Press, 1977.

Nozick, Robert. *Anarchy, State, and Utopia*. New York: Basic Books, 1974.

Rawls, John. *A Theory of Justice*. Cambridge, Mass.: Harvard University Press, 1971.

Wolfe, Alan. *The Limits of Legitimacy*. New York: The Free Press, 1977.

Is an adherent of democracy more likely to believe that justice is fairness or goodness? We could look at the writings of democratic theorists to answer this question, but we would be disappointed. Were we to read John Locke or Robert Dahl, we would feel certain that democracy is consistent with Justice as Fairness alone. But then we might read Jean-Jacques Rousseau or Karl Marx to discover that democracy is consistent with justice as Goodness alone. Like **politics**, **democracy** is a contested concept and many sophisticated thinkers disagree on its essential meaning.

Nevertheless, people do have preferred visions of democracy. On the whole, Americans and American political scientists believe that democracy consists of a set of fair processes similar to those that exist in America. But some Americans and American political scientists argue that democracy is more closely related to egalitarian community life, which is basically absent in America. In other words, people who are basically satisfied that America is a democracy tend to define democracy in procedural terms akin to Justice as Fairness; people who believe America is undemocratic tend to define democracy in communitarian terms akin to Justice as Goodness. Why is this the case?

Fairness and American Democracy

Since the founding of their nation, Americans have been nurtured on the procedural theories, concepts, and words of John Locke. The European forbearers of Americans engaged in violent conflict over various versions of the good society. Americans hoped to avoid this conflict by allowing individuals the right to pursue their private versions of goodness. America was to be a nation in which every individual had the opportunity and the right to define his or her own happiness. Government was not to create the good society; it was merely to arbitrate individual conflicts.

With this vision in mind, American institutions were framed according to the Justice as Fairness criteria. A few of America's political institutions aimed at allowing all individuals an equal right to pursue private goals and receive a fair decision in case of conflicts are: one person-one vote, regular elections, separation of powers, the ethic of bargaining and compromise, due process in the courts and the freedom of speech, assembly, and press. Moreover, the institution of American law was framed to protect private property, contracts, and investment choices to promote fair dealings in the economic sector. And throughout American culture, the notion of fair play (e.g., sportsmanship) came to prevail. In children's games, accusing another participant of playing unfairly (e.g., breaking the rules, cheating, etc.) is tantamount to moral condemnation. As such, children reproduce the Justice as Fairness attitude prevalent in America.

Today, much if not most of American political discussion focuses on the fairness of procedures or activities. Political dirty tricks, partisan judicial behavior or police brutality are often considered serious, reprehensible acts even if done to achieve good ends. Procedures that deny equal rights to people because of race or sex are often condemned as unfair despite the fact that many people do not want blacks or women to play a more prominent political role. And on the whole, Americans of all ideologies hope to achieve their diverse goals through electoral coalitions, lobbying, court battles, and winning public support rather than through **illegal** means of **usurpation.** America is unique in this respect. Most other nations have substantial groups of dissidents willing to forsake established procedures to attain their goals, but America has few such groups. Taking into account America's tremendous wealth, it is not surprising that the United States has had one of the most stable political systems in recent history.

This brief history and analysis helps explain why most Americans and American political scientists equate Justice as Fairness with democracy. If everyone has a fair chance of being heard and registering their opinions, and if everyone has a fair chance of defining and achieving personal happiness; then America must be a de-

mocracy because the people are politically equal and sovereign. No individual or group has the right to usurp power. All that need be worked out is a system by which people can translate their varied and diverse views into public policy. In America, this translation is achieved through two systems of public representation.

The first system of representation is open elections. Through elections, regulated by the Constitution and a number of laws aimed at guaranteeing fairness, people select candidates who represent their wishes and who translate those wishes into public policy. Unfortunately, this mechanism has several major weaknesses. How are elected officials to be held accountable between elections? How are an amorphous mass of votes to be converted into a specific public message? How are elected officials to be sensitized to the intensity of voters on particular issues? The electoral process does not deal well with these questions. A second mechanism of representation is necessary.

In America, any group of people who believes its representatives are not reflecting its views, or are not properly following its electoral mandate, or are not sensitive to voter intensity, has the right to register its preferences and complaints. This right is exercised informally. Groups can put pressure on representatives by giving or withholding campaign funds, by amassing public opinion in support of or against representatives, by providing or withholding pertinent information from representatives, or by badgering representatives constantly. These pressure groups add a new dimension to public representation. Nevertheless, any particular pressure group is likely to find itself opposed by another pressure group. For example, during recent school busing controversies, school board members felt pressures coming from both pro-busing and antibusing groups.

Consequently, America's electoral system is complemented by the *pluralism* of open group competition for influence. And because these competing groups also play a critical role during elections, the electoral system may also be considered a pluralistic arena. Pluralism is a fair system of representation because no individual or group is barred from the competition and no individual or group has a right to monopolize the competition. Formal elections and pluralist competition form the core of American representative democracy.

Those people who believe that America is a democracy are likely to define democracy in terms of pluralism. Furthermore, because American pluralism and American political norms are so thoroughly entwined with the notion of fairness, there are good reasons why an American pluralist would prefer to view Justice as Fairness. If American democracy is just and is based on fair competition (in elections and among groups), does it not follow that justice must be primarily related to fairness? Yes, answer most defenders of American democracy.

Goodness and American Democracy

Not all Americans equate Justice as Fairness with American democracy. Since the founding of the nation, there have always been those who have argued that America's sense of fair

play has masked substantial and un-democratic inequalities. Let us see why.

There has always been the question of how really fair are American procedures at any particular moment. How fair is the electoral process when particular groups are legally prevented from participating? At one time or another, the poor, minorities, and women have not had the right to vote. And even when they have had the right to vote, poll taxes, literacy tests, or resident requirements effectively prevented them from doing so. In these and other ways, large groups of Americans have been prevented from engaging in politics or from running for office. Similarly, the fairness of America's economic system has been repeatedly questioned. How fair is economic competition when a few corporate giants monopolize materials and markets, fix prices, and exclude new competitors? The critics, of course, respond that fairness is more of a theory than an actual practice in America. Why?

The gap between theory and practice results from well-placed groups using their positions to secure further advantages. Since the wealthy, white and male Americans have dominated the political system from the very beginning, they have used their power to maintain their position. Since a few corporate giants emerged, they too have used their position to exclude potential challengers. These groups constitute the historical American elites intent on maintaining their more-than-equal powers, and they are intent on winning an unfair share of political and economic benefits in America.

Critics who have pointed to this gap between theory and practice in American democracy sometimes suggest that reforms can narrow the gap. After all, voting rights are more widespread today than ever and government is regulating economic giants more fully than ever—but there is still some distance to go before fair competition is restored. Other critics suggest that the gap is so wide that nothing short of civil disobedience and violent conflict will narrow it. But no matter how reformist or revolutionary these critics may be, they agree on one thing: America can become more democratic only if greater fairness in competition is realized. In other words, these critics, along with the pluralists, equate democracy with Justice as Fairness.

Second, however, there has always been an alternative group of critics who argue that even the fairest procedures, in theory or practice, do not constitute democracy. Fair procedures, at best, provide equal opportunities, but democracy is a matter of equal results. By this criterion, America is and always has been undemocratic.

Consider the three examples below. In all cases, assume that procedures are perfectly fair. Then notice that despite equal opportunities, the results of competition are likely to favor one group.

1. You are an American Indian living among 30,000 other American Indians in a particular state. You campaign for office on the basis of Indian rights and demands. Virtually every Indian in the state supports you and some non-Indians do as well. Nevertheless, you experience tremendous difficulty in getting campaign funding, access to the media, and consideration as a viable candidate.

You lose the election. After all, your 30-40,000 supporters constitute a small percentage of voters in the state. The same holds true for black candidates and chicano candidates. Consequently, while minorities are an important segment of state population, they do not succeed in getting one representative of their own into office. Once again, state government posts are filled by whites.

Because whites basically control campaign funding, the major parties, and the media, they can usually block the candidacy of minority candidates. Because minorities rarely constitute a majority of voters in broad geographical districts, they rarely can win over white candidates. The result here is that even though minorities make up a substantial portion of the population, they are unrepresented. Of course, it is conceivable that a minority candidate can win an election with the support of white backers. But because this candidate is so indebted to white backers, he will be more likely to represent white interests than represent minority interests.

2. You yourself are relatively wealthy but are elected to office on a platform aimed at helping poor people. Like all representatives, you will be pressured by many groups. Since groups representing the wealthy tend to be better organized, more fiscally sound, and more influential, a good part of your time will be occupied with these groups. They will offer you financial support, sophisticated policy alternatives, and even favorable public opinion if you support their interests.

But, if you oppose them, they will cut off financial support and organize a media campaign against you.

What can your poor constituents offer or threaten? Very little. Concerned with everyday survival, the poor lack the time, resources, and education to develop a cohesive viewpoint, to organize pressure, or to keep a close watch on your actions. Consequently, when you confront an issue which pits the interests of the poor against the demands of the wealthy, you find a way to please everyone: offer the poor, symbolic or token rewards, but support tangible policies in the interests of the wealthy. You can later rationalize how this is really in the long-term interest of the poor.

In this example, even the representative sympathetic to the poor ends up supporting the interests of society's privileged. The wealthy have the resources and infuence necessary for converting their demands into political reality. Although a few representatives may be able to withstand such pressures, they are unique. Regardless of fair procedures, the poor tend to be underrepresented and the wealthy tend to be overrepresented in America.

3. Under unusual circumstances, lower class Americans are able to use fair electoral and pluralist procedures to elect their own representatives and to pressure them into defending their interests. We must now consider the ability of a lower class representative to exert political influence over policy.

If our lower class representatives number very few, as is likely to be the case, what influence will they have in state legislatures or national govern-

ment? They will most likely be placed on insignificant committees chaired by representatives who will stymy their efforts. Their few votes will not be enough to allow them to raise their issues, let alone call votes on them. At best, they might exert minimal influence during close votes on issues which concern other representatives. In sum, their ability to exert influence on behalf of their lower class constituents will be minimal.

This example summarizes and concludes the other two examples. Minorities, poor people, and ordinary workers have little chance of exerting much influence in America. The barriers to electing their own candidates, of getting officials to represent their interests, or of getting their own representatives to be effective are usually prohibitive, despite all the fair procedures in the world. These examples illustrate the critics' point that fair procedures have undemocratic results: wealthy, white males continue to reap the lion's share of political benefits.

Critics with this perspective are likely to emerge from or identify with the plight of the poor, the minorities, and the women of America. They explain the inequality of results in terms of (1) the vast economic inequalities which allow the privileged to exert undue influence and (2) historical racism and sexism. They conclude that Justice as Fairness implies continued political impotence for the poor, minorities, and women. Certainly, a system where such systematic inequalities exist must be considered *elitist*.

What can appropriately be called a democracy? A system in which everyone can exert equal influence and benefit equally from political decisions is only possible when people have the same economic resources to bring to politics, when people do not compete with one another nor discriminate against one another but feel a mutual concern, and when people think and act on the basis of their common human situation. Only under these circumstances is it likely that equal voice will result in equal benefits.

Of course, this vision of democracy is consistent with the notion of Justice as Goodness. Democracy is the good society. Were America to become more democratic, Americans need be less concerned with procedures and more concerned that basic human needs be fulfilled and warm human relationships be developed. Consequently, those who believe America is not democratic because It Institutionalizes "fair" competition rather than communal relations have good reasons for believing that justice is goodness.

Political Values and American Democracy

Those who view America as a pluralist arena of electoral and group competition have good reasons for believing that justice is fairness which, in turn, gives them good reasons for preferring the politics as conflict-resolution model. So too for those who view American politics as elitist; they have good reasons for believing justice is goodness and for choosing the politics as community-building model. Let us add a third tier to our two logics:

	Logic I	Logic II
Definition of Politics	Conflict-Resolution	Community-Building
	↑	↑
Political Values	Justice as Fairness	Justice as Goodness
	↑	↑
American Politics	Pluralism	Elitism

Again, the arrows indicate that people with particular views of American politics have good reasons for adopting a particular set of political values. Those who basically accept Logic I hold a set of political preconceptions which allows them to view America as democratic because it has fair procedures for resolving conflicts peacefully. Those who cluster around Logic II have a set of political preconceptions which impels them to view America as elitist because it supports political and social inequalities inconsistent with egalitarian community life.

Neither Logic I nor Logic II is superior in any absolute sense. Each logic is a set of systematic preconceptions that Americans and American political scientists bring to their political studies. To the extent that these preconceptions are ignored, adherents of each will have a difficult time talking to those who support the alternative model. To the extent that we can elucidate these models, we can better understand how we go about studying politics.

Let us now examine the history and recent developments of the pluralist vs. elitist debate which was popular in the 1960s.

Selected References

Friedman, Milton. *Capitalism and Freedom.* Chicago: University of Chicago Press, 1962.

Galbraith, John Kenneth. *The New Industrial State.* New York: Signet Books, 1967.

Garson, G. David. *Power and Politics in the United States.* Lexington, Mass.: D.C. Heath, 1977.

Heilbroner, Robert L. *Between Capitalism and Socialism.* New York: Vintage, 1970.

Katznelson, Ira and Kesselman, Mark. *The Politics of Power.* New York: Harcourt, Brace, Jovanovich, 1975.

Milbrath, Lester. *Political Participation.* Chicago: Rand McNally, 1965.

Pateman, Carole. *Participation in Democratic Theory.* London: Cambridge University Press, 1970.

Wolff, Robert Paul. *The Poverty of Liberalism.* Boston: Beacon Press, 1968.

4

AMERICAN POLITICS: PLURALISM AND ELITISM

CHAPTER FOUR Is American politics pluralistic and therefore democratic? Or is it elitist and therefore substantially undemocratic? Consider the following story. Assume that the rules are perfectly fair in the sense that they apply equally to everyone. Do both sides have an equal chance of winning? Or does one side have an opportunity to win but have little chance of success? How you and political scientists answer these questions will reveal a good deal about your preconceptions and theirs.

THE LANDLORDS VERSUS THE TENANTS* Imagine that you are one of many elderly, retired tenants in the Elysian Towers apartment complex. Like your neighbors, your major income source is monthly social security checks. Occasionally, you also receive a small check from your children. Although low, this income is adequate for your needs: food, clothing, health care, and rent. Your apartment is old but it is well maintained. Your neighbors sometimes complain about the apartment complex, but they generally agree that Elysian Towers is a nice place to enjoy one's Golden Years modestly. You agree with them.

One day, Elysian Towers' tenants receive a notice that the apartment complex has been sold to a major real estate corporation. A ripple of excitement and fear moves through the complex. New landlords generally mean improvements but also rent hikes. You confide to your neighbors, "Well, I suppose we'll all have to tighten our belts a bit more. But life will just go on as always."

One neighbor is less stoical. Mrs. Adams complains, "Who knows how much the rent will go up? I can't afford much more than I pay now!" You try to reassure her but to little avail.

Within days, you notice men with blueprints circulating between apartment buildings; within hours, rumors circulate among the elderly tenants. A new electrical system, new plumbing, and new utilities are being installed. The landscaping will be improved. But who will pay for all this? The answer arrives in the mail with the effect of a bombshell. The new corporate owners are not only raising rents, but they are doubling, and in some cases tripling, the rents. Attached to each notice is this explanation:

We, the management, regret to inform you that such rent increases are necessary and beyond our control. Rising real estate costs, property taxes, and maintenance fees mean substantial increases in our overhead costs. In addition, our engineers tell us that major improvements must be made lest the buildings deteriorate and fall below strict city housing standards.

*This story is a fictionalized account of actual events in Venice, California during the mid-1970s.

We do hope you stay at Elysian Towers. But if you decide to vacate, you are legally bound to give us thirty days notice. The new rents will go into effect one month from today.

There is a great uproar among the tenants. Some swear they will neither pay the increases nor move. Others call their children for advice or money. Still others express their anger and frustration with little idea of what they will do. And a very few tenants immediately give their thirty days notice and go out searching for new lodgings.

Within a week, signs are posted around the complex inviting Elysian Towers' tenants to a tenants' meeting in a nearby church. Many tenants attend but for different reasons: some for lack of other entertainment, some for curiosity, and some with the hope that effective strategies can be developed to alleviate this crisis. The dull buzzing of elderly voices dies down as the chairwoman announces that a local attorney has volunteered his time to speak to them. In a slightly condescending manner, which approximates the way younger people address the elderly, the attorney begins his "lecture."

"We live under a system of law," he says. "The law is enacted by our elected representatives and in this case the law is clear. Landlords have the right to charge whatever rent they wish for the use of their property. But, the law is never perfectly rigid. It is subject to new interpretations in light of new circumstances. My feeling is that you people have some chance of fighting this outrageous rent hike in a court of law." The attorney then goes on to explain a number of legal technicalities, a possible courtroom strategy, and a set of possible outcomes. He concludes, "I cannot guarantee a successful outcome but I believe we have some chance of winning."

Your neighbor, Mrs. Adams, immediately asks to be recognized and the chairwoman does so. Mrs. Adams prefaces her remarks with a poignant statement, "This is nonsense. We have about the same chance of winning in the courtroom as a baby deer has of eluding an expert marksman in an open field." Having won the audience's attention, this very articulate old woman defends her statement. "It takes a great deal of time and money to fight in the courtroom. While tenants who are mostly retired have time, they have little money because they live on small, fixed incomes. Could such people afford to hire an attorney to pursue a court case which may last months and even years if it enters the appeals stage? Now consider the financial resources of the competition. A big corporate real estate company can afford to and usually does maintain a slew of high-priced lawyers. And such a company can afford to prolong the case through all sorts of legal maneuvers. Old people may have time today, but they may be dead tomorrow. What good will a court victory be in that case?" she asks. A number of tenants nod in agreement with Mrs. Adams' arguments.

"And why do you suppose the law already favors landlords?" she continues. "Most lawmakers have the time and money to engage in politics. Many are landlords themselves or have wealthy friends in real estate who contribute to their campaigns. And the same holds true for the judges who hear cases on landlord-tenant disputes. Lacking time, money and important connections, most tenants exert no influence on the law and its administration. Sure, we have the right to compete with them, but they have the ability to win!"

You are not yet convinced by her argument. You point out that tenants do win sometimes. Various community groups have lobbied legislatures and won important reforms extending tenants' rights. And the attorney adds that the same community groups could be mobilized to support Elysian Towers' tenants in the courtroom. The competition between landlords and tenants may not be perfectly fair but, with public support, the tenants have a real chance, he says.

Mrs. Adams is not convinced. She says she is aware of the fact that some legislation protecting tenants' rights has been enacted and is aware of cases in which tenants have won favorable decisions over landlords. But, she warns, the tenants must not be fooled by these token gains. They promote the illusion that every group in America can be equally influential, but the fact remains that politicians and judges continue to ignore the needs of old people and tenants by making decisions which ultimately protect and increase the profits of landlords.

"If you are correct, Mrs. Adams," you ask, "then what alternatives do we have to a courtroom case?"

"One alternative is merely to recognize that large numbers of Americans are powerless and dominated by the wealthy. At the very least, such recognition allows us to see our subordinate position, dispel any notions of democracy, and act accordingly. In this case, we pay the increase or move out without wasting money on the courts only to make our personal situations more precarious," Mrs. Adams replies.

"And the second alternative?" you ask.

With a tired smile which reveals both her age and youth, Mrs. Adams responds. "The second alternative is to organize ourselves and perhaps start a rent strike. Let the landlords try to evict us. Imagine the public support and the ensuing storm of protest in the community when the police try to remove us (physically) from our homes. And if we are evicted, let us reorganize and move ourselves back in. Only then will legislatures and courts take us seriously. Are the police and courts going to imprison a large number of old people for claiming the right to a decent home at a reasonable cost? I doubt it. People power makes change possible."

Now assume that you are interested in protecting your rights as a tenant. Do you agree with the attorney that the most significant factor in this crisis is that you and other tenants have an opportunity to defend yourselves in the courtroom and to defeat the landlords? Or do you agree with Mrs. Adams that, despite the law and the courts, old and poor people are basically dominated by the wealthy; and therefore that, some form of illegal protest may be justifiable and more effective in defending your rights? If you take the first viewpoint, it is quite likely that you see American politics as a pluralist arena of fair group competition. If you take the second position, you implicitly assume that elitism dominates political decision making in America.

AMERICAN PLURALISM
Group Competition in American Politics

Virtually all politicians and political issues in America are surrounded by several groups competing for influence. This is also true for the judicial system; judges dealing with controversial issues such as civil rights or religion are usually set upon by many groups who hope to win favorable decisions. Even the modern notion of bipartisanship assumes that these groups are central to American politics. Bipartisan support for an issue means that some groups have *temporarily* suspended competition. The norm, however, is competition of interests.

Groups compete for political influence in at least three arenas. First, they offer various forms of support to political candidates who are favorable to their interests. Second, they pressure political officials in the hope that political decisions will be made in their favor. Third, they mix support and pressure to get bureaucrats to interpret and administer decisions in their favor. Group competition is democratic in the sense that all people are free to organize, support, and pressure to achieve their goals. With pro and con groups exerting constant pressure, all sides of an issue are raised, and all interests are recognized; thus, compromises can be worked out.

There are two related prizes to be won in group competition. The first prize is the placement of a group's issue on the already crowded American political agenda. Thousands of demands are made on political officials each year; they cannot possibly deal with them all. Consequently, groups must continually press their issues forward merely to politicize them—to make them an object of political debate and decision. Not many years ago, the saying of prayers in public school classrooms was taken for granted; it took much time and effort on the part of some groups to raise this as a political issue. Once a group wins a spot on the political agenda, a second prize may be won: election of a group's candidate, a favorable decision, or perhaps a favorable interpretation of a past decision. A group may win this second prize, but its victory is never complete. Competitive groups may attempt to defeat another group's candidate, get a reversal on the decision, or obtain a reinterpretation of the decision. Because group competition is never ending, constant vigilance is necessary to protect a group's interests. Many groups hire lobbyists who have offices in Washington or state capitals or near city governments to make sure that old victories are not forgotten and to press for new victories.

The constant tumult of American group life raises an important question. How do Americans live peacefully with one another if they constantly engage in group conflict? Group theorists provide several answers. One important factor is that although all Americans have the opportunity to engage in group competition, many do not. And even those who do so participate in the competition in minimal ways. The typical group member occasionally reads group publications and rarely attends group meetings. He relies on group leaders to represent his interests. Consequently, his involvement in the everyday competition of groups is minimal; it is unlikely to affect his friendships with members of antagonistic groups.

A related factor is that people who join groups often join several groups. Having multiple group membership improves the possibility that an individual's losses as a member of one group will be offset by his gains as a member of another group. Moreover, having multiple group membership implies that one's opponents on one front today may be one's allies on another front tomorrow. Finally, multiple membership increases the likelihood that members will feel cross-pressured; a member of both the Catholic Church and the American Civil Liberties Union will very likely be ambivalent on the abortion issue and will therefore be less upset by any particular ruling.

Although these factors are important in keeping group competition within peaceful boundaries, one other factor is perhaps most important: groups rarely suffer total victories or total defeats. A group that supports a losing candidate knows it will have another chance in the next election. The outcome of group competition over decisions is often the result of bargaining and compromise; most competitors win something, though less than they initially hoped for. For example, early labor organizers demanded the right to unionize for better wages and benefits and for greater control over industry. Early manufacturers' organizations demanded the end to unionization. They demanded the right to determine wages and benefits, and to have total control over industry. After years of group competition, a compromise was worked out: workers would have the right to unionize, but owners would maintain control over industry. Both sides won partial victories and suffered partial defeats. And because both sides maintained the hope of winning greater victories, they basically continued to abide by the rules of peaceful competition.

During the 1950s, most political scientists characterized American politics as a combination of fair procedures and group competition. On the one hand, American politics consisted of a set of formal procedures for political competition: election, representation, legislation, enforcement, and "blind" justice. This formal system was neutral in the sense that all people had the right to compete according to the rules of the political game. On the other hand, American politics also consisted of a set of informal procedures, according to which, groups could organize, use their resources, their expertise or their voices to politicize and influence decisions, and to fairly compete with other groups. Although political scientists recognized that some groups had obvious advantages over their competitors, they believed that virtually all groups that persisted, amassed public support, and skillfully presented their position, had the ability to win partial victories. This understanding of American politics became known as "pluralism."

The pluralist consensus among American political scientists was dramatically challenged in the 1960s. Issues such as poverty, racism, and war seemed to split the polity into two opposing camps: the Establishment and the anti-Establishment. The Establishment counseled people to be patient, to make their demands through normal procedural channels, and to trust the intentions and ability of leaders to formulate compromises. Rather than protesting in the streets, the poor, the minorities, and the antiwar people should organize into pressure groups, work towards the election of favorable candidates, and lobby legislators. The message was that those who play by the pluralist rules of competition can *eventually* win.

However, the anti-Establishment people viewed the situation quite differently. Why do politicians continually speak about eradicating poverty in America and yet do so little about it? Why does racism persist a hundred years after the Civil War? Why do the American military and major defense contractors push for war so readily? The answers to these questions were forthcoming when the questions were condensed and rephrased: Who benefits from continued poverty, racism, and war? President Eisenhower had already cautioned Americans to beware of a "military-industrial complex" —the corporate, political, and military elite who profit from policies antagonistic to the public interest. C. Wright Mills, in the book *The Power Elite*, suggested that major political decisions were not a result of group competition. Rather, American policy making was a product of a small group of wealthy, white protestants who occupied dominant positions in the American economy, government, and military. Pluralism was a mask which blinded Americans to the real centers of power.

Defenders of American pluralism were beset by two problems. First, how could they explain the division of American society into two opposing camps (both of which were occasionally willing to employ violence) instead of into a plurality of groups peacefully competing? This was not difficult. A closer look at the Establishment versus the anti-Establishment people revealed a plurality of groups underlying these labels, as well as shifting coalitions among these groups. Conflicts between young and old, white and black, student and worker, urbanite and suburbanite, male and female occurred between and within the two opposing camps. The only thing unique about the 1960s was the levels of violence involved. But the fact that the violence diminished in a relatively short period of time indicated the strength of American pluralism, e.g., students would rather vote for George McGovern than carry on illegal demonstrations. If anything, the defenders of pluralism emerged from the 1960s with a tremendous sense of their rightness; despite tremendous pressures, fair procedures and group competition withstood.

The second problem was the more difficult intellectual question posed by people like C. Wright Mills. How could pluralists explain the fact that those who occupy major positions of power in America tend to come disproportionately from the upper class? The pluralists' initial response was to ignore the question and to criticize the critics. If the elite rule America, then how can one explain the victories of groups outside the elite? What evidence is there that upper class people agree on policy? Why can they not represent other Americans? The point of these questions was mainly that the pluralist understanding of American politics may be imperfect, but it is certainly more valid than the alternative.

By the 1970s, the defenders of American pluralism began to take their critics even more seriously. They could not deny the fact that the elite, an unrepresentative cross section of the American population, did dominate political decisions. Furthermore, they could not effectively deny the fact that some groups in American society continually win political influence while other groups, try as they may, rarely win more than politicians' wrath. In trying to account for these two facts, defenders of American group competition developed the new theory of pluralism.

The New Pluralism The new theory of pluralism contains the following ideas and logic:

1. American politics can be characterized as "imperfect" competition between a plurality of groups.

2. Groups lacking the resources, organization, and skills necessary for effective competition can become competitive with some government compensation.

3. Government compensation must not favor disadvantaged groups. Rather, it must raise disadvantaged groups to the point where these groups can help themselves.

4. At this stage, groups must expand their resources, organizations, and skills themselves. They are now accountable for their own gains or losses.

5. In as large a society as America, it is inevitable that group competition will take the form of an group elites competing with other group elites.

6. Elite competition is democratic to the extent that competing elites are accountable to their respective memberships.

7. With compensation for disadvantaged groups and elite accountability, American pluralistic competition becomes less "imperfect."

One implication of this logic for American politics in the 1970s and 1980s is a faith that pluralistic competition is actually becoming less imperfect. Let us see why.

New pluralism theorists understand that some groups in America have distinct advantages over their competitors. Some groups have established a virtual monopoly of influence in their own arena; consequently, it is very difficult for new groups to enter those arenas. For example, the American Medical Association (AMA) has already won such great influence that dissident physicians or researchers have very little chance of placing their concerns on the political agenda. And if they try to compete, the AMA can use its power over medical licensing, medical schools, and the media to quell dissidence.

In addition, some groups already have immediate access to the resources necessary for winning group competition. Other groups sorely lack these resources. For example, groups which advocate greater free enterprise and less government regulation can usually get resources from major corporations, major political figures, and the media. But, groups demanding greater rights for welfare recipients have tremendous difficulties obtaining access to resources; welfare recipients are poor, welfare bureaucrats are often unsympathetic, politicians avoid such sensitive issues, and newspapers have little interest in publicizing such demands. The result is that issues like lesser or greater government regulation have been salient in American politics while issues like the rights of poor people rarely make it on the public agenda.

The new pluralists believe that fair competition requires that all groups have access to the means of competition. Otherwise, some groups would be unable to register their demands, receive public recognition, or have any chance for success. While they hope that groups lacking access to the means of competition can gain access by themselves, the new pluralists are realists. They know disadvantaged groups require some government aid. Indeed, they look at the "welfare state" as a source of aid for both individuals and groups unable to compete in the economic and political marketplace. Their hope is that with minimal state welfare, both individuals and groups will soon become self-sufficient.

Government welfare to groups may take two forms. First, government may directly subsidize disadvantaged groups. It may provide monetary subsidies to help stimulate group organization, publicity, and activity. It may create or expand government agencies to represent the interests of disadvantaged groups. Or government might provide these groups with the services of professional organizers, lawyers, ombudsmen, or bureaucrats. All these government services are aimed at making the pluralist arena more competitive.

Second, government may enact and enforce restrictions for groups who already monopolize or who bring extraordinary resources to particular arenas. Restrictions may range from protection of dissidents or "whistleblowers" (insiders who reveal group corruption) to limits on group spending in political campaigns. Such restrictions promote greater diversity and greater competition in politics; it is the "antitrust" side of the political marketplace.

Government welfare, whether in the form of subsidies or restrictions, must be severely limited to ensure government neutrality. If government does more than help disadvantaged groups enter the competition, it unfairly favors the demands of those groups. If government enacts undue restrictions on already successful or influential groups, it unfairly undercuts those groups' popularity. Because the line between helping the disadvantaged enter the competition and favoring the disadvantaged is blurred, government officials must proceed cautiously lest they overstep the bounds of Justice as Fairness.

As group competition becomes less imperfect, we expect to find new groups representing new interests entering the pluralist arena. This has been the case in recent years. Ecology groups, feminist groups, and a host of others have been able to enter the political marketplace despite the opposition of established groups. Moreover, these later entrants have been able to win partial victories which demonstrate the growing vitality of American pluralism.

Many of these groups have benefited from government support and continue to do so because they are still relatively disadvantaged. The new pluralists expect that these groups will rely less on government aid as they become more self-sufficient and competitive. When this stage is reached, these groups and their supporters alone will merit praise for their victories and blame for their defeats. These groups, already compensated for previous disadvantages, will be solely responsible for their own public support or lack of it.

Even as American politics approaches this stage (as the new pluralists hope and expect) it is still fair to ask if all citizens are really represented. After all, group competition is carried on by group leaders who are a highly distinct segment of the population. Leaders are disproportionately drawn from the ranks of wealthy, white male Americans. Can such an elite pretend to be able to represent the poor, the minority, and the female segments of America? Will not members of this elite manipulate group life in such a way as to benefit primarily wealthy, white male Americans?

The new pluralists have two responses. First, there is no reason to believe that a person's wealth, race, or sex necessarily dictates the nature of a person's ideas or activities. Wealthy people have no consensus about political issues; white people disagree about racial issues; and males often support womens' rights. In fact, it was a group of wealthy white males who were instrumental in supporting the Civil Rights Movement and in aiding poor minorities of both sexes. A person's background does not prevent him from representing other groups and from competing with leaders who have similar backgrounds but different viewpoints.

One of the reasons wealthy, white males have dominated leadership positions is that they have been very effective representatives. They have the time, the sense of effectiveness (efficacy), and skills to benefit their constituents. Moreover, they are generally more devoted to democratic norms than are others in the population and are therefore more likely to adhere to the rules of fair competition. To some extent, the poor, the minorities, and the women's groups should feel fortunate to have such leaders.

Once said, the new pluralists usually add a second response. They hope that more and more members of disadvantaged groups, with government help, will be able to assume leadership positions. More poor people should represent the interests of the poor; more minority people should lead minority groups; and more women should assume the top posts on women's issues. And again, the new pluralists believe that this has been happening in recent years. To some extent, the new pluralists have supported affirmative action programs to educate the poor, minorities, and women in law, medicine, and management. Group members have been increasingly represented and led by people from their group who have these skills.

Here we find one of the major differences between the old and the new pluralism. In the 1950s, many political scientists believed that special group and political leadership should be drawn from a select portion of the population. Compared to the average citizen, wealthy, white males were most devoted to democratic norms and most competent in political skills. Perhaps as a result of the agitation of the 1960s, political scientists have tended to raise their estimates of the democratic and skill capacities of American citizens. Consequently, they now suggest that more Americans should get actively involved in politics, represent themselves and others like them, and compete directly in political competition.

To the extent that more Americans from diverse sectors of society have gotten involved, they have been more able and willing to demand that group leaders be accountable and that government officials be neutral. Labor union members have challenged traditional labor union officials; new congressmen have challenged traditional congressional leadership. Groups like Common Cause continually watch political officials for evidence of partiality; groups like Nader's Raiders oversee consumer protection. Today the elites in and out of government know they are being watched and will be held accountable for their actions. Consequently, they are more likely to represent group interests and effectively compete with other group representatives. The new pluralists understand American politics as moving toward a stage in which greater group competition and greater leadership accountability is making imperfect competition less imperfect.

From this perspective, American politics is increasingly democratic. It is not dominated by a power elite because political influence is diffused among many groups and competing leaderships. Increasingly, political competition determines political outcomes and not the interests of any one particular group.

The New Pluralism and the Landlords-Tenants Dispute

If you accept the new pluralism characterization of American politics, you would probably support a courtroom contest to protect your rights as a tenant. You would base your support on two suppositions: (1) Even a disadvantaged group like relatively poor old people have some chance of competing against corporate landlords; (2) The court is a relatively neutral arbiter of conflicting group claims. When Mrs. Adams finishes advocating an illegal rent strike, you disagree with her. "Perhaps," you say, "our ability to win in the courtroom is much greater than you suspect." You then defend your statement.

You agree with her that your tenants' group is relatively disadvantaged. It lacks the resources to pursue a lengthy court battle; the law tends to be advantageous to landlord interests. Nevertheless, you add that there are a number of government programs that compensate for these disadvantages. First, there are a number of government programs that provide free legal aid to the poor and elderly. Second, there are at least a few sympathetic politicians and community newspapers that might be willing to publicize your cause and support you in the courtroom. Finally, it may be possible to go to a number of government agencies to attain the services of skillful landlord-tenant negotiators or even community organizers. "These programs will allow us to enter the courtroom with enough resources to compete effectively with the owners of Elysian Towers," you say.

Mrs. Adams says, "Even if you are right, our chances of winning the court battle is minimal. The court is certainly not a neutral arena. The judge is likely to be a wealthy man with real estate investments of his own. And the law he is supposed to interpret and enforce is biased toward landlords. Wouldn't you say the competition is stacked *against* us?"

You concede her points regarding the judge and the law. But you add two important factors. One is that recent legislation concerning conflicts of interest has been enacted. If the tenants' group discovers that the judge is himself a landlord or has investments in rental property, then the tenants' group has the right to get a new judge. Two, you remind Mrs. Adams that the volunteer attorney had told the group that the law is never rigid and is always subject to reinterpretation. Consequently, despite the fact that the law favors landlords, it is conceivable that a strong case can be made in defense of tenants' rights. Obviously there are no guarantees; you hope that the law will be changed. But in the meantime, you can assume that the court will be a relatively neutral arena of competition.

"There is one further contingency," you add, "that actually provides us some advantage over the landlords." If the tenants lose in court, they have to move out. Such a move may be inconvenient, even painful for some, but the tenants' lives will basically go on as always. However, if the landlords lose, the very basis of their corporate existence is called into question. A definitive ruling in your favor may set a major precedent restricting the rights of corporate land-lords to raise rents arbitrarily, to evict tenants who have inhabited buildings for years, or to tear down or modify tenants' homes without their consent. And even if the landlords win, the adverse publicity they would receive for their treatment of old people might spark a public movement to restrict their privileges. Fearing the prospect of a courtroom battle, the owners of Elysian Towers might back down.

"This is ridiculous," sighs Mrs. Adams. "How are you to discover if the judge has a conflict of interest? And suppose he does, do you think all your government 'helpers' are going to challenge one of their own? Although the law can be flexibly interpreted, isn't it usually interpreted in favor of the wealthy and powerful? Why should a corporate real estate firm back down from a court battle? They have so consistently won court battles that they must feel at home there. And even if your tenants' group were to somehow win a court battle, what would a victory mean? A decrease in the rent hike? Stalling the inevitable? A token or symbolic win useful for per-suading others that their courtroom losses are justified? For a person who is 'realistic'," she concludes, "you sure know how to pursue fantasies."

You see no sense in responding to her. You have already made your position clear. The other tenants at the meeting are also silent. Perhaps they too would like to pursue a court proceeding but are unsure of how to do so, what is expected of them, or the risks involved. They need a leader to get them involved. Having stuck your neck out this far, you offer to help organize a committee to map tenants' strategy.

AMERICAN ELITISM
The Illusions of Group Competition in America

There have always been Americans who have suspected and analysts who have argued that group competition in America is substantially different from what the pluralists (new and old) would have us believe. On the one hand, group competition is mainly an arena in which the upper classes work out their differences. The interests of the lower classes are rarely taken into account. On the other hand, the function of group competition is not to arrive at fair decisions. Rather, it is to legitimize decisions that have already been made by the leaders of the upper classes; the power elite. In short, group competition in America (1) serves to mask the fact that the lower classes have little political power (2) helps to solve disputes among the upper classes and (3) functions to legitimate the decisions of an informal power elite. The main implication of this analysis is that the political marketplace and the government are tools for promoting upper class interests.

This "elitist" analysis of American politics became increasingly popular, though never widely accepted, in the aftermath of the Civil War. This was the famous epic of the Robber Barons when the Rockefellers, Morgans and Carnegies amassed vast fortunes. Many people noticed that the government helped subsidize these fortunes by providing capitalists with land grants, tax breaks, or by selective enforcement of the law. Meanwhile, the new industrial workforce and the old small farmers were experiencing tremendous hardships with little help forthcoming from government. How could one explain this without arguing that government was a tool of the wealthy?

By the end of the nineteenth century, workers and farmers had organized into groups to compete with the capitalists for political influence. The Progressive and Populist movements brought together many lower class groups, under middle class leadership, to counter government officials and policies which gave the wealthy unfair advantages. They ran candidates for political office; they demanded reforms ranging from restrictions against political corruption to equal subsidization of the lower classes; they challenged judicial administration and especially the hated injunction often used to prevent the lower class from organizing, striking, or boycotting. Here then was a real test of pluralism in America. Could lower class groups actually compete on an equal basis with wealthy capitalists?

Many Americans, then and today, answered yes. Since the beginning of the twentieth century, thousands of bargains and compromises have been struck between the lower and upper class interests in America. On the one hand, the lower classes have won new democratic rights, greater welfare benefits, and important regulations restricting the privileges of capitalists. On the other hand, the upper classes have maintained many of their prerogatives, have won government contracts, and have helped engineer enough social peace to allow them to continue amassing profits. Certainly lower class groups believe that they have not won enough and that decisions have favored capitalists too much; but upper class groups also feel that they have lost too often and that their opportunities are too restricted. But that is the way of compromises. Consequently, groups from both sectors of American society continue the competition.

Some Americans interpreted these events much differently. Because many of these lower class Americans were labelled aliens or socialists or both, their more radical analysis was often disregarded. Nevertheless, millions of Americans supported the candidacy of Eugene V. Debs of the Socialist Party for the American Presidency. And multitudes of workers joined unions affiliated with the very radical International Workers of the World. Adherents of a radical analysis of American politics found their way into important local offices and labor union positions well into the 1930s and 1940s. Their alternative interpretation, although always a minority analysis, was taken very seriously in the 1960s. By this time, many Americans and scholars argued that the reforms won by lower class groups had primarily benefited upper class interests; the pluralists significantly overestimated the ability of lower class groups to compete effectively. On the whole, the welfare state subsidized the welfare of the rich.

Who has reaped the greatest benefits from the reforms of the twentieth century? Consider the following: On the one hand, anti-trust laws were passed to prevent the growth of economic monopolies detrimental to competition. On the other hand, those laws have rarely been used to stem the tide of monopoliziation but as a barrier to unionization. Unions can be defined as a trust or a monopoly of workers. Or consider the right to collective bargaining. In return for this right, capitalists gained a stable workforce and unions were responsible for disciplining dissident workers. This was a considerable gain for the largest corporations. It allowed them to take advantage of technological advances and plan for the future. Although workers won wage and benefit gains through collective bargaining, the cost of those gains was less control over the workplace and higher prices for consumer goods. Accordingly, the right to collective bargaining pacified the workforce and increased the largest capitalists' profits. Small business, nonunion workers, consumers, and the poor paid the price.

One can look at many other reforms only to find that, on the whole, the reforms provided few tangible benefits for the lower classes and tremendous windfalls for the upper classes. For example, many government agencies created to regulate big business are controlled by big business. Democratic reforms such as primary elections or woman's suffrage have weakened the party system and made candidates more dependent on private wealth. Woman's suffrage increased the number of white, middle class voters when the lower class people were using the vote more effectively. For the lower classes, most of these reforms were symbolic victories; for the upper classes, they were tangible victories.

How did the upper classes maintain their tremendous political power and get legislatures to enact reforms to their benefit? They did so through a power elite. One sector of the American upper classes took responsibility for seeing that its own members or representatives filled the most important positions in the economy, government, and military. Various members of the power elite would meet to discuss which policies would be beneficial to the long range interests of the upper classes. They would see to it that their policy decisions become national policy. Herein lay the real hub of political power in America, a hub far removed from the illusions of group competition. Nevertheless, group competition was still important. It was a basis for persuading Americans that government served their interests, even when it did not.

This theory of the power elite gained widespread credibility in the 1960s. Major studies were done, showing that local elites dominated local governmental decisions and that national elites controlled national policy. As this theory gained credibility, the advocates of pluralism raised some very difficult questions. First, how do members of the power elite win political positions if elections are the basis for filling those positions? And even if the wealthy do predominate in important political decisions, is there any reason to believe that they do share a coherent view of the interests of the upper classes? After all, some capitalists support high tariffs and others low tariffs, some more government regulation and others less government regulation. Moreover, why is it that the so-called power elite has lost some very important battles to the lower classes? How could a representative of consumers such as Ralph Nader win a case against General Motors if corporate leaders have such immense political power? These were difficult questions. Their basis was that the power elite theorists had presented a conspiratorial theory of American politics without providing the necessary evidence.

In response to such questions, the theorists developed a much more subtle and sophisticated analysis of American politics. I call it "the new power elite theory." It has found an increasing number of advocates in recent years.

The New Power Elite Theory

The following points summarize the basic logic underlying the new power elite theory:

1. Those who occupy the highest positions in the economy have a self-interest in maximizing their political power.

2. They can use their resources to maximize their political power in three ways.

    a. They can self-consciously use their wealth and influence to control government positions.

    b. They can merely follow the profit motive. When threatened by unfriendly political powers, they reduce their investments causing recessionary trends. To avert recession, political powers must restore a healthy investment climate favorable to economic leaders.

    c. They can compete with other groups in the political marketplace. Because their superiority in resources is quite great, they will dominate that marketplace.

3. By maximizing their political power, economic elites "dominate" but do not totally control political decision making.

4. Their dominance approaches total control when the citizenry are persuaded that the good of the nation rests on the profits of the largest economic concerns.

5. Their dominance diminishes to the extent the citizenry recognizes it, considers it illegitimate and struggles against it.

6. When their dominance is maximal, economic elites are free to pursue whatever policies they deem necessary for enhancing long-term profits. When their dominance is minimal, they will support reforms which undercut threats to their power and which often enhance their power.

Let us further investigate this logic to understand how the new power elite theorists and the new pluralists differ in their view of American politics.

A very few individuals and families control the major corporate and financial institutions in America. They hold controlling blocs of stock, chairmanships of the board, and directorships of the largest economic institutions. They hire the managers of these institutions and either directly or indirectly control major investment decisions which affect the lives of all Americans and people of other nationalities. While members of this economic elite have many disagreements, they all share one article of faith: private control of the economy and private accumulation of profit must be protected at all costs.

The immense economic power of this elite has two key implications. First, a very few people make decisions which shape the options of most Americans. The elite's control over investments determines what kinds of energy sources will be available to Americans and limits options in housing, food, clothing, health care, and so forth. The elite's control over management determines how millions of Americans will spend their workday or if they will work at all. Their control over the media, educational institutions, advertising, and entertainment industries determines what kind of information is available to Americans and what kind of leisure activities will be promoted. If political power is considered the ability to influence the behavior of others, then the sheer economic power of this elite is also a form of political power.

A second implication concerns the importance of government to this economic elite. In the abstract, government is a potential danger. It could exert forms of public control over heretofore private economic decisions. It could restrict corporate profits in the name of public good. On the other hand, government is also a potential ally to the economic elite. It could enact favorable tax policies or buy corporate goods. It could pay for the transportation, communication, and educational costs necessary for maintaining a corporate economy. And government could help legitimize the vast inequality of wealth which is both a need and a by-product of a corporate economy. If most Americans believe that government is safeguarding their interests when, in fact, government is augmenting the power of elites, then Americans would be satisfied with *symbolic* reassurances while the economic elite reap *tangible* rewards.

From the perspective of the economic elite, government can never be neutral. If government supports elite interests, it can protect and extend corporate profits; if it does otherwise, it is a potential threat to corporate decision making and profits. And this threat alone makes it very difficult for the economic elite to engage in long range planning—a necessity in our advanced technological society. Consequently, members of the economic elite have a direct class interest in controlling governors and governmental decisions. But how is such control possible in a *democratic* polity?

One way is for the economic elite to use their wealth and influence to (1) formulate elite policy and (2) make certain that governmental positions are filled with people willing to pursue elite policy. Members of the economic elite meet periodically at directors' meetings, social gatherings, or in private policy-formation groups. Here they iron out differences among themselves, decide on what policies are in the long-term interest of the economic elite as a whole, and hire intellectuals to help inform them of policy alternatives. Furthermore, they perpetuate their sense of class by sending their children to exclusive private schools which nurture a favorable ethic of upper class cohesiveness and responsibility. Their leaders, the power elite, then solicit and use upper class wealth to maximize favorable political influence. Using tactics ranging from illegal bribes to legal campaign contributions, the power elite put forth their members for elective and appointive offices. Or the power elite win the compliance of other elective and appointive officials by offering them lucrative future positions. Or, the power elite finance costly media campaigns to gather public support for officials they favor or to stimulate public distrust of officials they consider dangerous. In a multitude of ways, the power elite generally succeed in filling political posts with officials willing to pursue policies favorable to the upper class.

The second means of maximizing political power does not assume a cohesive upper class consciousness nor a conspiratorial effort to fill political positions with upper class members or representatives. It is more indirect. When political officials pursue policies favorable to the economic elite, top economic officials feel confident that the political atmosphere is favorable for their new investments. These new investments stimulate national economic growth, new goods, more employment, greater social mobility, and higher wages. With this economic boom, political officials can claim partial responsibility and thereby enhance their own political influence or their chance for reelection.

But when government officials are less than friendly to economic leaders and pursue policies the power elite deem dangerous, economic investments at home may slack off. Corporate officials may decide it is more profitable to invest abroad. This is likely to stimulate economic sluggishness, fewer goods at higher prices, more unemployment, less social mobility, and tighter wages. Many citizens may blame public officials for pursuing recessionary policies. Meanwhile, upper class control of the media will allow power elite members to pinpoint the blame on key public officials. As a result, the political influence or chances for reelection of key public officials is diminished; and public officials feel tremendous pressures to restore a healthy investment climate favorable to the power elite. Without direct intervention in government, the power elite still get their way.

The third method by which the power elite win political influence is partially contingent on the success of the first two methods. To the extent that the power elite have captured many government decisions and have used investment policies to ward off potential challengers, they can enter the field of pluralist competition. On the one hand, their vast resources and control over the media gives the power elite some assurance that their concerns will get on the public agenda. On the other hand, with friendly politicians in office, the power elite are virtually assured that political decisions will be favorable to their interests. Pluralistic competition then is mainly symbolic: many groups compete for a place on the agenda and favorable decisions, but one group in particular, the power elite, tends to win an inordinate number of times.

These three methods of political influence add up to upper class political domination but not to total political control. Occasionally, key political posts are won by people willing to challenge corporate priorities. Periodically, public officials have challenged recessionary threats with innovative policies that the power elite consider dangerous. And sometimes, anticorporate groups are able to get their demands on the public agenda and win favorable decisions. But these are the exceptions according to the new power elite theorists —very important exceptions to be sure. Without these exceptions, it would be extremely difficult, if not impossible, for members of the power elite to convince Americans that decision making in America is competitive and therefore democratic. Moreover, without these exceptions, members of the power elite would have little stimulus to reexamine or reformulate their policies in light of new social pressures. These exceptions serve as a barometer of difficulties which the power elite must confront to secure their domination.

When confronted with public support for officials or policies the power elite believe dangerous, they must outline reforms which will satisfy moderate opponents and isolate their more radical opponents. For example, members of the power elite are often at the forefront of reform movements aimed at creating regulatory agencies. The creation of these agencies usually reassures the moderate public that its interests are being protected; these agencies usually function to stabilize competition in their particular domains and to profit the largest industries involved. And it is not unusual for these agencies to become tools of the industries they are supposedly regulating. The moderate public is appeased, corporate interests are enhanced, and the few dissidents remaining are isolated. The dissidents can then be labeled extremists or even criminals, depending on their actions. If all goes well, the power elite appear to be progressive and their dominance is reinforced by reforms.

On the other hand, if power elite members and their supporters cannot formulate, agree upon, or support such reforms, their dominance is weakened. In the economic sector, they may face uncontrollable wildcat strikes, high rates of absenteeism by workers, and radicalized demands for workers' self management. In the political realm, they may find it increasingly difficult to control elections, the appointments of antagonostic officials, or the enactment of unfavorable policies. However, none of this means that they do not remain dominant; a few unruly workers or unsympathetic politicians do not undermine upper class influence. Rather, they are symbols or omens of future difficulties which the power elite must face if they are to sustain their dominance. The new power elite theorists generally believe that, if these difficulties multiply drastically, members of the power elite will exert their political influence to support authoritarian control over the citizenry; private control and profits are more important to the power elite than is democracy.

How then do the new power elite theorists answer the new pluralists' questions? First, they argue that members of the upper class win political power through their immense wealth and control over investment decisions. Their political power takes the form of getting their own members or representatives elected or appointed to office, or by using recessionary threats against those already in office. Second, upper class people generally do agree on major policies formulated in private groups or resulting from the common need for a healthy investment atmosphere. Disagreements on minor policies are often worked out on the basis of private groups, common needs or, to some extent, pluralistic competition. Third, the fact that the power elite have lost some offices or decisions does not prove the pluralists' case. Rather, these losses help members of the power elite promote the illusion of competition and also serve as barometers for accommodative changes. Members of the power elite, when faced with public dissidence, will give in to or even promote some public demands, in ways which do not challenge their own privileges but do undercut more radical demands. Thus, Ralph Nader can beat General Motors in one or two small contests, but General Motors will continue to dominate the American auto industry with little interference.

Once said, the new power elite theorists admit that there are many areas of conflict where no upper class consensus exists. The dominance of the upper class is not at stake on issues like abortion, school busing or even capital punishment. Therefore, various members of the upper class can be found on both sides of these issues. Here, there is some reality to pluralistic competition. However, on issues which directly affect upper class dominance, the power elite will usually unite and prevail despite the illusion of pluralistic competition. Because this is the case, America is certainly less than democratic despite its fair procedures; the outcomes continue to favor a very small but powerful sector of American society.

The New Power Elite Theory and the Landlords-Tenants Dispute

Assume that you believe that the new power elite theory is essentially correct. You and Mrs. Adams would then agree on two points: (1) The wealthy tend to dominate political decisions and (2) your tenants' group has little chance of winning a courtroom contest. Do you then agree with her that it is not worthwhile to pursue a courtroom contest and that a rent strike would be a more appropriate form of political action? Not necessarily. Your continued conversation might move along the following path.

"We agree," you tell Mrs. Adams, "that we have very little chance of winning a legal battle. It would be difficult for us to get public attention. And despite some flexibility in the law, we know that legislatures and judges continue to defend the landlords' right to make profits above the tenants' right to lead decent lives. The best that we could reasonably expect from the court is a slight delay in rent hikes on some procedural grounds. What then are our options?"

You suggest that by simply moving out you become part of the problem. As long as people do not protest, landlords will continue to treat tenants as instruments for profits rather than as people. If you do not protest but quietly move out, you basically leave the problem for others. And if others follow your example, the problem will continue to get worse. There must be another option. Mrs. Adams agrees and suggests you give more serious consideration to her rent strike plan.

You suggest that there are major difficulties involved with it. "First, if we pursue an illegal rent strike, we are likely to alienate the more moderate community groups whose support we might find useful. Second, we will alienate many Elysian Towers' residents who, for one reason or another, would not be willing to engage in illegal actions. Consequently, the real estate corporation will be able to divide us; they'll offer to cut back rent increases for the more moderate among us and evict the rest of us. Once we are evicted, the others will eventually give in to increased rent hikes over time." Mrs. Adams is not yet convinced; so you continue.

You suggest that another option is to pursue a legal rent strike. The law covering this area is very tricky. You would have to hire a lawyer to oversee the whole process. And in any event, a legal rent strike would put you back in the courts where you both agree your chance of winning is slender at best. Again, Mrs. Adams displays signs of disapproval and impatience and finally asks, "Are you saying that we have no feasible options?"

"No," you respond. "Let's look at a courtroom battle again." You suggest that your tenants' group has little chance of winning a competition against landlords in the short-run, whatever the strategy. But the tenants' group can contribute to the long-run struggle against corporate dominance.

"How?" Mrs. Adams asks.

"Let's go to court," you say. "We will get all the community help we can to publicize our plight and to get financial support for our court battle. Instead of fighting to win a losing cause, we will use this support as an educational device. We will dramatize the injustice of corporate dominance by using ourselves as a concrete case. We will force local politicians to commit themselves to support tenants' rights or to face difficult electoral challenges. We will force judges to recognize our rights or reveal the bias of the judicial system. Our courtroom can become a platform for spreading the idea that people's lives should take priority over the profits of a few people."

"What happens then?" an audience member asks.

You answer that it is possible that, if you dramatize the issue in this way, many other people will support it. For example, environmental groups have recently promoted the idea that people's need for a healthy environment is more important than some corporation's profits. Perhaps those groups will support you. Some trade unions and student groups might give their support also, for similar reasons. In the long-run, your court action will have been one step toward the start of a movement of people opposed to corporate dominance in America.

Mrs. Adams interrupts and says, "Not so fast! You are forgetting your own argument about accommodative reforms. Corporation directors and their political officials will probably appoint a commission to look into the problems of renters. Our supposed coalition could be fragmented if some members suggest that we wait to hear commission results and other members demand that we continue political protest. In that case, the result would be that we will have been forced out of our building with no real change having occurred."

"And what of your option, Mrs. Adams?" you ask.

"My way," she says, "forces people to commit themselves. An illegal rent strike with community group support will set an example for everyone else. When the police force comes to throw us out, this action will show, not only that the corporations control political power in America, but that power rests on their police forces, and not on the consent of the people. Education takes place in the streets, not the courtrooms," she concludes.

Finally, another neighbor in the audience directs a question at both you and Mrs. Adams. He says, "You both believe we have little chance of winning. What makes you think that we can fight this?"

Mrs. Adams is exhausted by this time; so you respond, "History is the history of change. Unless we make an effort to direct change in egalitarian directions, elites will direct it in their direction."

But your neighbor continues, "You may be right. But what about us today? Do we move out? Or do we stay and fight with little chance of keeping our apartments?"

"Let's fight," you say. "We are old people with time on our hands. A fight will fill in that time in useful ways. Maybe in the process, we will get to know each other better."

SUMMARY AND CONCLUSION In the last chapter, I described two sets of political values. In this chapter, I have described two theories of American democracy: (1) New Pluralism and (2) New Elitism Theory. Again, these two theories of American democracy represent a clustering of viewpoints for understanding American politics.

The new pluralists are likely to adopt a justice as fairness set of values because it is consistent with their understanding of American politics. They see that American politics is constituted by competition between various groups. While this competition is imperfect, they hope that government can help underprivileged groups compete in the political marketplace and render competition less imperfect, i.e., fairer. To the extent that they already see this happening, they believe America is basically democratic.

On the other hand, the new power elite theorists are more likely to see justice as goodness because this set of values is consistent with their understanding of American politics. Despite fair procedures in America, they see the inordinate wealth and economic control of a relatively few Americans as the most significant factors in American politics. These factors allow a power elite to dominate, but not totally control, political decisions in their interests. The reforms enacted generally serve to accommodate moderate dissidents and isolate radicals; and they often enhance the influence of the power elite. Only when Americans recognize the power elite's control of the "marketplace" and power elite's ability to use government to serve their particular interests will Americans be able to see how undemocratic the nation is. Consequently, Americans must work toward creating a society in which the community of human needs takes priority over the profits of the very few. According to the standards of justice as goodness, only then will a truly democratic America be realized.

Which theory of American politics is right? Certainly both theories are reasonable; they both systematically account for many of the basic facts of American political life. I cannot answer this question beyond saying that the two theories account for the same facts in different ways. But, I can consider another dimension which explains why some people might prefer one theory to the other. This is the comparative dimension.

SELECTED REFERENCES

Bachrach, Peter. *The Theory of Democratic Elitism: A Critique.* Boston: Little, Brown and Co., 1967.

Braverman, Harry. *Labor and Monopoly Capital.* New York: Monthly Review Press, 1974.

Cook, Terrence and Morgan, Patrick, eds. *Participatory Democracy.* San Francisco: Canfield Press, 1971.

Dahl, Robert. *After the Revolution?* New Haven, Conn.: Yale University Press, 1970.

Dolbeare, Kenneth. *Political Change in the United States.* New York: McGraw Hill, 1974.

Domhoff, G. William. *Who Rules America?* Englewood Cliffs, N. J.: Prentice-Hall, 1967.

Fowler, Robert Booth. *Believing Skeptics.* Westport, Conn.: Greenwood Press, 1978.

Greenberg, Edward. *The American Political System.* Cambridge, Mass.: Winthrop Publishers, 1977.

Halberstam, David. *The Best and the Brightest.* New York: Random House, 1973.

Kelso, William Alton. *American Democratic Theory: Pluralism and Its Critics.* Westport, Conn.: Greenwood Press, 1978.

Pennock, J. Roland and Chapman, John W., eds. *Participation in Politics.* New York: Lieber-Atherton, 1975.

Szymanski, Albert. *The Capitalist State and the Politics of Class.* Cambridge, Mass.: Winthrop Publishers, 1978.

Truman, David B. *The Governmental Process.* New York: Alfred A. Knopf, 1955.

Most of the terms we use to study politics require a comparative referent. It makes little sense to say that America is a pluralist democracy unless we have some comparative idea of what an elitist or authoritarian society is like. To view American politics as elitist necessitates some idea of a less elitist or nonelitist political system. Similarly, people's interests are *private* only in comparison with their *public* ones; people are *free* only to the extent that they are not *unfree*; or political systems are *open* or *tolerant* only in comparison with others which are *closed* or *intolerant*.

Often, the comparative referent for the terms we use is unspoken but generally understood. For example, when we say that Carol is a political activist, we mean she engages in activities which go beyond David's once-in-four-years vote. Or if we say the President is unpopular today, we imply that he is unpopular compared to yesterday or compared to past presidents. In many cases, our unspoken comparative referent is so obvious that it need not be specified. But in the study of politics, there are many cases in which the comparative referent is the crucial factor.

Is it appropriate for us to consider John F. Kennedy as a *democratic* leader compared to Mao-Tse-tung, an *elitist* leader? On the one hand, Kennedy won his office through a formal electoral process; Mao came to power on the basis of a violent revolutionary struggle. On the other hand, only a small percentage of American people actually voted for or expressed support for Kennedy; the vast majority of Chinese have affirmed their support for Mao in various other ways. Perhaps it is not appropriate to use Mao as Kennedy's comparative referent because the contexts of their political activities were so radically different. What may constitute democratic or elitist leadership in one culture might not be applicable in another culture.

If we are to understand why some Americans believe their political system is a pluralistic democracy while others view it as elitist, we must investigate their comparative referent points. And we must be sensitive to the appropriateness of those referent points. In theory, there are an infinite number of possibilities here. One could compare American politics to French, European, Asian or African politics today, or maybe to American politics yesterday, or even to possibilities in America and elsewhere tomorrow. On the basis of some of these comparisons, America will appear highly pluralistic; on the basis of other comparisons, it will look quite elitist.

Recent Historical Comparisons

Suppose we were to compare American politics today to the Nazi politics of the 1930s and 1940s. Relative to the Nazis, Americans resolve their conflicts quite peacefully according to fair processes based on group competition. The Nazis' use of physical coercion, arbitrary edicts, and centralized control went far beyond the boundaries of American norms and practices. After World War II, many citizens and political scientists chose Nazi Germany (or Stalinist Russia) as their major referent for understanding American politics. Not surprisingly, America appeared to be highly pluralistic to these people.

Now consider American politics in light of an ideal future characterized by communal consensus, shared economic abundance, and equally shared political influence and benefits. Relative to this ideal future, modern American politics exhibits a high degree of coercion, unfair economic competition, and high levels of political inequality. Compared to the ideal, America is politically elitist. In the 1960s, comparative referents like this one were the basis of many citizens and scholars' critiques of the American political system. Indeed, some went so far as to claim that both Nazi Germany and modern "Amerika" were fascistic compared to what they could and ought to be.

Americans and American political scientists continue to use both comparative referent points today, though with less frequency than in the 1950s and 1960s. For some, America is virtually heavenly when compared to the most repressive regimes in modern history; to others, American politics is hellish compared to the ideal. The first kind of comparison is based on this strategy:

To the extent that American politics avoids reproducing characteristics associated with the worst of all possible worlds, it is pluralistic. Or, it is a "realistic" democracy.

The second kind of comparison is based on an alternative strategy:

To the extent that American politics reproduces characteristics associated with ideal values, it is approaching communitarian democracy. To the extent that American politics remains distant from fulfilling this ideal, it remains elitist.

These two alternative strategies of comparison are often found side by side in most political analyses and in most political movements.

Consider the Civil Rights Movement. Some black leaders emphasized how far blacks had come since the days of slavery. They feared that past gains could be lost if blacks demanded too much too quickly. Consequently, they often counseled patience and moderation to avoid a white backlash. Other black leaders preferred to stress how far blacks have yet to go before attaining full equality in America. They counseled the need for extensive demands and activism in order to move toward their ideal. Similarly, in the ecology movement and in the women's movement today, there are moderates who stress protecting past gains and radicals who prefer rapid movement toward future ideals. The moderates tend to see American politics as relatively pluralistic compared to the past; the radicals view America as relatively elitist compared to future possibilities.

When major social groups have such divergent referent points, for better or worse, political stability is weakened. Some see tremendous pluralism where others see oppressive elitism. Some say *liberty* and mean *not slavery*; others say *liberty* and mean perfect *political equality*. Unable to perceive the same political world and unable to talk out differences, these social groups are ready for prolonged political struggles.

Although many Americans today do hold such divergent referent points, the gap has somewhat narrowed in the "practical" 1970s. Fewer Americans look to tyrannical pasts or to ideal futures; more political analysts are comparing American politics to politics elsewhere today.

The American Nation and Other Nations

One school of thought today is that it matters little if we compare American politics to the politics of Europe, China, Africa, or anywhere else. The specific comparative referent is less important than the method we use in comparing nations. Let us briefly outline the preferred method through an illustration.

We arbitrarily decide to compare American politics to the politics of newly emerging socialist nations in order to see which is most pluralistic. Drawing on our own understanding and experience with pluralism, we suggest that the existence of a competitive, multiparty system is a prime indicator of pluralism. Conversely, the existence of a noncompetitive, one-party system indicates minimal pluralism or maximal elitism. Our assumption here is that without interparty competition, one particular group will most likely dominate the political arena.

Now we survey the various levels of American politics: federal, state, and local. We discover that two parties, but sometimes more than two parties, compete with one another for political office on virtually all levels. It is extremely rare when only one party offers a candidate. Next we survey the newly emerging socialist nations. We discover that one-party systems are the rule in these nations; some have elections with only one candidate running for office, while others dispense with elections altogether. On the basis of this indicator, it is quite clear that the American political system is pluralistic relative to the political systems of newly emerging socialist nations.

We may continue these comparisons using other familiar indicators: centralization of political power, tolerance of dissent, guarantees of civil rights, and so forth. Were we to do so, we would quite likely reinforce the strength of our earlier finding: American politics is pluralistic relative to newly emerging socialist nations.

At this point, we may want to specify what particular factors explain why American politics is more pluralistic. It occurs to us that a capitalistic economy may be more consistent with pluralism than a socialist economy. To test this, we apply our indicators to all capitalist nations and to all socialist nations. Again, we would quite likely discover that capitalist nations tend to have multiparty systems whereas socialist nations are more likely to have one-party systems. Using our other indicators, we may feel confident in concluding that capitalist nations are comparatively pluralistic and socialist nations are comparatively elitist.

At this point, we subtlely introduce a political strategy. If we are to protect American pluralism and avoid elitism, we must be careful to protect American capitalism. Moreover, we might take a short step and recommend that American foreign policy be geared toward protecting international capitalism against growing socialist movements. In this way, we can move toward a world in which American pluralism is protected by pluralism abroad.

This method of comparison may be labeled Cross-National Comparison. We ask a specific question comparing several nations according to familiar indicators. We rate nations according to our indicators and make a tentative statement of results, e.g., America is more pluralistic than emerging socialist nations. To isolate the factor which explains this difference, we try comparing all nations on the basis of our indicators. We then make a general statement of our results, e.g., capitalist nations tend to be more pluralistic than socialist nations. Finally, on the basis of our general statement, we make appropriate policy recommendations. In an unsystematic fashion, many Americans employ this method; in an extremely sophisticated and technologically advanced fashion, many political scientists use it well.

Nevertheless, there is a major bias in the way this method is generally used: the American political system almost always appears to be pluralistic compared to other nations. Briefly, the reasons for this are as follows. First, it required a rather specific kind of history, the development of a specific kind of political culture, and a tremendous level of economic abundance for America to lay claim to its degree of pluralism today. The specific historical circumstances of most other nations, their radically different political cultures, and their lack of economic abundance make high levels of pluralism almost inconceivable to

them in the near future. This means that our units of comparison may not be appropriate: we are comparing a mature, advantaged nation to neophyte disadvantaged nations.

Second, and more important, it nevertheless remains questionable if America is relatively pluralistic on the basis of findings such as those outlined above. After all, we have used indicators of pluralism which are familiar to Americans; but our indicators may be unfamiliar and unacceptable to people in other cultures. While the multiparty versus one-party indicator may make sense to us, it ignores a number of factors which others believe to be more significant. When they look at our Democratic and Republican parties, they may see two parties which offer basically the same platforms. In this instance, there is no significant competition. However, when they look to their own one-party system, they may see mechanisms internal to the party which assure that workers, peasants, and other social groups have a say in candidate selection. If we use "American indicators," then America will always appear to be pluralistic; if we adopt indicators others believe are significant in their cultures, America may appear quite elitist.

Finally, if we base our policy recommendations on inappropriate comparisons and biased indicators, we will very likely put the American political system in the position of being the world-wide standard for pluralism. To the extent that other nations are like America, we will consider them pluralistic. To the extent that they are different, we will almost automatically assume they are elitist. In these circumstances, we begin to fulfill the role of a Don Quixote: leaders in the struggle to make the world less elitist. However, from the perspective of those in other political cultures, we may look more like the Ugly American: imperialists using our vast power to get others to conform to our image.

Cross-national comparisons do not inevitably lead to this result but in practice they tend to do so. Therefore, I believe it is fair to say that people who make comparisons on the basis of these strategies and cross-national comparisons are likely to adopt a model of American politics which is pluralistic.

The American Culture and Other Cultures

Analysts who believe cross-national comparisons are biased, often explain this bias by focusing on America's political culture. Since Americans usually assume that politics is conflict-resolution, that justice is fairness, and that American politics is pluralistic, they often do not see how this system of beliefs colors their comparisons. They are quite content to compare themselves to others on the basis of their own assumptions because (1) they often believe their assumptions are the only true ones and (2) they often believe that somehow or other every rational person shares them. To eliminate this bias in comparisons, some analysts suggest we must focus our attention on comparing differences in cultural preconceptions. Only then will we be able to gauge the significance of political institutions and behaviors.

First, we must be willing to question the *truth* and *universality* of our own cultural preconceptions. For example, most Americans believe that their two-party system is an important basis of American pluralistic democracy. The only question asked here is, "In what way is the two-party system an important aspect of pluralism?" However, we might ask, "Is a two-party system helpful or harmful for nurturing pluralism?" It is at least conceivable that some forms of one-party systems or some forms of multiparty systems are more likely to nurture pluralism. A two-party system tends to produce moderate candidates who do not represent some significant groups in society; a one-party or multiparty system may be more likely to provide representation for more or all groups in society. If we do not consider these possibilities, we will use indicators which assume that America is pluralistic, rather than ones which will help us examine if America is pluralistic.

Second, we must steep ourselves in the histories and cultures of those political systems we would compare to America. Many cultures have belief systems in which politics as community-building, justice as goodness and an elitist view of America predominate. To shed our biases, we must be willing to look at American politics through these alternative cultural lenses. Moreover, we must try to understand the significance of political institutions and behavior elsewhere through the eyes (and culture) of those who participate in them. For example, do the people of newly emerging socialist nations see their one-party system as a stimulus or a hindrance to greater pluralism in their own terms? What we may see as a hindrance, they may view as a stimulus.

This ability to question our own preconceptions and to temporarily view the world through alternative cultural lenses is the basis of Cross-Cultural Comparison. According to this method of comparison, the analyst must attempt to understand as many perspectives as appropriate before comparing political systems. This presents two problems. One is that it is extremely difficult and time-consuming to examine one's own cultural preconceptions, let alone the cultural preconceptions of those in another political system. Furthermore, one must then consider subcultural preconceptions in one's own system as well as the other system in comparison. Consequently, comparisons by this method tend to be limited to a few political systems at any one time.

Consider the difficulty of supporting just one relatively simple comparative statement: American voter turnout is lower than French voter turnout. What does this mean? On the one hand, we must ask a slew of questions regarding the significance of voting in America.

Do Americans believe voting is a significant political act? Does voting have much effect on policy decisions? Is voting a symbolic act of national unity? Do nonvoters disproportionately come from one subculture or another? Is there psychological pressure on Americans to vote?

In order to merely get an idea of the significance of a low voter turnout in America may require an in-depth study of the history and function of voting among many groups in America. We must ask the same questions regarding the vote in France. To give reasonable answers, we must become thoroughly acquainted with

French history, belief systems and subsystems, reward and punishment patterns, political institutions, and so forth. After all this we may feel confident enough to make a modest statement such as:

America's low voter turnout has little significant effect on American pluralism as long as Americans have the opportunity to vote. However, in French political culture, a low voter turnout would indicate tremendous dissatisfaction with the options afforded by the political system.

Moreover, this relatively modest statement would be highly controversial because it is so interpretive.

A second problem is how one isolates the factors which explain similarities or differences between political systems. One certainly cannot survey all nations to see if one factor is more closely associated than another with the difference under question (e.g., to see if capitalism or socialism is more closely associated with pluralism). The reason is that each of these factors may mean different things in different political cultures. In one socialist nation, a one-party system may be a step toward greater pluralism; in another socialist system, a one-party system may be a step toward greater elitism. Consequently, cross-cultural analysis tends to limit one's ability to make broad general statements which can be used as the basis for policy recommendations.

The major implication of this method is that its user is more likely to see American politics as elitist. The person who examines his own American prejudices is more likely to see problems in America than those who do not recognize their prejudices. Moreover, the person who at least temporarily views America through the lenses of alternative cultures is more likely to be sensitive to the ways in which American political and economic elites resolve conflicts in their own particular interests. We must remember that nearly half the world's people live in socialist political cultures which emphasize (but not necessarily practice) an egalitarian community free from the extraordinary political power of wealthy capitalists. This cross-cultural sensitivity is especially likely to lead to an elitist view of American politics if the user is also attracted to the goal of building an egalitarian community.

	Logic I	*Logic II*
Definition of Politics	Conflict-Resolution	Community-Building
	↑	↑
Political Values	Justice as Fairness	Justice as Goodness
	↑	↑
American Politics	Pluralism	Elitism
	↑	↑
Comparative Politics	Cross-National	Cross-Cultural

Let us now consider more fully the differences between cross-national and cross-cultural comparison before we assess the significance of our two logics of political preconceptions.

American Politics and Comparisons

Those who compare American politics to politics elsewhere, according to the cross-national methodology, are likely to adopt a pluralist view of America. Those who do their comparisons on the basis of cross-cultural analysis are more likely to view American politics as elitist. Noting this, we can now add a fourth tier to our two logics:

Selected References

Bill, James A. and Hardgrave, Robert L. *Comparative Politics: The Quest for Theory.* Columbus, Ohio: Merrill, 1973.

MacIntyre, Alasdair. "Is a Science of Comparative Politics Possible?" In *Philosophy, Politics and Society: Fourth Series*, edited by Peter Laslett, W.G. Runciman and Quentin Skinner, pp. 8-26. New York: Barnes and Noble, 1972.

Polsby, Nelson, Dentler, Robert A. and Smith, Paul A., eds. *Politics and Social Life.* Boston: Houghton Mifflin, 1963.

Surkin, Marvin and Wolfe, Alan, eds. *An End to Political Science: The Caucus Papers.* New York: Basic Books, 1970.

5

COMPARATIVE POLITICS:
DON QUIXOTE
AND THE UGLY AMERICAN

How do we compare the American political system to other political systems? Do we make broad generalizations on the basis of familiar indicators only to distort the uniqueness of others' histories or cultures? Or do we immerse ourselves in others' histories and cultures in order to make highly subjective interpretations? Consider the following story. You are placed in a hypothetical situation where you must make some comparisons. Can you avoid stepping into the role of Don Quixote, savior, or the Ugly American, oppressor?

ABROAD WITH THE PEACE CORPS You have just finished your studies in agricultural engineering. You realize that you have led a somewhat sheltered existence and would like to travel some before starting a career. But you are short of money. Joining the Peace Corps seems like the perfect alternative: they will pay for your travel and you can use your education to help others. You volunteer and are accepted into the program.

You undergo three months of intensive training in a Peace Corps school in the United States. You learn about the language, history, and culture of the Southeast Asian nation to which you will go. More important, in your view, are your lessons on the specific agricultural problems of the nation. The major problem is irrigation. The extremes of a wet and dry season mean that the rice fields are consistently flooded; then parched. Your job will be to develop an irrigation system able to drain flood waters during monsoons and water the fields during droughts. With your educational background, you feel confident that you can meet this challenge.

You arrive at the capitol city of the Southeast Asian nation. You are briefed on the specific nature of the irrigation problem and then board a bus for "your" village. There you are met by the Peace Corps volunteer you will replace. She shows you to your lodgings and spends a few days introducing you to village officials. She also talks about the difficulties she has encountered. Everyone has been verbally supportive of her ideas, but then they refuse to implement them. She mentions something about religious "mumbo jumbo" being the major barrier to change. You listen attentively, but decide that you will begin your experiences without being prejudiced by her preconceptions or experiences. She leaves the village.

During the following weeks, you divide your time between talking to village people and surveying the rice fields. You hear stories of past floods and droughts and begin to develop a master irrigation plan. It has three basic components. First, a series of drainage canals must be dug to carry off excess flood waters. Second, a reservoir must be excavated on a nearby hillside to catch water during monsoons and serve as a water source during droughts. Third, a system of pumping stations will be necessary to keep the waters flowing in or out depending on the season. The plan **106** is by no means ideal but it is practical and beneficial.

Your next step is to check the availability of necessary equipment and supplies for the irrigation system. The drainage canals can be dug by hand, but for the reservoir you need a bulldozer. More important, your plan is contingent on getting a series of small but sophisticated pumps. You send out letters on these matters only to discover how slow and inefficient the local mail system is. You finally decide to travel to the capitol city. After some incredible delays and bureaucratic mixups, you discover that a village near your own has a bulldozer. And to your surprise, you find out that an American foreign aid agency will finance, import, and transport the pumps you need. You make the necessary arrangements.

On your way "home," you stop off at the village where the bulldozer is. The owner is quite willing to rent it to your village. The costs include a rental fee, a driver's wages, and a guarantee that some of the excess rice be marketed in the bulldozer owner's market stall. This seems fair enough. You make a verbal agreement and return to your own village.

You tell the village elders you would like to speak with them at their next meeting. They agree. At the elders' meeting, you present your plan, timetable, and list of benefits to villagers. The elders listen politely, ask an occasional question; then dismiss you. They will consider your plan. A few weeks pass and you are becoming anxious. Finally, the elders reconvene and invite you to the meeting.

They profusely thank you for your efforts. They very much like the idea of digging drainage canals and will soon organize the work crews, which you may direct. However, instituting your pumping system and hiring the bulldozer are quite out of the question. Their pumping system is old but adequate and the hillside for the reservoir cannot be disturbed. You explain to them that your plan will succeed only if all parts are implemented. The drainage canals will be inefficient without a more advanced pumping system, and the drought problem will not be solved without the reservoir. Both the pumping system and the reservoir could be constructed with little cost to the village. Again the elders listen politely, but seem to ignore all you have said. They ask, "When will you be ready to direct the digging of the drainage canals?" Somewhat exasperated, you avoid this question and leave the council meeting.

You evelute the situation as follows. The elders support the drainage canal plan because it is merely a variation on something villagers have been doing for centuries. They refuse the pumping system because of a fear of technology. Finally, they reject the reservoir because of some kind of religious ritual related to the hilltop. Taking all this into account, you develop a more modest irrigation plan based on the traditional manual pumping system. You modify the irrigation canal plans and you select a new hilltop for the reservoir. This plan is less efficient than the first but certainly more efficient than their present one is.

You present this plan to the village elders. Again, they support the drainage canal plan; again they reject the reservoir idea, despite the fact that you have selected an alternate hilltop. But now they question your affirmation of the traditional pumping system. Apparently, a village bicycle mechanic has developed a new sort of pump: one sits on a makeshift bicycle and pedals; the pedals turn the gears of a pump apparatus. The elders all agree that the new pump is ingenious and should be integrated into the irrigation system. You examine the apparatus. While it is slightly more efficient than the traditional pumps, it is probably not efficient enough for your modified system. Moreover, the costs for producing these pumps would be relatively high when you could get a sophisticated pumping system for free. Ignoring your assessment, the village elders ask how many of these ingenious new pumps would be needed. Again, you avoid their question and leave feeling confused and frustrated.

You return to your lodgings with many questions. Why can't these people understand that they need a *whole* irrigation system? Why do they refuse to consider the need for a reservoir? Why are they so enamored with that simplistic bicycle pump? Why don't other villagers challenge the elders' decisions? In pondering the answers, a more immediate question crosses your mind, "Why stay here if I cannot accomplish anything?" At least back in America these decisions are made more rationally. You then understand that you can answer these questions only by comparing decision making in this village with decision making in America with which you are more familiar. But how do you make such a comparison?

You recall some lessons from your Peace Corps training sessions. You were told that peasant societies generally have authoritarian political structures based on traditional social relationships. Perhaps this explains why the elders would not even bargain or compromise with you, why most villagers accepted the elders' decisions, and why the elders refused to support innovation. But even if this general perspective is accurate, a number of points remain unclear. If the political structure is so authoritarian, why did the elders allow you to discuss your plan with other villagers as well as outsiders? And if peasants are so traditional, why did the elders support innovations like the new drainage canals or the introduction of the bicycle pumps?

You also remember another statement from your training course. Each nation and each village has its own way of understanding the world. Perhaps you do not know the history and culture of these villagers well enough to understand the basis for their decisions. But can you ever know enough? Not being born here, you will always be an outsider with foreign understandings. Not being a villager, you will never experience their history or culture as directly as they do. At best, you can study them, live as an outsider with them; then interpret their motives, intentions, and acts. But you know such interpretations are quite subjective.

At some point you must make a decision. If you decide that the general statement about peasant societies is applicable to your village, you will most likely do one of two things: try to teach villagers greater economic rationality or give up and leave. If you decide to learn more about the history and culture of the village, a number of implications may follow. You are opening yourself up to the possibility that alternative modes of understanding may be equally or even more acceptable than your American perspectives are. Furthermore, you may discover that Peace Corps members and other American agencies attempt to impose their own perspectives and values on foreigners. Implicitly, the first option places you in the shoes of an American Don Quixote striking down enemies which villagers see as windmills; the second option potentially awakens you to your own role as the Ugly American imposing your world's view on a nonreceptive audience. Whatever you decide, you will be acting on a decision which most Americans and American political scientists make when they compare American politics with other political systems.

CROSS-NATIONAL COMPARISON
Comparing Political Systems

There is no limit to the comparisons and contrasts which can link or divide political systems. At the most basic level, all political systems are comparable precisely because they are political systems. According to politics as conflict-resolution, all political systems are composed of individuals with differing interests who sometimes conflict; such conflicts are resolved by authoritative institutions and processes. Thus, the United States, tsarist Russia and ancient Athens all share these characteristics. Nevertheless, all political systems are necessarily distinct. Even if the United States and England had the exact same political systems on paper, the two systems would differ in geographic location, in the nature of their citizenry, and in population patterns, to name a few possibilities. And of course, no two political systems are exact replicas of each other.

A multitude of similarities and differences are readily available once we move beyond this basic level. For example, America and England share a literate citizenry, an advanced industrial economy, a legal system based on precedent, and a relatively independent judiciary system. Moreover, both political systems are based on a set of liberal values, electoral politics, and political secularism. But America has a president, a congress, and a history of racial conflict while England has a prime minister, a parliament, and a history of racial homogeneity (until recently). America has a two-party system and serves as the home base for many multinational corporations while England has three ideologically distinct political parties and few major multinational corporations. These comparisons and contrasts could go on forever.

Suppose that we were interested in one specific contrast: English labor unions continually conflict with government whereas American labor unions generally get along with government. How could we explain the relative labor-government conflict in England as opposed to the relative labor-government harmony in America? In other words, what differences between the English and American political systems explain the differences in their respective labor-government relations?

We might begin with a reasonable guess. Maybe there is some factor in a prime ministerial system which generates this conflict but is absent in a presidential system. A prime minister is chosen by the party with the most seats in parliament rather than by the electorate; thus he or she is likely to be a symbol of partisan party interests rather than a symbol of national unity. A president is chosen by the national electorate and is expected to be above party interests once in office. Consequently, when a prime minister calls for labor harmony, it is seen as a political ploy; when a president calls for labor harmony, it is seen as a national necessity. On the basis of this reasoning we surmise that prime ministerial systems are likely to encounter more labor challenges than presidential systems.

A friend now offers a different explanation. She says that the racial composition of the two political systems is the most significant factor. In England, it has been relatively easy for workers to unite and make demands on government because they are not diverted by racial divisions among themselves. Most English workers have been white. In America, however, the racial composition of the workforce is more mixed and worker unity is more difficult. The white workers who dominate the unions will comply with government leaders as long as those leaders guarantee them some job security when minorities demand more jobs. Our friend adds that labor-government conflict is likely to diminish in England as more and more minority members enter the English workforce. As in America, racial conflict among workers will make worker unity against government more difficult.

Finally, a second friend enters the conversation and offers another explanation. He believes that the different geographies of the two political systems is more important. America is a huge nation geographically isolated from the European continent; England is a small nation barely separated from the European continent. The sheer size of America makes labor unity quite difficult, while the isolation of America innoculates it against continental ideas of class conflict. England, however, is small enough for a cohesive workers' movement to develop and is close enough to the continent to be infected by radical ideas. At this point, there is a lull in our discussion; we are at a loss as to how we should establish a valid explanation.

An adherent of cross-national analysis may be able to assist us. He might suggest that we each do a study to determine how often our "pet differences" are associated with labor-government conflicts. First, we draw up a list of all the nations with prime ministerial systems and then another list of all the nations with presidential systems. We then see if prime ministerial systems generally are more closely associated with labor-government conflict than are presidential systems. Our first friend draws up a list of all systems where racial harmony is the rule and another of systems where racial conflict prevails. She checks to see if racially homogenous populations are more closely associated with labor-government conflict than are racially mixed populations. Lastly, our second friend divides the political world into relatively large nations isolated from the European continent and relatively small nations near the continent to determine if labor-government conflicts occur more frequently in one group than the other.

Our next step is to organize our information to answer our questions. Suppose we do the following:

	High Conflict	Low Conflict
Prime Ministerial Systems	10	10
Presidential Systems	10	10

Each box contains the number of nations which fall into our categories. When we organize our information this way, we can begin to answer our question. It appears that prime ministerial systems experience high and low labor-government conflict as often as presidential systems do. In other words, prime ministerial systems are not more closely associated with labor-government conflict than are presidential systems in our hypothetical example.

Assume that our two friends organize their information in the same manner. Friend One hypothetically discovers that labor-government conflicts occur more often when the workforce is of one race than when the workforce is composed of more than one race. In other words, a racially homogenous workforce is closely associated with labor-government conflict. Friend Two organizes his data and discovers that large, distant systems experience no more and no less labor-government conflict than small, nearby systems. Accordingly, we have discovered evidence that Friend One's explanation is most valid. Race may indeed be the most significant factor.

However, our first friend cannot remain satisfied for very long. It may be that religion, sexual practices, or technological factors are even more closely associated with labor-government conflict than race. Consequently, we must continue to test the possibilities in order to discover better explanations. Cross-national comparisons require endless testing.

The Logic of Cross-National Comparison

The logic of cross-national comparison is outlined below:

1. The units of comparison are generally political systems with national, geographical boundaries: nation-states.

2. The basis of these cross-national comparisons is always the significant similarities shared by the nation-states under consideration.

3. The immediate object of comparison is to explain the interesting differences between significantly similar nation-states.

4. These differences are best explained when they are highly associated or "correlated" with other factors or "independent variables" across many nation-states.

5. Very high correlations which hold true across many nation-states may be considered social scientific "laws."

6. The ultimate object of cross-national comparison is to generate very general social scientific "laws" which can be used to explain the differences among many nation-states.

This logic is the most complex of those we have considered so far. We must then investigate it in greater depth. However, since this particular logic moves us into the area of political science methodology, we will be reconsidering it in Part Two of this book.

To be consistent with the definition of politics as conflict-resolution, a political system may be defined as a *patterned* and *integrated* set of processes for resolving conflicts. By patterned, I mean that the processes of the system continually repeat and renew themselves. In the American political system, the process of elections is repeated at regular intervals and the process of altering elections is standardized by law. By integrated, I mean that the many processes which constitute a political system are related in a definite fashion. In the American political system, the Constitution defines how federal laws are related to local laws where the two conflict; so too with relationships among the various institutions of federal government. Thus, when we speak of the American political system, we know we are speaking of a patterned and integrated set of processes.

By this definition, there are an infinite number of political systems in the world: international political bodies like the United Nations, nation-states like Argentina, local governments like the Chicago City Council and bureaucratic agencies like the Internal Revenue Service. How are we to decide which political systems to compare? Some analysts suggest that this is an arbitrary decision. One can compare any type of political system with another, and many comparative analysts do. However, there are some advantages to using nation-states, which are political systems with definite national and geographical boundaries, as one's primary unit of comparison.

Subnational political systems, like local governments and bureaucracies, are patterned and integrated in very limited ways. At any moment, their procedures can be overridden, reformed, or constrained by the national political process. For example, when the United States Supreme Court declared school segregation unconstitutional in 1954, local government processes became inoperative or radically changed in certain cases. Moreover, local citizens or bureaucratic clients always have the option of disregarding local or bureaucratic decisions by appealing to the superior authority of the national government. During the 1960s, many Southerners blatantly broke local laws with the hope that federal judges would declare those laws void. When federal judges did so, the local officials' procedures were weakened. The point here is that subnational political systems are very temporary because of the existence of superior national authority; therefore they are not very autonomous.

International political systems have little recognized authority and are extremely weak. The United Nations or various treaty organizations may make demands on nation-states, but nation-states usually feel they have the authority and power to ignore these demands. Consequently, no matter how patterned or integrated the United Nations is, its decisions are in themselves "relatively" meaningless. They become politically relevant only when particular nation-states are willing to back them up with their national authority and power. If this is the case, we ought to focus on the nation-states themselves.

Nation-states are unique political systems in at least two senses. First, they are perhaps the most autonomous of all political systems. There is usually no recognized superior authority outside them and no competing authorities within them. On the whole, the nation-state's decisions are final and can only be appealed to the nation-state. This is not to say that the autonomy of the nation-state is unchallengable. Other nations may wage war against it and try to conquer it or some segments of the citizenry may try to overthrow it by revolution. In these cases, we generally conclude that the national political system is threatened with a breakdown. When a breakdown occurs, we can no longer speak of a *political* system because the processes of peaceful conflict-resolution have given way to violent confrontation.

However, the nation-state is unique in a second sense. Even when it is threatened with a breakdown, it tends to outlast the threat. The American political system was threatened during the Civil War; yet the system remained substantially the same after the Civil War. We cannot say the same about international or subnational systems. The League of Nations and many treaty organizations were short-lived; and many subnational political units which existed fifty years ago either no longer exist or are substantially different. In short, the nation-state is one of the most stable political units in the modern world. As a relatively stable unit, it is excellent for comparison.

It should be stressed that the autonomy and stability of the nation-state are only matters of degree. The Eastern European nations are examples. Their relative autonomy and stability is questionable because of the preponderant Soviet influence and because of the dramatic changes in their boundaries and political processes. Nevertheless, those interested in comparative politics generally choose the nation-state as a good, but not ideal, unit of comparison. They are justly labeled "cross-national" analysts.

All systematic comparisons of nation-states begin with the idea of similarities, for two reasons. First, unless there are significant similarities between our units, we do not know if the units are appropriate. Think back to Robinson Crusoe. We cannot compare his and an oak tree's intelligence because our units of comparison are not significantly similar enough; they do not both share a capacity for intelligence. Similarly, it might not be appropriate to compare modern America's and a primitive nation's systems of elections because the latter may lack a literate population or any system we may be willing to call an electoral system. In many cases, the idea of similarities is not a problem. In the sense that all nation-states are political systems, they all share a patterned and integrated set of processes for resolving conflicts.

Second, it is only by focusing on similarities that differences worthy of analysis become clear. Some people enumerate the similarities between the American and the European systems. And then they ask a question about differences: If the American and European systems are so similar, then why is American politics more stable than European politics is? Only the basic similarities make the question of differences interesting. A variation on this is to take two very different political systems, highlight a similarity; then consider a difference. Some people suggest that because the economic interest in industrial production is so similar between the United States and Russia, it is surprising that the two nations can sustain such different ideologies. Why is that the case? Again, only the similarities make comparisons of differences seem like questions worth asking. The object of comparative analysis is to answer these questions about differences. But how?

One possibility is through historical interpretation. One can examine various developments in the nation-states involved and suggest that a plausible answer can be found. For example, America's relative stability compared with France's can be explained by the following factors unique to America: the lack of a feudal heritage, an open frontier, the accommodative political institutions, the abundance of natural resources, the vast economic growth, and so forth. Each factor partially explains why Americans tend to be satisfied with their political system or why dissatisfied Americans tend not to threaten political stability. The absence of these factors in France implies that France lacks important structures which support political stability. This constitutes a *plausible*, interpretative answer.

However, the cross-national analyst must raise two questions at this point: (1) Despite their plausibility, how do we know that each of these factors actually contributes to American political stability? (2) Even if all factors do contribute, how do we know which are the most important? Historical interpretation is not adequate in itself. We must also be able to *test* the validity and the relative importance of each factor.

How can we test the importance of a broad frontier in terms of America's political stability? We could move to a more general level of analysis to see if the existence of a broad frontier contributes to political stability in most nations. If a broad frontier is associated with political stability world-wide then we have good reasons for believing it is an important factor in explaining America's stability compared with France (which lacks a broad frontier). Unfortunately, we cannot pursue this analysis because the existence of a broad frontier is unique in modern history. Indeed, one of the basic problems with historical interpretation is that it focuses on unique factors which cannot be tested world-wide. Consequently, while the importance of the frontier may be a plausible explanation, it cannot be tested.

Cross-national analysts are more likely to consider plausible factors which can be tested. Degrees of governmental centralization, industrial production, or proportions of literate citizens are factors which can be applied to all nations. To the extent that these factors are plausible, they can also be tested. Suppose that we believe that America's vast industrial production results in a relatively satisfied population unlikely to challenge politcal stability. How would we go about testing the validity of this factor?

First, we would ask, "are high levels of industrial production *generally* (across many nations) associated with relative political stability?" Second, we would *operationalize* (or stipulate a definition for) industrial production and political stability so that we could collect data (facts). We could define industrial production as the average gross national product (GNP) of a nation during the past twenty five years; we could define political stability as having few (less than five?) major political upheavals during the past twenty five years. Third, we can collect as much data as possible from as many nations as possible on GNP and political upheaval. How much data we collect depends on the time and resources at our disposal and the availability of the data. Fourth, we can organize the data in a way that allows us to see if a high average GNP is or is not usually associated with political stability.

Hypothetically, we discover that: (1) 80 percent of the nation-states with very high average GNPs have experienced less than five major upheavals during our time period, and (2) 80 percent of the nation-states with moderate or low GNPs have experienced five or more major upheavals in the same time period. We could summarize our findings by saying that high industrial production significantly *correlates* with (or is associated with) political stability on a world-wide basis. We could then use this correlation as evidence when we return to our America-France question: America's extraordinarily high GNP explains the absence of major political upheavals while France's moderate GNP explains the presence of political upheavals or political instability.

But how significant is the factor of industrial production compared to the factor of political centralization? Perhaps America's relatively decentralized political system means that dissatisfied Americans have many arenas for appealing decisions or promoting changes; and perhaps France's highly centralized political system means that French people have few arenas for promoting change and that they therefore are more likely to challenge political stability. Again, we would divide the world into centralized and decentralized political systems and see how closely political decentralization correlates with political stability. Suppose we discover that 95 percent of decentralized political systems experience few upheavals while 95 percent of centralized political systems experience five or more upheavals in our time frame. Returning to our America-France question, we might now want to say that while both political decentralization and high industrial production are associated with America's political stability compared with France's, political decentralization may be the more significant factor; both "explain" the difference between America and France, but one "explains" the difference better.

At this point, we must decide if our correlations actually answer our question. Perhaps we should test other factors (e.g., literacy rates) to see how closely they correlate with political stability. Or perhaps we believe that the combination of our plausible explanation and our high correlations allows us to say that these factors "cause" political stability. Or perhaps we believe it is necessary to test further the plausibility of our explanation. For example, we might ask if high industrial production is associated with favorable public opinion of the political system and if favorable public opinion of the political system is associated with political stability. Were we to test these relationships, we might conclude that:

(1)	(2)	(3)
High GNP →	Favorable Public Opinion →	Political Stability

In other words, high industrial production "causes" favorable public opinion which, in turn, "causes" political stability. (1) would be our *independent variable,* (2) would be an *intervening variable*, and (3) would be our *dependent variable.* Some cross-national analysts are unwilling to say that one factor (variable) actually causes another. In this case, it is always possible that political stability causes or enables a nation to maximize its industrial production. My point here is that the testing process—the process of answering our comparative questions—has no end. It does however have an implicit goal.

Imagine that we discover a correlation which is so high that it holds for virtually every case we can test. For example, suppose we discover that large organizations are *always* associated with elite leadership in the following manner:

If an organization has more than X number of members; then (1) elites will emerge as the basic decision-makers, (2) their lieutenants will transmit and justify their decisions and (3) most members will passively comply with those decisions.

Again, we test and retest this relationship and find that it is universally accurate. Our faith in it may be so great that we might want to consider it as a social scientific "law" akin to Newton's Law of Gravity or Boyle's Law in the natural sciences. We would then have a very powerful tool to use for comparative explanations.

Let us return to an earlier question. Given the fact that America and the Soviet Union both pursue maximal economic production, how can they sustain such different ideologies? Our hypothetical "law" provides the means to answer this question. Both systems are so large that, according to our "law," we would expect a system of elites, lieutenants, and passive followers to emerge. The lieutenants will promote an ideology to justify or rationalize elite decisions. The nature of the ideology, be it free enterprise or communism, is secondary to its function of legitimizing elite rule. The answer to our question then, is that they can sustain any ideology so long as it functions to legitimize elite rule. To fortify this answer, we could point out that both the American and Soviet ideologies have little effect on actual political decisions; both governments support mixed economies in which private and public decision making are often indistinguishable.

Furthermore, our general "law" is also a powerful tool of prediction. It tell us that regardless of particular ideologies, the growth in size of a political system will necessarily result in political inequality. Consequently, when American or Russian politicians tell us that the era of political equality is around the corner, we have good reasons for distrusting them. Political equality is conceivable only when a political system is below an optimum size. However, if political activists promote decentralization into small, interpersonal communities, we can predict that there will be some chance of establishing greater political equality. But, suppose we had a second "law" which says:

If a political system reaches an optimal size, it will continue to grow larger.

On the basis of this second "law," we can predict that plans for decentralization will fail and therefore political inequality will persist. If we were nevertheless interested in political equality, we would realistically guide our research to discover how "greater political equality" is conceivable in large organizations; and we would forsake utopian considerations of attaining "absolute political equality."

Many cross-national analysts believe that the ultimate goal of their studies is to begin to develop social scientific "laws" akin to those of the physicist. These laws could be tested in the world laboratory of politics and become the basis for scientific explanation and prediction. In other words, they believe that cross-national comparisons are the foundation for establishing a truly scientific political science. This is the ultimate goal; yet it is far from realization.

Cross-National Comparison and the Peace Corps

Assume that you accept the cross-national idea that peasants societies are generally associated with authoritarian political structures which are based on traditional social relationships. How might this general correlation or "law" help you explain your inability to promote the construction of a rational irrigation system? How will it help you decide on the appropriate actions? Your line of reasoning may be the following.

The authority of the village elders must be based on their role as the keepers of village traditions, long-lived political hierarchy, social rituals, and agricultural norms. As long as these traditions are unquestioned, the elders will maintain their political dominance. Consequently, it is in their self-interest to reject innovations in the social and economic systems.

They will accept the digging of new drainage canals because that represents a small change well within the boundaries of their traditional agricultural ways. But they will refuse the introduction of the new technologies of a sophisticated pumping system or tractors because that represents major changes potentially threatening to their authority. Moreover, they are unlikely to forge new links with outside communities—hiring outsiders' tractors or changing marketing patterns—because this would upset some traditional social relationships. After all, once villagers saw that changes in the social and economic systems are conceivable, would they not be more likely to consider possible changes in the traditional political order?

Your irrigation plan might also upset the religious order upon which leadership is based. The elders are also the village priests who protect religious shrines. Perhaps the surrounding hilltops have religious significance, which would explain why the elders refused to consider digging reservoirs. Once villagers realized that floods and droughts could be partially controlled by science rather than being accommodated by religion alone, would they not have another basis for challenging the elders' leadership? Indeed, scientific knowledge could easily become a primary instrument of dissidents.

Yet why did the elders accept the silly bicycle pump as a wonderful innovation? It may have served them as an ideological tactic to buttress their power. But why not resist it as another potentially disruptive change? In fact, why allow an outside Peace Corps volunteer to enter their village? Your presence is in itself a potential disruption. Perhaps the bicycle pump is being used as a moderate change which the elders can control, giving the illusion that you and technological improvement are helping the community when, in fact, you are not. Have you become the elders' pawn in a power game?

With this analysis in mind, you decide to leave the village. You have provided villagers with a rational plan for maximizing crop production and for increasing profits through new marketing outlets; you have given them a chance to enter the modern world. But their traditionalism blinds them to your "gifts." If they will not change their ways, despite the many benefits you could almost guarantee them, there is little reason to remain. Satisfied with your good intentions but dismayed by the villagers' stubborness, you take the bus back to the capitol city.

There you have a drink with an American foreign aid official. He tells you, "You should not feel bad. Although we can offer these people help, we cannot force them to take it."

"What's the use of even offering, if we know we will be rejected?" you ask.

The agent replies that your role as a Peace Corp volunteer must be seen as one part of a complex American effort to aid this nation. Through many avenues of aid and services, American representatives are promoting new views and new leaders aimed at bringing the nation out of the Dark Ages. In the long run, your presence and efforts add to this goal. "Eventually, this nation will be a politically developed nation capable of making rational decisions!" he says.

CROSS-CULTURAL COMPARISON
Comparing Political Cultures

Anyone learning a foreign language quickly discovers a number of words which have no obvious equivalents in one's native language. Most middle class white Americans have difficulty understanding the street language of American ghettos, despite the fact that it is English. To the middle class white: "That man is bad," means that the man is wicked or evil in some sense. A ghetto resident, however, might interpret the sentence to mean, that the man is good; he is willing to stand up to unjust authority.

The reason that translations and interpretations are so difficult is because words' meanings are intertwined with the speaker's culture. A Mexican "siesta" is not only the equivalent to a "nap" but involves a whole social ritual which is alien to Americans. A ghetto black saying "That man is bad" is using the word "bad" in an historical context of black slavery and oppression: If a slaveholder had a "bad nigger", he had a black slave unwilling to accept slavery, which made that slave "good" in the eyes of others unwilling to accept slavery. Unless one is acquainted with or experienced in foreign cultures or American subcultures, one is likely to misinterpret meanings.

The same holds true for interpretations of political actions; unless one is tuned in to the culture of the actors, one is likely to misunderstand the significance of the actions. This point is illustrated in the following example.

You are an American abroad for the first time. You observe people walking into a building labeled Polling Place. You follow them in. They go to a table and receive a slip of paper. On the paper are several boxes, some of which they check off. They then deposit their slips of paper in a container marked Ballots.

It is quite obvious to you that these people are voting. The next day, you read in a local newspaper that 98 percent of all eligible voters cast ballots in this election. You find this remarkable. In America, less than 50 percent of all eligible voters cast ballots in many elections. "These people certainly take their elections seriously," you remark to your travel companion.

Let us now look at the same set of actions through the eyes of a native of this nation. He knows that his food rations will be cut off if he does not go to the polling place; his civil liberties will be ignored if he does not check the "right" boxes on his slip of paper; and he knows he may be imprisoned if he does not deposit his slip of paper in the prescribed container. Finally, he also assumes that regardless of what people mark on their papers, the ruling elite will announce that their people won by an overwhelming majority. And when he reads that 98 percent of the voters went to the polls and voted, he might comment to a neighbor, "It's remarkable that 2 percent had the courage not to participate!"

We have two different interpretations of the same set of events here. Which is correct? As an American witnessing these events, it is almost natural for you to conclude that an election was taking place, and that people were voting for candidates by casting ballots. Certainly that is what this set of actions would signify to you in America. However, had you studied the beliefs of the people of this nation, you might have concluded otherwise. If these people engage in these acts because they fear the penalties for not doing so then there is really no "election," "voting" or "candidates." Each of these terms assumes an element of voluntarism and choice which are lacking in this instance. Were you more aware of the cultural context, you might be more likely to interpret these acts as coerced paper shuffling.

On the other hand, we might want to hesitate before we accept our native's interpretation of these acts. He might be part of a national subculture which perceives itself as oppressed, and thus forced to go through these rituals. Consequently, his own perceptions might be accurate when applied to his subculture but inaccurate when applied to the more general culture. In fact, most of the citizens of this country may have actually "voted" for their preferred "candidates" in a way common to Americans.

Still another possibility exists. Members of the dominant culture may take it for granted that they are free to vote or not vote, to choose their preferred candidates, and to be represented by candidates who win the most votes. But if they examine these assumptions, they might notice that they are inaccurate. Perhaps they would see that they have been subtly "brainwashed" to vote or that they have subliminally learned that all opposition candidates are evil. Upon examination, they might decide that with these psychological pressures they are no better off than are the subculture members oppressed by more overt pressures. In this case, they may come to describe their own actions as coerced paper shuffling rather than as "voting."

Every person is a member of one or more political cultures. A political culture is a set of shared beliefs which members usually take for granted. As an American, you probably take for granted the goodness of liberty. This assumption has been nurtured in you and other Americans since childhood, reinforced throughout your life, and ultimately ingrained in your psyche. By adulthood, the goodness of liberty seems perfectly natural. When you engage in political arguments, you usually try to show that your viewpoint enhances people's liberty. If your opponent agrees that it does indeed enhance people's liberty, the argument is over; for both you and your opponent believe that whatever maximizes a good like liberty must also be good.

This belief in the goodness of liberty is usually the basis of your interpretation of other nations. During the cold war, many Americans assumed that the Russian people would love to overthrow their communist "dictators" if only they had the opportunity. It was assumed that certainly they too craved liberty. And every time that Americans heard the voice of a Russian dissident, this assumption was reinforced. The thought that people could actually give voluntary support to Khrushchev, let alone Stalin, was inconceivable to most Americans. But from the Russian perspective it was inconceivable that the American people could voluntarily support their "capitalist, imperialist, war-mongering" elites. Is it possible for Americans to really understand Russian politics when they ignore the fact that many Russians do not believe in the American notion of liberty as naturally good? Indeed, is it possible for Americans even to notice this without understanding that their own political culture is only one of many, and maybe not even the best?

The influence of political culture on our perceptions poses immense problems for comparative analysis. If we compare American politics with the politics of other nations by imposing our assumptions on them, will we not bias our analyses toward the American side and distort the significance of events elsewhere? And when we gather statistics to compare many nations at once, will this bias and distortion not be magnified as we impose our own assumptions on the entire world? Finally, if we compare nation-states rather than political cultures, will we not distort the significance of political events for national subcultures or political cultures which cross national boundaries?

Cross-cultural comparison is an attempt to minimize the biases and distortions involved in cross-national analysis. It demands that the analyst be sensitive to his own preconceptions as well as to the political culture of others. It demands that generalities and laws give way to interpretive statements which take into account the particularities of the different systems of meanings and assumptions in political culture. It proposes a new understanding of the meaning of political comparison. Let us investigate that new understanding.

The Logic of Cross-Cultural Comparison

The logic of cross-cultural comparison can briefly be characterized as follows:

1. All comparisons across cultures are biased by the political preconceptions of the analysts.

2. Analysts can never fully shed these preconceptions, but they can become aware of them and become sensitive to the preconceptions of others.

3. Sensitivity to other cultural preconceptions requires study of the norms and history of other cultures.

4. Analysts may then compare political actions across cultures by specifying the similarities and differences in the alternative cultures' patterns of significance and change.

5. Patterns of significance and change are not amenable to quantification. Consequently, analysts may compare only a few political cultures at one time.

6. Explanations of similarities and differences in these patterns are interpretive. Interpretations are valid to the extent that are logical, systematic, and comprehensive.

Let us further examine this logic.

Socrates believed that "to know thyself" is the first step on the road to wisdom. Cross-cultural analysts agree. Americans and American political scientists are born and nurtured into a political culture with specific preconceptions. We may now state that those preconceptions are generally the same ones underlying Politics as Conflict-Resolution, Justice as Fairness, and Pluralism. Americans tend to accept the naturalness and necessity of individual conflicts, regularized procedures for settling conflicts fairly, and group competition as a means of developing and legitimizing those procedures. The extent to which Americans accept these preconceptions varies; nevertheless, most Americans tacitly assent to them as the basis for political knowledge.

These cultural preconceptions necessarily bias people's understandings. As I have noted throughout this part of the book, these preconceptions shape what we consider to be political, appropriate political action, fair resolutions, and legitimate demands. When we evalute and compare our own political system with the political system of other cultures, we tend to project our own preconceptions on others—even though they may view the political world quite differently. A slightly fictionalized account of an actual event might illustrate this.

When Richard Nixon made his historic trip to China, he was accompanied by a host of American reporters, some of whom knew little about Chinese culture. One of these reporters did a "man-in-the-street" interview with a young Chinese woman. He asked, "Do you have any boyfriends?" This may be an appropriate question to ask in America, but it breaks a number of Chinese cultural taboos; it is the equivalent of asking an eight-year-old girl, "How many boys do you fornicate with weekly?"

The Chinese woman was very embarrassed and quickly replied, "I have no boyfriends. I spend all my spare time studying the works of Marx, Lenin, and Mao!" Within her own cultural context, she was signifying that one should not ask such questions in public. Not cued in, the reporter took her literally and analyzed her statement as a manifestation of Chinese communist propaganda.

There are at least two ways to minimize our own cultural biases when comparing our own politics with others' politics. First, we must become conscious of our own biases. We must attempt to step outside our everyday modes of understanding in order to examine the conceptual lenses which distort our vision. If we can do this, we may realize that many of the things that we believe are "natural" may be "conventional" assumptions shared by Americans alone. For example, most Americans believe that the pursuit of private profit is perfectly natural to human beings; however, were one to explore 4,000 years of recorded world history, one would quickly discover that most peoples have considered the pursuit of private profit as quite unnatural. It is mainly a convention of modern times in Western capitalist nations.

The second, and related, method of minimizing our biases is to immerse ourselves in other cultural modes of understanding. On the one hand, we can live in other cultures, befriend people from other cultures, or maximize our daily intercourse with those who are immigrants in our country. Moreover, we can do the same for the many subcultures which exist within any nation. On the other hand, we can vicariously experience other modes of cultural understanding by (1) temporarily suspending our own preconceptions and (2) empathetically studying the history and lives of peoples of other cultures. We can explore new languages and customs and imagine what it might be like to have been born into cultures different from our own. Indeed, because our preconceptions are shaped in our own cultures, it takes a large dose of imagination to view the world through the eyes of others.

Nurturing this cross-cultural sensitivity is a necessity, if one hopes to do valid comparative analysis. This sensitivity is necessary for testing the equivalence of the units of comparison. For example, within the context of modern America, the two-party system functions as a means of selecting candidates for political office. In Mozambique, Africa, the present one-party system mainly functions to mobilize passive sectors of the population to participate in politics. Were we to assume that the Mozambiquan party system functioned as our own does, we would most likely conclude that it is an extremely authoritarian means of selecting candidates; we would most likely ignore its function of stimulating a greater public role in decision making. A cross-cultural sensitivity would allow us to see that the party systems are not wholly equivalent; their varying significance for their respective systems must be considered in order to avoid distortions.

Furthermore, cross-cultural sensitivity alerts analysts to the importance of historical change. The formal structures of political systems may be stable for long periods while the cultural significance that people attach to those structures may change drastically. Notice, for example, that although American political institutions have changed little in the last 200 years, the everyday lifestyles of modern Americans are drastically different from those of their parents and grandparents. If the analyst is to capture the significance of political acts, he must also capture a sense of the historical trends which define the cultural context.

Prior to the twentieth century, the American party system was instrumental in mobilizing new groups to participate in politics. However, when many of these new groups participated in bringing about radical changes, the nature of the party system changed, though its structure was not altered much. During the twentieth century, the party system became less significant as a mobilizer of new groups and more significant as an administrator of elections: the party system provided campaign workers, sought electoral funds, and brought out the vote. After World War II, the function of the party system changed again. Today, candidates organize their own campaigns, rely on the media to win popularity, and seek out their own private financing. In an historical sense, today's party system functions less to administer elections than to legitimize the outcome of elections.

Compare this historical trend to the Mozambiquan situation. Once under European colonial rule, the Mozambiquan people were systematically excluded from political influence. Today, their one-party system is making systematic efforts to reverse this situation by overcoming historical patterns of passivity and by increasing public participation. At this point, we might wish to compare the American and Mozambiquan party systems. Both systems potentially mobilize citizens to participate in politics, but they are historically different. The American party system functions less and less as a means of involving people in politics, while the Mozambiquan party system, despite the lack of party competition, functions more and more as a means of political involvement. With this historical understanding, we may at least consider the possibility that a one-party system may be more democratic than a multiparty system may be, under specific circumstances.

Cross-cultural comparative analysis is mainly a matter of outlining similarities and differences in patterns of significance and change across cultures. Cultural significance and change are not readily subject to quantification. Industrial production can be measured by GNP, but how can one "measure" norms and history in numbers? There is no obvious answer. One must investigate in depth the cultural notions of significance and the historical changes of each particular system of interest. In order to compare the American and Mozambiquan party systems, even as briefly as we have done above, we are required to evaluate the functions that those systems serve for their peoples at various times. We must immerse ourselves in the complexities of the motives, intentions, and interests underlying people's political actions if we are to do a valid comparative analysis. Every unit of comparison is a puzzle we must sort out and then reconstruct.

Two implications follow. One is that to compare many political systems or aspects of political system at one time will result in gross distortions. We have already encountered some difficulty comparing the American and Mozambiquan party systems. Imagine what would happen if we compared 130 "party systems" simultaneously. We would have to lump together the "party systems" that serve radically different functions in their respective cultures. Some systems that serve primary religious functions would be included with those that serve symbolic functions, or those that serve competitive functions would be included with those that serve military functions. To call them all "party systems" is to ignore the possibility that people in different cultures may see very little relationship between any two of these systems. Furthermore, to call them all "party systems" is to imply that they all share something in common, but do they? If we impose an American answer by saying that they are all instrumental in candidate selection, we might be pointing to a factor which has little significance for some "party systems" and virtually no significance for others. Without a cross-cultural sensitivity, we impose our own idea of significance on others and thereby distort our understanding of the world.

A second implication is that we can only study a few political cultures at any one time. We know we cannot study all "party systems" simultaneously without biasing our understanding. Now, we must see that the process of understanding our own culture and our own preconceptions is a long, arduous process; the attempt to see the world through the eyes of a member of another culture is even more difficult. Consequently, if we wish to compare just two political cultures, we must spend considerable time understanding the complex patterns of meanings, norms, and changes which characterize those cultures. The thought of doing this for 130 cultures is virtually inconceivable. Cross-cultural comparisons must be modest in scope.

It is this modesty which distinguishes cross-cultural analysis from cross-national analysis. The cross-cultural analyst knows that he can never fully shed his biases or see the world through the eyes of one born into another culture. Rather, he exerts his maximal efforts to approach these impossible goals only to gain a better understanding. At best, he can claim justifiably that his comparisons are good interpretations. They logically and systematically account for similarities and differences across cultures. But he knows that there are other logical, systematic interpretations of similarities and differences. For example, as he highlights his understanding of the similarities and differences between the American and Mozambiquan party systems, he knows that others are developing interpretations which are based on the religious significance of the party systems, or the economic significance, or the psychological significance. Knowing this, the cross-cultural analyst must only claim that his is a reasonable comparison.

Cross-national analysis rarely assumes such modesty. It assumes that it is only a matter of time until general social scientific "laws" can be discovered that will explain the similarities and differences across all political systems for all times. Differences in cultures will fall away before the explanatory power of these "laws." Until we reach this plateau of knowledge, we must try to perfect the indicators and the tests that allow us to choose, among plausible interpretations, the interpretation best supported by the evidence. In brief, the cross-cultural analyst believes that good interpretation is the end of analysis; the cross-national analyst believes that good interpretation is the beginning. Let us now see how the cross-cultural approach would influence our Peace Corps dilemma.

Cross-Cultural Comparison and the Peace Corp

Suppose you applied a cross-cultural analysis to elucidate your particular Peace Corps experience. Rather than leave the village, you decide to stay another year to become better acquainted with local norms and trends. At the end of the year, you summarize your experience in a diary:

For hundreds of years, local peasants have engaged in traditional forms of agriculture: intensive labor and uncertain rice production. Although this mode of production is often inadequate for meeting local dietary needs, it has the virtue of strengthening community self-reliance and autonomy. Villagers depend only on themselves and each other; outsiders are considered potential threats to village life. Even in years when there are record crops, villagers avoid selling the surplus outside the local marketplace in order to avoid the threat of outsiders.

The people in this village are very concerned about a number of changes which have taken place in nearby villages. In one village, a tractor was introduced and rented out for a nominal fee. Those who could afford the nominal fee, hired the tractor which helped plow their fields and harvest their crops more efficiently than ever before.

As a result, those who invested in the tractor had record high yields. The tractor operator then informed his clients that even higher production could be assured by the introduction of new strains of rice and fertilizer. When his clients complained that they could not afford all this, the operator offered to finance it. He would later be repaid with a portion of the expected surplus. Those who accepted this also recorded high crop yields the next season.

Then the village's problems began. The operator raised his fees and the wealthy peasants became indebted to him. These debts could be paid off, he suggested, if the wealthy peasants would expand their production across larger land areas. The peasants said that this was impossible; village land has been divided in traditional ways for hundreds of years. One could not alter this. The tractor operator said that this was not his problem; he had his own creditors to pay.

Consequently, the wealthy peasants devised a plan to redistribute local land in their favor. Instead of providing free rice for the poor local peasants, as had been done traditionally, they offered the rice only if the poor peasants gave them access to their land. In turn, the wealthy peasants would "loan" the tractor, new rice strains and fertilizer to the poor peasants. With little alternative but starvation, the poor peasants complied. Soon thereafter, the tractor operator raised his rates and demanded payment on some of his loans. He apologized but explained that prices in the capitol city had raised his expenses. Again the wealthy peasants responded, this time by "persuading" village elders to let them use the common lands—hilltop areas set aside for the poor to cultivate during hard times. Gaining access to this land allowed the wealthy peasants to increase production further and make the poor more beholden to them.

The wealthy peasants' "persuading" took the form of a threat: If we do not get access to commons land, we will default on our loans. In this case, the tractor operator would sell the land to outsiders; thus the poor peasants would be unable to depend on these outsiders for help. In the interest of village peace and survival, the elders consented.

The long-term result of these events was: (1) the division of villagers into very rich and very poor peasants, (2) systematic village ties to an outside marketplace they could not control, (3) the loss of the elders' traditional political power, (4) the disappearance of traditional forms of mutual aid, and (5) a great deal of antagonism among village members. The relative equality of villagers and the relative autonomy of village life were destroyed. Although rice production did increase, the surplus was controlled mainly by outsiders like the tractor operator or by a few very rich villagers. Most community members were no better off economically and many were worse off—they had lost their lands.

You then continue your diary by relating this story to your own experiences:

I now have a better idea of why my irrigation plan was rejected. The elders were interested in increasing crop production; that is why they were willing to have a Peace Corps volunteer come to their village and why they supported the new drainage canals and the bicycle pump. These innovations might increase production without necessarily making the village less egalitarian or autonomous. But, renting a tractor to dig a reservoir, introducing a sophisticated pumping system, or marketing surpluses elsewhere were all dangerous ideas because each of these "innovations" would put important aspects of village life under outside control. Moreover, I now understand why the elders refused to consider excavating a reservoir on local hilltops. These areas are reserved for the poor villagers' use (for growing crops or grazing animals) during droughts or floods. A reservoir would upset this traditional use of common lands.

Finally, my suggestion about marketing the expected surplus crops must have been particularly ominous to villagers. Their agricultural system is not based on a profit motive; it is based on a cultural desire to provide subsistence for all villagers *and* to maintain village cohesiveness. The villagers take this so much for granted that they do not speak of it; they assume that everyone sees agricultural production this way. Because my preconceptions were the exact opposite of theirs, I had difficulty understanding. Moreover, their virtual unanimity on this issue makes me now realize that the community elders are not authoritarian figures; they are more like guardians of village norms. Though they are not elected, it is thoroughly understood by the villagers that this is their responsibility. If they do not meet it, they are expected to resign.

Your diary ends here. Your decision to stay or leave is now more complicated. On the one hand, you understand better why your irrigation system was rejected, though you still believe your plan could have been useful. On the other hand, you are not certain that you will be comfortable taking a job back in America. You may be asked to develop pesticides, which do increase agricultural productivity, but cause long-term health damages to agricultural workers and consumers. You have changed: once you took efficiency and profit for granted, but now you see them as conventional norms among other conventional norms which people elsewhere treat as more significant.

SUMMARY AND CONCLUSION
Don Quixote and the Ugly American

In Chapter 4, I described and analyzed two theories of American politics. In this chapter, I have described two ways of comparing America to other systems of politics: (1) Cross-National Comparison and (2) Cross-Cultural Comparison.

Cross-national analysts tend to compare nations by searching for generalities that can be made for many nation-states, that can be tested, and that can be applied to particular questions. The virtue of cross-national comparison is that it provides the analyst with some basis for deciding which, among many plausible interpretations of national similarities and differences, is most valid.

The danger of cross-national comparison is that it allows the American analyst to bias his comparison in favor of America. By treating America as one nation-state among many, the analyst ignores the fact that America exerts tremendous influence over other nation-states. By ignoring this, the analyst is unlikely to see that many of the "problems" of other nations are rooted in their relationship with America. In addition, by ignoring the cultural differences of nations in order to quantify data, the analyst ignores the possibility that this data may have significantly different meanings for members of other cultures; he is likely to invest his data with meaning derived from his own American culture. In many cases, the result is that those who do cross-national comparisons tend to assume values which make America appear relatively pluralistic; they are likely to adopt a pluralist view of American politics.

Cross-cultural analysts try to examine their own American biases and empathetically understand how the political world appears in the eyes of people from other cultures. Their greatest virtue lies in their sensitivity to the historical and cultural complexity of political institutions and actions. They are likely to develop a multi-dimensional understanding of politics based on modest statements of similarities and differences between cultures. And they are apt to be sensitive to the ways in which their own political system is limited and elitist.

The danger of cross-cultural analysis is in the opportunity it gives to those people in America who are disenchanted with their own political system. It tempts people to eschew the biases of American political culture, only to adopt contrary biases of other political cultures; it tempts people to develop unreasonable interpretations by not providing a well-defined set of criteria for distinguishing valid interpretation from invalid interpretation. Consequently, among cross-cultural analysts we are likely to find at least a few who use the method more as a justification of their opinions and less as a tool of understanding.

I suggest that neither mode of comparison *necessarily* implies that its user must become an American Don Quixote or a critic of the Ugly American. Political scientists who study comparative politics rarely go to either extreme, though examples of both are readily found. To repeat an earlier point; I am speaking of tendencies. Cross-national comparisons more readily portray America as a world-wide standard of pluralism; cross-cultural comparisons more readily sensitizes one to American elitism.

Is one mode of comparison superior to the other? Although I will once again argue that there is no absolute basis for preferring one to the other, this argument is more complex than earlier ones. Above all else, most American political scientists prefer cross-national comparisons because they believe that these are more scientific. Nevertheless, some political scientists disagree; they argue that the alternative is more scientific. To examine this debate is to examine what we may mean by a "science" of politics. Part Two of this book is devoted to this examination.

But before we can begin Part Two, we must consider how our two preconceptual logics affect our ability to understand politics. As we shall see, the particular logic that we have been nurtured on will affect what we consider to be "scientific."

SELECTED REFERENCES

Almond, Gabriel and Verba, Sidney. *The Civic Culture*. Princeton: Princeton University Press, 1963.

Apter, David E. *Introduction to Political Analysis*. Cambridge, Mass.: Winthrop Publishers, 1977.

Geertz, Clifford. *The Interpretation of Cultures*. New York: Basic Books, 1973.

Greene, Thomas H. *Comparative Revolutionary Movements*. Englewood Cliffs, N.J.: Prentice-Hall, 1974.

Gurr, Robert T. *Why Men Rebel* Princeton: Princeton University Press, 1970.

LaPolombara, Joseph. *Politics Within Nations*. Englewood Cliffs, N.J.: Prentice-Hall, 1974.

Mannheim, Karl. *Ideology and Utopia*. Trans. L. Wirth and E. Shils. New York: Harcourt, Brace and World, 1936.

Marx, Karl. *The Economic and Philosophic Manuscripts of 1844*. Edited by D. Struik. Translated by M. Milligan. New York: International Publishers, 1964.

Miliband, Ralph. *The State in Capitalist Society*. New York: Basic Books, 1969.

Mills, C. Wright. *The Sociological Imagination*. London: Oxford University Press, 1959.

Ryan, Alan, ed. *The Philosophy of Social Explanation*. London: Oxford University Press, 1973.

Sansom, Robert L. *The Economics of Insurgency in the Mekong Delta of Vietnam*. Cambridge, Mass.: MIT Press, 1970.

Schurrman, Franz. *Ideology and Organization in Communist China*. Berkeley: University of California Press, 1966.

Wallerstein, Immanuel. *The Modern World System*. New York: Academic Press, 1976.

Weber, Max. *The Methodology of the Social Sciences*. Glencoe, Ill.: The Free Press, 1949.

Are there reasons for preferring the cross-national mode of comparison to the cross-cultural mode? Or are there reasons for preferring the latter to the former? The answers to these questions return us to our starting point, that is, the appropriate definitions of politics, and also allow us a final opportunity to evaluate our two logics of political preconceptions.

The Limits of Politics

The ultimate aim of cross-national analysis is to yield social scientific laws which can be used as the basis for policy recommendations. The idea, however, that laws of human political behavior are conceivable, let alone capable of being discovered, implies severe limits for policy recommendations. The physicist may discover laws of atomic behavior and use his knowledge of those laws to make recommendations, but he assumes that the laws are unalterable. Consequently, his recommendations must not overstep the boundaries of laws he cannot change. Similarly, if laws of political behavior exist, then the political scientist may be able to discover them and use them to good ends; but he cannot make policy recommendations which overstep the boundaries of human political possibilities as de-

fined by those laws. He must accept human behavior as it exists today.

Let me illustrate this with an example. Assume that you and several friends organize to advance the goal of women's equality. Your group is quite small. After some discussion, you arrive at a consensus concerning your new organization: everyone will share in responsibilities and everyone will participate equally in group decisions. As a group, you all hope to experience egalitarian nonsexist relations and to promote them in society.

Your organization flourishes. Victories are won. New members join. Donations come pouring in. Success, however, is accompanied by growing-pains. You discover it is inefficient for everyone to share in the ever growing responsibilities: mailings, research, speaking engagements, lobbying, coalition meetings. Should everyone continue to share in all tasks or should you hire secretaries to do mailings, have your most skillful researchers do research, assign your best public speakers to publicity and so forth? Surely specialization and a divison of labor would be more efficient. Another growing-pain ensues. The original members want to continue sharing tasks; the new members believe specialization would best serve group goals. Discussions on the topic are interminable and yet little consensus is formed. What is to be done?

According to many political scientists who believe political behavior is lawful, there is really no choice here. First, the growth of organizational size necessitates the development of a leadership able to set priorities and to resolve conflicts peacefully. Without this leadership, not only will group activities be inefficient, the survival of the group itself is endangered. If members have no formal means of conflict resolution, some will use coercion to have their way and forcefully establish leadership, or others will simply resign and seek membership in competing groups. Second, this means that organizational efficiency must take precedence over ideological beliefs. Unless specialization and a division of labor are developed, organizational inefficiency will render the group less competitive with more efficient groups. Either a new, efficiency-oriented leadership will emerge or the organization will perish in all practical terms.

Given these "laws" of leadership and specialization, these political scientists would recommend that the old egalitarian mode of organization give way to the newer, more efficient leadership orientation. While it might be nice to dream of a large egalitarian organization pursuing egalitarian goals, it is impractical to try to realize it. The attempt to do so is likely to result in the end of the group. Realistically, group membership must live with the paradox that they need to participate in a hierarchical organization in order to pursue the goal of sexual equality. Like atomic behavior, the laws of political behavior constitute the basic facts of life—for better or for worse.

If it is not its nature, an atom cannot suddenly zoom off in any direction; if it is not its nature, a human being cannot eliminate the inevitable conflict which accompanies human organizations. Regardless of a person's contrary beliefs, histories, cultures, ideologies, or religions, he cannot create a large, egalitarian organization. He cannot build a society-wide community. The scope of people's political actions is limited by their nature.

It is precisely this notion of people's limited political potential which lies at the heart of our first definition of politics as conflict-resolution. Adherents of politics as conflict-resolution assume that it is people's nature to conflict with other people, as if it were a law engendered by cross-national analysis. The choice of nonconflict is not as open as we might desire. What choices are open? We have already specified three major choices: (1) Are conflicts to be resolved violently or peacefully? (2) If peacefully, are the procedures for resolving conflict to be fair or unfair? (3) If fair, are procedures to be subject to pluralist group competition or elitist manipulation? In short, it is the belief in the limits of people's political potential which unites adherents of the four models which constitute Logic I. Adherents share a belief that policy recommendations aimed at greater peace, fairness, and pluralism are acceptable, especially in terms of American politics; policy recommendations aimed at egalitarian community, the good society, or perfect social and political equality are irresponsible, utopian, and potentially dangerous. Those who attempt to create a political system which oversteps the bounds of human nature, usually end up promoting violence, intolerance, and vicious brands of elitism themselves.

Are there good reasons for preferring the cross-national mode of comparision? For people who emphasize the limits of people's political potential, the answer is a clear yes. Cross-national political analysis aims at revealing the laws which define the limits of political behavior. In turn, these laws are useful tools for promoting "realistic" policies based on people as they are, not on people as they might be.

With this in mind, we may now give a substantive label to Logic I. It is "Political Realism." Its adherents are hardheaded people who avoid the sentimentality of dreamers in order to promote reforms that yield concrete results. The aim of these reforms is to develop a limited political system which can peacefully and fairly resolve conflicts in ways which allow groups maximal influence in the pluralist arena. We may now draw our final diagram of the Logic of Political Realism.

THE LOGIC OF POLITICAL REALISM

The Logic of Political Realism tends to be a closed circle. Once one adopts one of its four models, there is a logical *tendency* to adopt its other three models. The basic link is the notion that people's political capacities are limited. The role of political science is to discover those limits by developing laws of political behavior. These laws then become the basis for limited policy recommendations. In America, these policy recommendations are limited to greater peace, fairness, and pluralism; greater community, goodness, and socio-political equality are unrealistic dreams. In sum, the politics of those who adhere to the logic of political realism is *reformist* at the very most.

It is beyond the scope of this book to do a detailed analysis of which people will be likely to accept the limits of political possibilities, adopt the logic of political realism, and recommend reformist policies. I can, however, ask a few suggestive questions.

1. Is it not likely that "pragmatic" and "business-oriented" Americans will be most sensitive to the limits of politics? After all, they deal with today's concrete realities and cannot be worried about grand future possibilities. They, if anyone, know the world of human conflict and competition.

2. Who, if not politicians, are most likely to accept the logic of political realism? They know best of all that small changes can be won through hard work, bargaining, and the compromising of various interests. Moreover, they know that their political futures are endangered if they become too dedicated to long range, ideological goals. In recent years in America, Goldwater and McGovern proved this poignantly.

3. Despite popular beliefs to the contrary, is it not likely that those who benefit most from the present state of politics recommend reformist policies? After all, political and economic elites suffer few losses in moderate reforms and they often benefit. But, surely they benefit from the absence of more radical demands.

4. And is it not in the interests of political and economic elites to use their offices, prestige, and resources to persuade the population that they too should be political realists and have much to gain by doing so? If elites succeed in this effort, then they need not be concerned with radical demands that threaten to damage their particular interests.

These questions suggest that those who are most privileged in America and have the most to lose by major changes are likely to accept the logic of political realism. Moreover, to the extent that the privileged are able to persuade others that they too have a stake in the present political system, it is conceivable that most Americans will have preconceived notions of political realism. This may have been the case for many Americans during the "quiet" 1950s.

The Opportunities of Politics

Cross-cultural comparisons assume the possibility of almost infinite human diversity. People's political perceptions, motives, intentions, and beliefs invest their actions with a wide range of meanings. Historical and cultural variation not only point to some of these possibilities; they also indicate that change is an ever present phenomenon in people's political existence. Nevertheless, amid this diversity and change is a basis for human harmony. Within particular social groups, cultures, and historical situations, people share structures of perceptions, motives, intentions, and interests. Some analysts go as far as to argue that historical diversity and change are the basis for an emerging human harmony: Once individual fought individual and tribe fought tribe; today, vast numbers of people live together in large societies. Perhaps we are moving toward an historical stage upon which people can develop their diverse capacities in harmony with others.

Both the persistence of diversity and change, and the historical potential for human harmony indicates that all "laws" of human behavior must be suspect. Laws are generalities, based on past behavior, which state that some relationships among people are unchangeable and which set arbitrary limits on the infinite possibilities for future political action. Laws support the assumption of human limits at the very moment when we witness limits being lifted. Who, for example, could have predicted that a consistently anticommunist Richard Nixon would be the one to open relations with the People's Republic of China?

People are not like atomic particles. They may occasionally behave according to lawlike patterns, but their similar behaviors may have different meanings. Moreover, those different meanings may explain why people break up their own lawlike patterns with experimentation and new structures. Unlike the physicist's laws, the social scientist's laws must be treated like old habits. It is often easier than not, to continue the old ways; yet people have always changed the old ways to explore the possibilities of the new. We must remember that the physicist deals with *natural objects;* the political scientist investigates *conscious subjects.*

We can illustrate this by returning to our example of your women's equality group. Suppose that your small group has grown and has experienced the growing-pains described earlier. Now also imagine that you have learned from others' experience and are sensitive to the pressures toward hierarchical leadership and specialization. Can you "break these laws?"

Maybe. Although the pressures are, of course, very real, the fact that you are conscious of them might provide you with some leverage. You might suggest the following course. Rather than accept hierarchical leadership and specialization, why not decentralize the organization into small groups akin to the original one? On the one hand, this will allow all members to continue to experience egalitarian relations within the group. On the other hand, It will not necessarily inhibit the organization's overall ability to promote sexual equality. These small groups will serve as embryonic examples of equality. These small groups might be more effective in involving people directly in the struggle for sexual equality than would be a hierarchical organization. Although contributions alone help, contributions combined with active support are even better. Finally, when the combined weight of the entire organization is needed, the small groups could form a coalition which aggregates their influence.

This plan's benefit is that the ethic of egalitarian community can be realized, within the organization, without necessarily inhibiting organizational effectiveness. Nevertheless, obvious problems will arise. Having grown up in a competitive society, new members will have difficulty adjusting to consensus decision making. Even if small groups are able to reach a consensus, their consensus might be quite different from that of other groups. Moreover, coalition activity may be stymied by some groups which feel certain that their interests must take priority over other groups. Yet, no matter how many possible conflicts we can imagine, we are only dealing with problems. If people become aware of these problems, there is a chance of solving them. There will be failures, but this only indicates the difficulty of solution, not the impossibility of it. If members maintain an experimental attitude, it is just possible that they will succeed in developing an egalitarian organization that will effectively pursue egalitarian goals.

How do we discover the possibilities for political action? Merely to state that there are limits forecloses experimentation. But that which is realistic or practical has a way of changing. Only a very few years ago, many people believed it was "unrealistic" to believe that women could vote, hold jobs, and have significant political power. These beliefs are becoming more anarchronistic. Today, it may be "realistic" to believe that women are capable of a great deal more than men are, as women demonstrate their extraordinary abilities to keep house, raise families, and participate in the social, economic, and political worlds. Few men have matched the achievements of the single, working mother.

This notion of people's untapped and unlimited political potential lies at the heart of our second definition of politics as community-building. Despite tremendous conflict, politics is characterized here as a diverse effort to tap people's potential to live together harmoniously. According to justice as goodness, it is even conceivable that this harmony, based on egalitarian relationships, can overcome trends toward elitism. For American politics, this means that we must highlight that elitism; thus we can face and overcome it. In short, what unites the adherents of the four models of Logic II is the shared belief in people's immense capacity to live together as family members of a common species.

Because adherents to Logic II emphasize human potentials, they are unlikely to limit their policy recommendations to what is presently considered realistic. On the one hand, they might agree with the political realists that greater peace, fairness, and pluralism are warranted. On the other hand, they clearly disagree with the realists that change is limited to these reforms. Policy recommendations to nurture greater community, move toward the good society and eliminate socio-political elitism are also warranted. And these policy recommendations, as radical as they may be, are not utopian; they are serious experiments aimed at controlling change for the better.

We may now give a substantive label to Logic II. It is "Political Opportunities." Its adherents are people interested in better understanding the past and present, in order to expand future opportunities. Adherents may be radical reformists or radical revolutionaries, depending on the particular context. The realm of politics is as broad as people's political potentials are. All aspects of society which affect people's ability to develop egalitarian communities are political. Let us diagram this Logic of Political Opportunities.

THE LOGIC OF POLITICAL OPPORTUNITIES

The Logic of Political Opportunities is also a closed circle in the sense that, once one adopts one of its models, there is a logical *tendency* to adopt its other models. The basic link connecting the models is the idea that people's political potentials are great, if not unlimited. The role of political science is to explore the diversity and change of politics in order to understand how people's political possibilities can be expanded. Policy recommendations are essentially recommendations to experiment with new possibilities. In America, in particular, policy recommendations directed at overcoming political and economic elitism are the steps toward greater harmony and equality. Those who adhere to the logic of political possibilities are usually less interested in incremental reforms and more interested in major structural changes.

Once more let me ask a few questions to suggest which people are likely to emphasize political opportunities.

1. Is it not likely that the young people will be most interested in exploring political opportunities? Their age alone sensitizes them to change that is a norm of youth. They may be more experimental and flexible in trying out alternatives because they are not locked into a specific career pattern.

2. Will not those people who are alienated from "politics as usual" be most likely to accept the logic of political opportunities? They have the opportunity and distance necessary for seeing political problems and considering a broad range of solutions because they are not directly tied into political interests or the present political system.

3. Who else is likely to benefit most from major structural changes, if not the least privileged in society? Poor people, exploited working people, minorities, and women conscious of socio-political inequalities perhaps have the most forceful reasons to support major changes. They are most likely to benefit.

4. Is it possible, however, that the "realistic" education of youth, of the alienated, and of the least privileged will lead them to believe that "reformism" is their only alternative? Perhaps not. An education at odds with people's everyday experiences tends to be less compelling than otherwise. And education is always a two-edged sword. Although education can be an instrument for propaganda, it can also be a basis for critical inquiry.

In America, these questions suggest that the youth, the alienated, and the least privileged are those most likely to accept the logic of political opportunities. These groups have some reasons for rejecting the more common logic; they often have a subculture upon which the alternative logic can be built. The political activism and counterculture of the 1960s may have been a manifestation of this.

Political Preconceptions and Political Science

The two logics developed in Part One should be considered as clusters of assumptions, perceptions, and values. For most people, these clusters remain at the preconceptual level: they are not systematically articulated or defended. The clusters constitute political common sense and are the basis of political opinions.

In America, most people are nurtured on the logic of political realism; they participate in processes which reward political realism, and they receive a continuous stream of media cues which reinforces that realism. As long as preconceptions of realism are taken for granted, rather than articulated and examined, most Americans will accept them. Indeed, it will seem quite natural.

Nevertheless, as more and more Americans become dissatisfied with their political system, which may have been the case in the 1970s, preconceptual realism will be questioned. Youth will be ambivalent and perhaps seek new modes of understanding and action. Alienated Americans may cling to their old preconceptions, with the hope that as individuals they can attain a modicum of success. But if the individual safety hatch closes, they too may seek alternative political perspectives. Finally, those least privileged in America are those most likely to adopt the preconceptual assumptions of the alternative logic. More so than other Americans, they live in subcultures which give greater weight to the importance of community life.

Political scientists also support particular clusters of assumptions, perceptions, and values. Because they are nurtured on, involved in, and affected by the American context, they too are most likely to adhere to the logic of political realism. Political scientists, however, can be dissatisfied with their political system and identify with the young, the alienated, and the less privileged. To the extent that they do, they are more likely to find the logic of political opportunities sensible.

Political scientists support either logic in two distinguishable ways. First, they systematically articulate their understandings of politics. The models and countermodels presented in Part One represent political scientists' conscious articulation of political preconceptions. Second, because they have articulated these preconceptions, political scientists can compare and defend them. Since the Age of Enlightenment the scientific argument has been the strongest defense of a viewpoint. If one of our two logics is more scientific; then we can say that one preconceptual logic of politics is more valid.

My argument will be quite different. I believe that poltical scientists are attached to a set of political preconceptions just as other people are. Political scientists are able to articulate their preconceptions more systematically than most people are, only because they are more conscious of them. They are not less attached to them. Political scientists choose to adopt a notion of science which they find useful, that is, the one most consistent with their political preconceptions.

In Part Two, I will argue that political realists are likely to choose a notion of science similar to that of the physicist; those who focus on political possibilities have good reasons for choosing an alternative notion of science. Neither one "scientific" methodology nor the alternative is necessarily more valid; both are useful to the extent that they help solve problems which emerge out of political scientists' differing preconceptions. Consequently, I will suggest that there are at least *two* systematic and useful political sciences. One is more useful to moderates interested in incremental reforms; the other is more useful to those interested in fundamental changes. Political science and politics are inextricably tied.

TWO

One's political preconceptions need not necessarily affect one's study of politics. One's position in political controversies does not necessarily determine that there is one superior method of study. Conceivably, the reactionaries and the revolutionaries are equally interested in an accurate picture of the political circumstances that they hope to change for their respective ends; both have an interest in adopting the *best* method for political analysis. Nevertheless, there are good reasons why people with particular preconceptions or positions in controversies tend to use one type of method while their antagonists use another. This is the subject matter of Part Two.

In the twentieth century, a general consensus has been reached on the best method of analysis, namely, the "scientific" method. Most political scientists want to replace political guesswork with systematic, scientific analysis just as astrology was replaced by astronomy. And most political activists hope for some scientific degree of certainty in the likely outcome of their actions. However, the definition of the "scientific" method is itself the subject of controversy.

What is the "scientific" method? For some, it is a set of specific steps for generating and testing knowledge. Terms such as theory, hypothesis, operationalization, quantification, validity, and reliability form the basic components of the steps. For others, there is no single, specifiable scientific method. Some scientists follow the step-by-step process, while other scientists imaginatively reconstruct events in ways that make more sense to them. Both perspectives on science include systematic logic and rigorous testing, but both approach the problem of understanding quite distinctly.

Are natural scientific methods justly adapted to the study of politics? Some analysts answer yes. As natural objects do, people behave in patterned and predictable ways that can be described and understood in terms of general laws of human behavior. Other analysts disagree. They assume that people can and do change their behavior patterns for a variety of reasons. For example, it may be that masses must attract one another, but people may consciously decide to move toward or away from one another. Political scientists ought not to search for general laws; they must develop their own scientific way of interpreting the meaning of human actions.

In Part Two, I will suggest that there are two predominant methods of analysis in political science today. The first is based on the following assumptions:

1. There is a single scientific method aimed at generating and
testing laws of human behavior.

2. This method is readily adaptable to political studies because both natural and human behavior is patterned and predictable.

In Chapter 6, I will consider this method of political studies more closely. I will briefly examine the "Logical Positivist" justification for studying behavior, the "Behavioralist" method for political analysis, and the "Post-Behavioral" revisions.

The second predominant method of political studies is based on the following, contrary assumptions:

1. There is not one scientific method but several, involving imaginative reconstructions of seemingly disconnected information.

2. Rather than adapt any one of these methods to the study of politics, the analyst must use those which help her interpret the meaning of politics from different perspectives.

In Chapter 7, I will consider this approach in greater detail. I will examine the "Phenomenological" notions of meaning and action, the criteria used in the "Interpretive Approach," and provide a concrete example of the Marxist variation of this method.

Which of these methods is more accurate or more scientific? Which is most useful for understanding politics? I will suggest that these questions cannot be answered in the abstract. Rather, we must think for what purposes are these methods accurate, scientific, or useful. Conceivably, the first and second method provide adequate understanding for some purposes.

Near the end of Chapter 6, I will suggest that the modern Post-Behavioral method tends to be accurate, scientific, or useful for adherents of the Logic of Political Realism. In brief, the Post-Behavioral method generates knowledge that is consistent with political realism and that provides political realists with a basis for involvement in moderate reforms. By demonstrating the systematic links between the Logic of Political Realism and Post-Behavioralism, I will have established what I call *Political Science I.*

Alternatively, near the end of Chapter 7, I will argue that the modern Interpretive Approach tends to be accurate, scientific, or useful to adherents of the Logic of Political Opportunities. This method is consistent with the political opportunities perspectives. It provides adherents with the knowledge necessary for broadening political opportunities. By demonstrating systematic links between the Logic of Political Opportunities and the Interpretive Approach method, I will have established what I call *Political Science II.*

There are two political sciences today. Both claim to be scientific; both have norms of systematic logic and rigorous investigation; both suggest that the alternative political science distorts rather than reveals the political world. Is it possible that there are two relatively distinct ways of scientifically understanding politics? In Chapter 8, I will argue that not only is this possible, but it is a norm in the natural sciences. For example, there have always been scientists interested in establishing general laws of the universe; but they have always been accompanied by scientists who have a greater interest in interpreting the constant changes in the universe. Their scientific interests have differed as have their methods of investigation. Modern political science, in some sense, reproduces these age old divisions.

Chapter 9 is a summary and conclusion of the major arguments in this book. It will reconstruct the logic underlying the two political sciences, consider the possibilities for other political sciences, and develop a notion of "political adequation" which relates the means of understanding to the ends of understanding.

6

**POST-BEHAVIORALISM:
POLITICAL SCIENCE I**

CHAPTER SIX Post-behavioralism is a method for studying politics as well as an attitude toward the study of politics. It is a method in the sense that it prescribes a set of steps central to any study of political phenomena. It is also an attitude which "realistically" holds that the study of politics can never be totally isolated from the surrounding political environment. This method and attitude constitute the primary approach to political studies among American political scientists today.

In this chapter, I will trace the scientific logic and the historical development of post-behavioralism. Included here are brief discussions of the methodological focus of political science, the Logical Positivist requirements for doing science, the behavioralist revision of those requirements, and post-behavioral analysis today. In brief, this chapter is an analysis of how the study of politics came to be seen as a science by practicioners.

I will conclude this chapter by suggesting that adherents of the Logic of Political Realism have good reasons for adopting Post-Behavioralism as the most sensible and scientific method for studying politics. This particular link between a set of preconceptions and a method constitutes what I call Political Science I. The next chapter will consider Political Science II.

THE FOCUS OF POLITICAL STUDIES: ACTUAL BEHAVIOR If one wishes to understand a political system or an aspect of politics, where does one begin? Does one investigate what people have said about politics? Does one consider not what people have said about politics, but how they have felt? Or does one simply observe the actions of people in politics? The following story illustrates some of the advantages political analysts see in observing actual behavior.

Imagine that you have been commissioned to analyze the politics of the planet Jupiter. Upon boarding your interplanetary vehicle, you map out your strategy. You will go to the Jupiter central library, pour over the planet's major political documents, and draw a chart of the official power structure. You will then do an analysis of the debates, reasons, and compromises which led decision-makers to legitimize the official power structure.

After months of study, you construct the following chart:

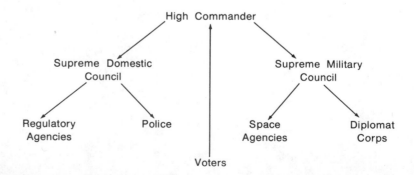

According to the Jupiter constitution and law, voters elect a new High Commander every ten years. The elected High Commander appoints a 25-member Supreme Domestic Council which advises him on planetary matters and which administers his edicts. The Supreme Domestic Council delegates some of its administrative authority to the appropriate regulatory agencies and police forces on Jupiter. The High Commander also appoints a 25-member Supreme Military Council which is expected to advise him on interplanetary policy questions. Once the High Commander makes interplanetary policy decisions, the Supreme Military Council administers the decisions through its subordinate space agencies (e.g., Office of Space Technology or Space Guards) or Diplomat Corps. At the end of ten years, a new High Commander is elected.

At this point, you might investigate the norms that justify this official power structure. Why should the High Commander have such a long term? Why should the Supreme Domestic Council have only advisory and administrative authority, and not legislative authority? Why should the Supreme Military Council have as much authority as the Supreme Domestic Council? To answer these questions, you might refer to early constitutional debates or look at past justifications offered by political leaders. Once you feel confident that you understand the official power structure and its justifications, you are prepared to compare Jupiter's politics to the politics of other planets.

Feeling that your analysis is now complete, you show it to a Jupiter friend who, you hope, will correct any small errors you have made. Your friend conscientiously reads your study and comments that you have all your facts straight. "But," she adds, "your whole study is a fantasy!" Shocked by this, you ask for further explanation.

She says that your chart and analysis of norms accurately reflect the *official* power structure but not the *actual* political behavior which takes place. For example, the Director of the Office of Space Technology, an agency "officially" subordinate to the Supreme Military Council, is "actually" the second most powerful person in government. The Director has used her position to win control of the dominant political party, to develop a loyal corps of supporters in other agencies, and to use advanced technological devices to spy on her potential antagonists. The Director, Janus Ehoov, is so powerful that the High Commander, let alone her ostensible superiors on the Supreme Military Council, dare not cross her. Knowing this, the last three High Commanders have sought her support as an important ally in government circles. With her support, the High Commander has greater assurance that his edicts will actually be carried out by bureaucrats. Your friend goes on to enumerate other ways in which the official power structure does not reflect actual power relations among individuals in government.

You are obviously surprised. You object that Jupiter's constitution and laws give both the High Commander and the Supreme

Military Council the *right* to fire Janus Ehoov whenever they wish. Your friend laughingly responds, "Yes, they do have the *right* but not the *might*." It would be extremely dangerous to fire Janus Ehoov because she has enough influence among government personnel to see that the High Commanders' edicts or Supreme Councils' administrative rulings are sabotaged. As a result of her spying operations, she has enough information to damage the careers of many high government officials.

On the basis of this new information, you may want to redraft your chart and alter your study of Jupiter's politics. Your new chart might look something like this:

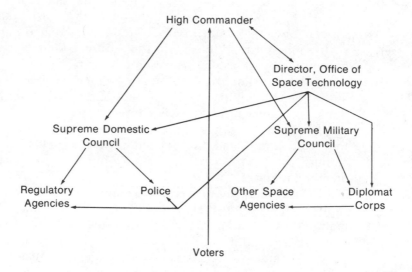

Despite this chart's differences from the official power structure, it better represents the actual patterns of behavior among individuals involved in Jupiter politics.

If you refocus your studies on actual political behavior, you might discover further discrepancies between what "should" be, according to official documents and norms, and what "is." Perhaps the reason conflicts between the Supreme Domestic Council and the Supreme Military Council are won by the latter is that Jupiter depends on Saturn's raw materials. After all, it is the Supreme Military Council's agencies that oversee relations with Saturn; relations which ultimately determine if there will or will not be an energy shortage on Jupiter. Once you systematically discover the major patterns of political behavior on Jupiter, you may end up revising your chart to such a great extent that it bears little resemblance to the official power structure.

Were you studying politics during the first half of the twentieth century, your major focus would have been on the official documents

and norms which constitute the theoretical basis of various governments. Your major emphasis would be on describing official power
structures and interpreting justificatory norms. Nevertheless, a
number of your colleagues might have suggested to you that the
official power structure and norms do not necessarily reflect actual
power relations. Constitutional norms are often not practiced; unof-
ficial groups are often able to wield political influence, and officially
subordinate agencies continually limit the power of superiors. By the
end of World War II, political scientists who believed studies should
be on actual political behavior were dominant in the profession.
Their significance in the last two or three decades has been (1) to
demonstrate the existence of a large gap between the norms of
politics and the practices of politics and (2) to develop a "scientific"
method for studying patterns of actual political behavior.

THE BEHAVIORAL METHOD Since the days of Socrates, political philosophers have concerned
themselves with the constitutions and norms that justify particular
political arrangements. As long as political analysts investigated
these political arrangements in terms of official constitutions or
prevailing norms, they looked to political philosophers for guidance.
What "ought" to be in politics and what "is" in politics were closely
related.

Once political analysts seriously noted the gap between what is
said in politics and what is actually done, they found the political
philosophers of little help; indeed, political philosophers were often
seen as a positive hindrance to the advancement of political understanding. Political philosophers speculate about values which may or
may not inform the behavior of political actors. But, if we are to
understand politics as it is realistically, as people experience in their
daily lives, we must forego speculation and analyze politics as it
happens, for better or for worse. At this stage, political analysts drew
a sharp line between political philosophy (with its focus on values)
and political analysis (with its focus on actual behavior). But how is
one to study actual behavior?

The most impressive model of study already existed, having
demonstrated its worth in the natural sciences. Over hundreds of
years, natural scientists had developed methods for studying observable phenomena ranging from microscopic particles to macro-
scopic worlds. Could one simply adapt their methods to the study of
observable political behavior? If so, then the studies of political
analysts could be considered "scientific," thus worthy of public
legitimacy.

Such an adaptation was no easy feat. Surely the behavior of
people differs from the behavior of atoms, chemicals, and so forth.
Natural objects lack moral norms or emotional imponderables; these

are factors which obviously affect human behavior. Are these differences not significant enough to make one question whether or not natural scientific methods can be applied to people? Interestingly enough, a group of language philosophers known as Logical Positivists answered these questions in a way which justified adapting the natural "scientific" method to political analysis.

Language,
Science
and Politics

Natural scientists and political analysts share one basic factor: both must communicate their understandings through the vehicle of language. As we shall see, it was upon this truism that Logical Positivists developed a basis for uniting natural scientific methods with political studies.

Logical Positivists posed the question: How do we know when we are using language intelligibly enough to communicate our meanings to others? They set down two criteria as an answer. First, the words in a proposition or sentence must represent observable phenomena in the world. In their eyes, there must be a *positive* correspondence between words and objects. Thus, the word "John" is intelligible because it positively corresponds to an observable person. The word "love" does not correspond to an observable phenomena; and therefore it cannot be communicated meaningfully. Second, words in a proposition which do not represent observable phenomena must represent *logical* relationships. In the sentence, "John is home," "John" and "home" represent observable phenomena while the word "is" represents a logical relationship between these phenomena. To say that "John is and is not home" is unintelligible because the relationship is illogical. Of course, most propositions are more complex than these, but the two criteria are still applicable. The most complex sentences can be communicated meaningfully only if they can be broken down into logical relationships and observable phenomena.

When we apply these criteria to common language, we discover that many of our sentences cannot be communicated clearly. When we use moral terms like *"justice"* or emotionally laden terms like *"happiness,"* we necessarily risk confusion. One cannot demonstrate the meaning of these words by pointing to something in the world and saying, "That is justice or happiness." At best, we can describe what we mean by these terms, but our descriptions involve using other moral or emotionally laden words that are equally unintelligible when communicated to others. The point here is not that *"justice"* or *"happiness"* do not exist; personally we may be able to experience them. Rather, the point of the Logical Positivists' argument was that such terms cannot be communicated with any precision. This is one reason why morality and emotions have been expressed through the symbolic (imprecise) language of poets.

When we make this distinction between communicable and noncommunicable language, we are better able to test the truthfulness of propositions. "John is home" can be tested by observing where John is, in relation to his home. But how can we test the proposition, "Justice is happiness?" We are never quite sure what these terms mean; we can only speculate about how they are related to one another. Whatever we conclude about the truthfulness of this proposition, our conclusions can only be subjective. For Logical Positivists, an objective test of truth was one that compared the words which picture observable phenomena and the phenomena themselves. Values, emotions, or subjectivity have no place here.

The implication of this linguistic analysis for investigators of natural and human behavior was simple: differences between objects in the natural world and people's behavior are insignificant for purposes of investigation. People may behave on the basis of moral or emotional motivations, but we cannot meaningfully communicate or test these factors. At best, we can make and test propositions about people's observable behavior, which is precisely what scientists do for natural behavior. Observation, precise language and logic, and testibility are the common basis of meaningful and scientific analysis.

With this in mind, the Logical Positivists formulated a "scientific" method that could be applied to all forms of investigation. The "Hypothetico-Deductive" method, which it is often called, includes the following steps.

First, all scientific propositions, known as hypotheses, posit clear and logical relationships between observable phenomena. One such hypothesis may be: "A match, when struck, will light." A match, the act of striking and the lighting of the match are all observable phenomena. Words like *"when"* and *"will"* signify a logical time sequence and relationship. Were we very precise in our meanings, we might specify more fully which objects are matches, how much time will elapse between striking and illuminating, and what flame temperature constitutes a lit match.

Second, we test our hypothesis against the behavior of matches, in the real world. In this case, we might repeatedly strike matches to see if they actually do light. To make our test more precise, we might check the chemical compositions of all matches ahead of time, invent a machine which strikes all matches with a constant pressure; and even use a light meter to test the luminosity of the flame. If, after numerous tests, we discover that the struck match always lights; then our hypothesis is true.

Suppose, however, that some matches do not light. After all, most scientific experiments do not have perfectly consistent results. Does this imply that our scientific proposition is untrue? Not necessarily. There may be extenuating circumstances that explain why some matches did not light. Perhaps some of the matches got wet because of a hole in the roof or a concentration of precipitation in our testing room. In future experiments we might try to control for wetness by fixing the hole in the roof or by controlling room humidity. Indeed, the more fully we can control our tests, the more confident we can be in our results.

The final step in this scientific method is to compare scientific propositions to the test results. Do the tests fully, or only partially validate the proposition? Are further tests necessary? If so, do we need to revise the hypothesis? Do the test results invalidate the proposition? By comparing our precisely worded hypotheses and our precise test results, we can slowly build up a storehouse of scientific truths that others can replicate (retest) and use to further scientific knowledge.

The Adaptability of the Scientific Method to Politics

In its original formulation, the Logical Positivists' scientific method seemed to formalize what natural scientists were already doing. There were, however, several reasons why political analysts could not yet adapt the method as stated. Decades of debate and some concessions by advocates of the scientific method seemed to remedy many of the ills barring the creation of a real political *science*.

One ill was the language of political analysis itself. It is virtually impossible to do political studies without using relatively vague terms like *government, community,* or even *politics.* People cannot use any of their five senses to observe government, community or politics. At best, one can observe the individuals who make up these institutions and who take part in their processes. If the scientific method required usage of language readily dissembled into observables, political analysis would be nearly impossible.

Critics pointed out that natural scientists also suffered on this account. For example, physicists could observe light but not light particles (photons) or light waves. These are theoretical constructs, which are quite useful in research, even though they cannot be observed. Were we to exclude such terms from the scientific lexicon, we would have to consider many major scientific discoveries linguistically meaningless. The Logical Positivists certainly did not want to imply this.

Consequently, they revised the scientific method in ways consistent with the use of such terms. They continued to advise scientists to select their terms cautiously to assure that they represent observable phenomena, but they allowed the use of theoretical constructs if the scientist specified what testing operations would represent those concepts. It was acceptable to talk about "photons" if physicists specified what laboratory tests measured "photons." By implication, it was acceptable to talk about politics if analysts (1) defined it as clearly as possible and (2) detailed which phenomena in the real world counted as politics. This concession allowed political analysts to use many traditional terms without the poetic license to speculate about morality under the guise of science.

A second adaptation difficulty was in the testing procedures. Political analysts lacked the precise instruments, the mathematical formulae, and the laboratory controls necessary to meet the Logical Positivists' testing standards. Physicists had developed sophisticated instruments to trace atomic motion, precise and complex mathematical language to describe and analyze natural relations, and laboratory controls for replicating experiments and eliminating extenuating circumstances. Consider the plight of the political analyst trying to understand the causes underlying revolution. He relies on some documentation and a lot of intuition in tracing various revolutionary movements; the contours of these movements are vague and not readily adaptable to quantification and mathematical formulation; every revolution seems unique and certainly cannot be replicated for scientific testing. The world is the political analyst's laboratory and he has little control over it.

Debate revealed again that the problem was not unique to political analysts, only the dimensions were. Sophisticated testing instruments are extensions of people's five senses; they can function to clarify, as well as distort observations. Furthermore, much of natural scientific testing does not involve quantification and mathematics. Darwin's theory of evolution is one example here. Finally, even the most sophisticated laboratory cannot be controlled for all possible extenuating circumstances; therefore the scientist can never be sure that he is retesting under similar conditions. Logical Positivists were forced to recognize the imprecisions and contingencies in all testing situations.

This concession had two major implications for political analysts. One was that they should, as much as possible, develop sophisticated testing instruments and mathematical precision. Political analysts responded by developing scientific surveys and by taking advantage of advanced statistical techniques. These techniques, in turn, allowed them to control statistically for possible extenuating circumstances. Another implication was that political analysts were still justified in studying the political phenomena that were not readily adaptable to precise testing. Although revolutions were still an appropriate topic of inquiry, now the inquirer had to be more sensitive to sharp definitions, quantifiable phenomena (e.g., numbers of revolutionary movements or the GNPs of nations threatened by these movements), and the possible extenuating circumstances (e.g., the political culture of a particular nation). General hypotheses could still be tested, but the test results, because of imprecision, had always to be communicated as tentative.

A third and related problem was in the evaluation of test results. Many questions that interested political analysts simply could not be retested many times for the certainty necessary for acceptable test results. Medical scientists perform thousands of tests before they are certain that a new drug will have a predictable impact. But virtually any proposition that political analysts make has limited test potential. One cannot hold the same election twice to satisfy the political analyst's desire to retest.

Critics of the Logical Positivists suggested that this was no less true for natural scientists. How many times need we drop objects to be certain that the theory of gravity is true? And what are the implications for the theory of gravity if we witness a feather floating away from the Earth's core? The critics' point was that no number of tests is sufficient to guarantee the truth of any hypothesis. More tests can always be done. New extenuating circumstances can always influence test results, and they can always be used to explain the "exceptions" to the general results. But if we did an infinite number of tests, these "exceptions" might ultimately be the norm, and our present norm might be the ultimate exception (i.e., 1000 straight successes today constitute exceptions when followed by 1,000,000 failures). We should always remember that 300 years of faith in Newton's theory did not prevent Einstein from challenging it.

Logical Positivists responded by eliminating the word "truth" from their vocabulary. They now spoke in terms of validity, confirmation, and falsifiability. Without going into subtleties here, the implication was that test results were further evidence in support of, or against a hypothesis. Indeed, test results are mainly a basis for saying that hypotheses are *probably* accurate. By introducing probability into the scientific method, Logical Positivists opened the door to the political analysts who wished to say that, "If America has a President, he or she will *probably* be a man," or "If a revolution occurs, it will *tend* to occur when economic prosperity suddenly diminishes." Consequently, even though political analysts could not do repeated experiments or control all contingencies, the Logical Positivists eventually justified their efforts to make probabilistic generalities on the basis of limited evidence. Using statistical techniques, political analysts could even specify degrees of probability, just as the surgeon does when he tells the patient, "This operation has a 75 percent chance of success." Although certainty would be preferable, high probabilities are the most we can realistically expect from any science.

These concessions were generally accepted among philosophers and practicioners of science; political analysts were prepared to enter the fold. Controlled use of language, more sophisticated testing techniques, and tentativeness of results were to be part of the basic scientific rationality underlying the study of political behavior. Putting moral theory and speculation behind them, the new behavioralists claimed the prestigious mantle of being the true political scientists. By the 1950s, they wore that mantle proudly.

The Behavioral Approach

The behavioral approach to the study of politics can be characterized by a series of steps. Those who follow these steps can be considered political *scientists* because: (1) they do not let their personal values interfere with their research, (2) they employ the scientific method, and (3) they develop general political knowledge which, although not certain, is the most reliable knowledge about people's political behavior. Let us briefly examine each step.

1. Theory Construction. Virtually all political inquiry begins at this level. We intuitively suspect that there exists a patterned relationship among observable political phenomena. The source of our suspicions is irrelevant. We might then consult others to see if they share our suspicions and if they have done any related theorizing or testing. Finally, we organize our suspicions into a general theory which posits some sort of logical relationship among the phenomena that interest us.

For example, suppose we suspect that poverty is a systematic cause of much criminal activity. We have heard that crime rates are higher among low income groups; perhaps we ourselves have been victims of impoverished criminals. After reading some material written by experts on poverty and crime, we are convinced that poor people will go to any extreme, including crime, to assure themselves of enough food, clothing, and shelter for basic survival. We then systematize our suspicions into a set of logical statements that posit a patterned relationship and that posit the reasons why these relationships might hold.

At this point, we must decide precisely what kind of relationship we wish to investigate. We might want to say that poverty is a *necessary* cause of high crime rates among social groups. This would imply that only impoverished groups engage in high levels of crime; wealthy groups never do so. Or we might want to say that poverty is a *sufficient* cause of high crime rates. This would imply that all impoverished groups will engage in high levels of crime; other groups may engage in high levels of crime for other reasons. Finally, we may only wish to suggest that poverty is highly *associated* with high crime rates. By foregoing the question of causality, we leave open the possibility that groups with high crime rates tend to become impoverished (i.e., crime is not a very effective way of making a living). Our testing procedures and the evaluation of test results will depend on which kind of relationship we are interested in.

It is extremely difficult to demonstrate either necessary or sufficient casuality in political studies, but less difficult in many natural science studies. Suppose we wished to test if poverty is a necessary cause of high crime rates. We might discover high levels of poverty and low crime rates, but this would only indicate that other factors may have been absent. If we discover high levels of poverty and crime rates, we might suspect that high drug usage (also associated with poverty) may be the real causal factor here. And we should not forget the possibility that criminals may generally be poor because they have been unsuccessful and imprisoned. Because the natural scientist is better able to control for time factors (which came first?) and extenuating circumstances in a laboratory, he has some advantage in establishing necessary casuality.

Demonstrating sufficient causality is equally difficult for political analysts. Suppose we discover that poverty and high crime rates are always associated. Does that mean that poverty is a sufficient cause high crime rates? Not necessarily. Other factors, which we are unaware of, may also contribute to high crime rates. Some of those factors may even be sufficient causes of high crime rates; poverty may contribute very little. Again, the laboratory scientists can add or subtract factors in different time sequences in experiments; the political analyst cannot suddenly eliminate poverty to see if the crime rate drops or add greater drug use to see if the crime rate increases.

Consequently, theory building among political analysts usually consists of: (1) positing necessary or sufficient casuality with extreme tentativeness, or (2) merely positing a high association among factors. The former is more difficult to do but provides fuller explanations of political behavior. The latter provides little explanation but good predictive ability. If we know, for example, that poverty is highly associated with high crime rates, we may not be able to say why, but we can accurately predict that poor people will have greater contact with the police than will wealthy people.

2. Hypothesis Formation. Theories make political studies interesting; hypothesis formation makes political studies possible. With our theory in hand, we ask, "If this theory is true; then what kind of testible propositions would most likely follow?" For example, if we have formulated a theory specifying that poverty is a sufficient cause of high crime rates, we might logically deduce the following hypothesis:

If people become impoverished, then they will be more likely to engage in criminal activity.

Our reasoning is that if poor people do commit crimes to enhance their chances for survival; then those who suddenly lose their economic security will also enhance their chances for survival, by engaging in crime if necessary. If we can do tests to show that our hypothesis is valid: we will have garnered further support for our theory. Of course, we could have deduced numerous other hypotheses to test; this is our option; but limited time and resources often foreclose that option. Again, on the basis of logic, we choose hypotheses that we think will best substantiate our theory.

3. Operationalization. We must now provide specific definitions for the terms in our hypothesis so that we can test them in the real world. This is known as operationalization.

In common usage, the word *poverty* can mean many things. For some, it is being unable to afford decent food, clothing, shelter, and health care. For others, it is making money below a certain income level. For still others, it means no longer being able to take three Hawaiian vacations a year. In our theory, we should have specified which kind of poverty we are interested in; this specification would be our "nominal" definition that clarifies our meaning. Suppose we nominally defined poverty as being unable to afford decent food, clothing, shelter, and health care. We still do not necessarily know how to go about determining who can afford these things. What is "decent?" Do we take an individual's word that he cannot "afford" these things?

At this point, we must commit ourselves to an "operational" definition of poverty. After much thought and debate, we may decide to stipulate, for purposes of our study, that a poor person is a member of a family with a combined income of less than $7000 per year. Similarly, we can stipulate that we will count engagement in criminal activity as convictions recorded in official court documents. We realize that no operational definition fully captures the nominal meaning. Some members of families earning less than $7000 per year may be extremely wealthy, retired people living off of past earnings and investments; many people who engage in criminal activity are not caught, convicted, or listed in court documents. Nevertheless, in order to test, we must develop some operational definitions and know their limits.

4. Data Gathering. With operational definitions in hand, we can begin to collect the appropriate facts. A number of important contingencies are involved here. Are the data available? Perhaps we cannot find statistics on the number of people who fall below our $7000 level or statistics on their particular crime rates. Perhaps we can find the data, but it would take an immense amount of time and resources to do so. Are the data available in the form we desire? Maybe the government statistics are based on different operational definitions of poverty. Maybe data on criminal indictments are more readily accessible than data on criminal convictions. The researcher must inevitably face these and other contingencies. At some point, the political analyst must decide whether he is to keep his operational definitions, spend the time and money to gather the appropriate data, or revise his definitions so he can gather data more easily.

Furthermore, the researcher must decide precisely which data are appropriate. In the case of our hypothesis, he must obviously gather data on persons who have recently (how recently?) fallen below the $7000 level and on their conviction rates. But with whom does he compare these people to determine if their criminal involvement rates have gone up, down or remained the same? He may look at the specific individuals involved and compare their crime rates before and after they became impoverished. Or he may figure their crime rate and compare it with the crime rate of all people above the poverty level, or to people just above the poverty level. Again, these decisions will help determine which data need to be gathered.

Finally, the researcher must decide how much data should be collected. Should he collect data on *all* individuls who have fallen below the poverty level in the last five years? Or should he use a statistical technique called random sampling to collect data on representative individuals in this group? There are many, many choices to be made here—some on a scientific basis and others on the basis of the researcher's personal time, interest, and resources.

5. Data Analysis.   What do we do with our data? The choices range from very simple operations to extremely complex ones. The availability of computers makes even more complex data analysis possible with limited time and resources.

In the case of our hypothesis, we may simply want to see if there is a high correlation between (1) people falling below the poverty level and (2) crime rates higher than those of people above the poverty level. We may get a little more sophisticated and compare our group's crime rate with that of people consistently below the poverty level. If we use a random sample, we might want to do statistical tests of significance. More complicated analyses can be done also. Political analysts often use techniques called multivariate analysis, factor analysis, and a host of more complicated techniques.

Political analysts have gone a long way toward developing precise mathematical terms and processes for getting as much out of their data as possible. As Logical Positivists have suggested, political studies in the behavioralist mode require a sophisticated understanding of statistics and computer technology. Yet these are all testing tools useful for analyzing and communicating reports of relationships in the real world.

6. Test Evaluation.   This is the point at which we compare the logic of our theory and hypotheses to the results of our real world tests. Our goal all along has been to see if our theory and hypothesis are supported or contradicted by behavior in the empirical world.

Suppose our data analysis provides evidence that the crime rate of people falling below the poverty level is only slightly higher than the crime rate of people above the poverty level. What are we to conclude? There are a number of possibilities.

First, we can suggest that these findings support our hypothesis. We should only expect a small increase in the crime rate because people do not shed their old law-abiding habits easily—even in the face of poverty. The fact that their crime rate increases at all is significant. In this case, we would also suggest that our hypothesis now supports our theory; thus, on the basis of our theory, we predicted that this would be the case and our tests have confirmed our predictions.

Second, we might suggest that further testing is necessary. Perhaps the difference in crime rates is so small because of several reasons: our operational definitions are not good ones, our data were inaccurately gathered or analyzed, or our sample was too small. We might suggest that other kinds of testing would be more appropriate.

Perhaps we should compare the crime rates of our test group to those of people far above the poverty level. Perhaps we should focus more closely on the crime rates of individuals who have fallen from extreme wealth into poverty. Perhaps, we should make a distinction between "blue collar" and "white collar" crimes. The possibilities for further testing are literally innumerable.

Third, we might suggest that our tests contradict our hypothesis but not necessarily our theory. We could argue that the differences in crime rates were so insignificant that they demonstrate no significant relationship between becoming impoverished and engaging in crime. However, this hypothesis is not really significant in terms of our theory. Perhaps people have to be impoverished for a long time, even generations, before poverty causes increases in crime rates. Moreover, falling into poverty may only be a necessary but not sufficient condition for increased crime rates. Perhaps poverty must be accompanied by the unwillingness of a person to accept welfare, which is common among "proud" working and middle class families who have lost their "shirts," before it will lead to higher crime rates.

Finally, we could suggest that both our theory and our hypothesis are falsified. There is no significant relationship between becoming impoverished and engaging in crime. To the extent that this is demonstrated, it means that, people who are poor do not necessarily engage in more criminal activity than others do. If we draw this conclusion, how do we explain the fact that crime rates among poor people are higher than among other groups? We speculate: Since poor people tend to be members of racial or ethnic minority groups, then maybe racial or ethnic discrimination causes higher crime rates. At this point, we are on the verge of constructing a new theory.

A number of points in the behavioralist approach should be highlighted here. Each step in this approach requires the researcher to make many decisions. Nevertheless, studies based on this approach, according to behavioralists, are essentially objective—the researchers personal political opinions should not influence results. Indeed, many behavioralist researchers argue that they have arrived at conclusions which they personally find morally objectionable. To the extent that this is accurate, behavioralists claim to be value-free scientists.

Furthermore, knowing they have made decisions at each step which some might consider objectionable, behavioralists demand that these decisions be published along with research findings. This provides objectors with a basis for testing the theories and hypotheses in less objectionable ways. Science, after all, is based on the intercommunication of many people using different means to achieve the same goal: political knowledge.

Finally, behavioralists suggest that researchers be open to the tentative nature of all findings. Test results can always be interpreted in a number of reasonable ways. Many consistent test results obtained by many different researchers provide strong evidence in support of particular theories and hypotheses; but strong evidence is not definitive proof of truth or falsity. Indeed, words like *definitive* or *proof* are usually dropped from the vocabulary of behavioral political scientists. Nevertheless, relatively value-free, open and tentative research in the behavioral mode is clearly superior to the moral and emotional abstractions of those who distort reality in line with their preconceptions and superior to their vague interpretations which omit precision and rigorous testing. Behavioralism is an imperfect method for political studies, but no one has discovered a more adequate substitute.

POST-BEHAVIORAL REVISIONS

Post-behavioralism, as noted earlier, is the major methodological approach used by American political scientists today. It has been necessary to consider the arguments of the Logical Positivists and the methods of behavioralists to provide an historical and analytical basis upon which one can understand the development of post-behavioralism in the 1970s. Criticisms of behavioralism in the 1960s were the foundations for revisions resulting in post-behavioralism today. I will consider the major criticisms and then develop the idea of post-behavioralism as a response to those criticisms. Note the similarities between these criticisms and the controversies discussed in Part One of this book.

Against Behavioralism

There was a growing feeling in the 1960s, especially among younger political scientists, that behavioralism was both a lot less and a lot more than its defenders claimed it was. In one sense, behavioralism was promoted as a sophisticated scientific method when it actually was simplistic. It developed a research method and technology which, in effect, confirmed things that were already obvious to laypersons. Behavioralists confirmed that American voters were relatively apathetic and that poverty was associated with crime; but any sensitive observer of American politics already knew these things. Behavioralists, however, had not really added to our knowledge of more complex questions.

In another sense, behavioralists ignored the politics around them by focusing on such simplistic questions. They had little to say about the practical political upheavals of the 1960s which surrounded them daily in their university or community settings. In their narrow quest to become scientists, they had lost sight of politics. For some, this meant that they had eschewed their traditional intellectual role of social commentators and critics; by ignoring the status quo, they had tacitly supported it in ways consistent with the Logic of Political Realism.

Consider the question of the nature of politics (discussed earlier in Chapter 2). The behavioralists had hoped to purge the language of political analysis of words which were vague, moralistic, or emotional; their hope was to develop a neutral language useful in scientific analysis. In many cases, they "accomplished" this by posing extremely narrow definitions of politics in terms of conflict-resolution; they restricted the scope of political science to governmental affairs and manifest individual behavior. In the name of science, they essentially reproduced the controversial preconceptions of the model of Politics as Conflict-Resolution. From the perspective of those who adhered to the alternative model of Politics as Community-Building, this new "scientific" approach was anything but neutral. It distorted the analysts' focus on significant questions of human sociality, cooperation, and community as future possibilities; it distorted the systematic links between politics and economics, history, and the other disciplines.

The behavioralists, in their hope to exclude norms, emotions and imagination from scientific analysis, implicitly attacked the notion of Justice as Goodness (discussed in Chapter 3). Words like *goodness* have no observable referents in the real world; their meanings cannot be communicated precisely and their validity cannot be tested by real world events. When someone presents an idea of the good society, he is only expressing his personal preferences under the guise of political science. For the behavioralists, there was no good society; there were only a multitude of individual, subjective preferences. The critics of behavioralism pointed out that this position actually assumed a moral relativism which was consistent with the alternative model of justice; Justice as Fairness. Implicitly or explicitly, most behavioralists believed that if there can be no objective moral values, then all individuals should be free to pursue their personal goals without undue constraint. While this seemed "logical" to most behavioralists, it actually involved a moral assumption: conflicts over the distribution of values should be solved by fair processes. And some behavioralists went as far as to specify that those processes included elections, competitive parties, representation, etc. For advocates of Justice as Goodness, this "scientific" logic was no more than an ideological adherence to Justice as Fairness.

In their studies of American politics, behavioralists were particularly sensitive to group conflict and competition, or to use an earlier label, pluralism (discussed in Chapter 4). It was relatively easy for them to observe elections or different interest groups vying for influence over the agenda and decisions. However, this approach generally implied that American politics was a relatively pluralistic system of fair competition. According to critics, this approach led to a number of major distortions. It ignored important nonbehavioral factors, such as, which issues were not discussed, which groups were excluded from the competition, what alternatives were not considered or what subtle pressures compelled decision-makers to ignore some issues, groups, or alternatives. For example, some government officials may have refused to consider campaigning against major corporate interests because they knew, though they might not have said so, that such a campaign would have endangerd their financial base. Because such actions were not overt or did not make it into the political arena, the behavioralists had nothing to observe. Nevertheless, the fact that some issues are not raised and some groups are not allowed into the competition is the basic critique of pluralism and foundation of elite analysis of American politics. Thus, the behavioralists' method implicitly viewed America as pluralistic and ignored elitist tendencies.

Finally, the critics challenged the behavioralists' comparative studies. Their narrow view of politics, their assumption of norms of fairness and their affirmation of American pluralism meant that they would bring American biases to their Cross-National studies (discussed in Chapter 5). Their general theories and hypotheses were based on American norms; their testing procedures and evaluations interpreted data in ways consistent with those American norms. For the critics, the behavioralist's comparative studies were little more than "scientistic" rationalizations for American Don Quixotism. The Cross-Cultural comparison which sensitizes analysts to possible problems with America and to possible differences in other nations was excluded from the behavioralist's approach.

In summary, the critics believed that the behavioralists had, under the guise of science, reproduced all the controversial preconceptions in the four models that constitute our Logic of Political Realism: Politics as Conflict-Resolution, Justice as Fairness, American Pluralism and Cross-National Comparisons. Behavioralism ultimately implied a political realism which accepted the limits of politics and people and ignored broader possibilities for change. It was not surprising then that the behavioralists had either ignored the upheavals of the 1960s or had tacitly considered the dissidents to be unrealistic utopians.

How had an apparently neutral method of analysis become a justification for a set of controversial political preconceptions and (as some would have it) a rationalization for the American status quo? One suggestion was that a neutral methodology had been appropriated by people who used it for biased ends. Adherents of the Logic of Political Realism constructed theories aimed at affirming the superiority of American politics; they developed hypotheses about narrow issues which ignored major American problems. Given their American bias, they had little trouble getting financial support from corporations and government to pursue such research. At times, they used their skills to do "counterinsurgency" studies or other studies which would facilitate American elites' interests abroad. Moreover, their control over political science departments, grant-giving agencies, and professional journals allowed them to reward those who used behavioralism for similar ends and to punish those who used it otherwise.

A second suggestion was that the behavioralist method was not or could not be fully neutral. Those who hope to generate and test broad generalities inevitably distort particularistic experience where uniqueness seems to be the norm. And no matter how clear or well defined one's concepts are, they will virtually always be impregnated with the value biases of one's own culture. Furthermore, the behavioral method demands that researchers spend a great deal of time developing precise and sophisticated testing techniques. Thus, behavioralists tend to become "numbers crunchers," often more concerned with quantification, testing, and computers than with actual politics. From this perspective, the method produces methodologists who are "above" politics: their concern will be with generalities and numbers which tend to be supportive of prevailing values. And by foregoing the traditional intellectual role of political and social critic, the behavioral political analyst tacitly assents to the status quo.

By the 1970s, many political analysts, including those who considered themselves behavioralists, became sensitive to these issues. They continued to believe in behavioral methodology as the most scientific way of studying politics. But they now called for greater tolerance, greater relevance, and greater humanitarianism. The behavioralist method should be used flexibly by critics and supporters of the present American political system. It should be used, not only to develop basic generalities, but also to help us better understand everyday politics. And behavioralism should become an intellectual tool for helping us achieve a freer, more open society, cognizant of the multitude of needs and problems which are present in America. For these political analysts, the criticisms of the 1960s served as a stimulus to developing the Post-Behavioralism of the 1970s.

Post-Behavioralism Today: A Response to the Critics

In 1969, the president of the American Political Science Association, David Easton, initiated debate over what he called "The Post-Behavioral Revolution." Behavioralism had been a methodology for studying politics, which grew up too quickly, and had recently experienced major growing-pains. The 1970s was to be a time when proper adjustments had to be made to guide the methodology toward maturity. Meaning many things to many people, post-behavioralism was less a revolutionary overthrow of behavioralism and more a sophisticated revision of how the scientific method should be adapted to political inquiry. Below I shall outline the main contours of the revision process of the 1970s.

First, post-behavioralists have conceded that the behavioral adaptation of the scientific method is not value-free. Which theories are constructed? What hypotheses are deduced? How are concepts defined and operationalized? Which tests are performed? How are results evaluated? These are all questions that leave room for subjective judgment. In many cases, these decisions are made according to conventionally shared norms of political analysts; but in many cases they are made according to the researcher's value basis. Either way, the objectivity of behavioral science is called into question.

Although this is a problem that can never be totally eliminated, it can be controlled. Now, political scientists should engage in discussions over values and imaginative possibilities to generate a broader range of theories and hypotheses. When stipulating their own definitions or when making research decisions, political scientists should openly concede the subjectivity involved and consider some of the alternatives that they reject for one reason or another. The idea of self-conscious consideration of the values and implications of one's assumptions and decisions has become pervasive today. This will create an atmosphere of scientific openness and tolerance. Barriers between normative political theorists and empirical researchers will break down. And barriers between those who adhere to Justice as Fairness and those who adhere to Justice as Goodness will break down as both openly employ the behavioral scientific method to substantiate or explore their own theories. The only limit on this intellectual pluralism is that all theories and hypotheses must be rigorously tested against actual experience.

Second, the post-behavioralists now call for greater flexibility and tolerance in the goals of political research. On the one hand, all scientific research concerns the search for general patterns of behavior that go beyond the idiosyncracies of the moment. This "basic research" is the foundation for building a storehouse of knowledge, which can later be used to explain particular events. Such research should be continued. On the other hand, "basic research" should be complemented by "applied research" and by the study of concrete, everyday political questions. Political and social problems like racism, sexism, and poverty should be examined, along with the more abstract questions of democracy, authoritarianism, and development. A consequence of this two-pronged research would be the simultaneous development of laws of political behavior and of possible solutions to the concrete problems that are especially salient at any particular historical moment.

Third, the post-behavioralists take an additional step by adding that both basic and applied research should be put to the service of humane values. Rather than simply conclude their research with the bare results, analysts should include some discussion of how these results can be used to expand the range of choices and alternatives in the political world. Sensitive to the fact that political analysis is often a tool for elites who can afford to hire professionals, post-behavioralists suggest that consumer groups, environmental groups, and other public interest agencies also sponsor research to serve public ends. While we may not be able to agree on which "humane values" should be fostered by research, we can certainly agree that the values of dominant groups alone should not be the only ones to benefit from research.

These first three revisions collectively aim to accomplish the same goal by solving a problem in past uses and abuses of behavioralism. That goal is to ensure that political scientific inquiry openly avows its own limitations and is accessible to all groups in society. To the extent that this goal is realized, the criticism that behavioralism serves the interests of the status quo alone and those who benefit from the status quo, will be weakened. Meanwhile, the door is now open to those who do not support the Logic of Political Realism; so they can enter the scientific marketplace and test their assumptions against empirical experience. This competition between supporters of the different logics will now be open and resolved according to scientific tests, rather than by speculation and ideology.

A fourth revision concerns the testing process itself. Although post-behavioralists, like behavioralists, continue to insist that theories and hypothesis be subjected to rigorous testing procedures, they now issue several new warnings. They warn researchers to remember that all testing involves subjective decisions; thus political experimenters must be more tolerant of those who make different decisions lest they forget the tentative nature of scientific inquiry. Another warning is for researchers to remember that quantification, sophisticated mathematical formulae, and computer usage are only tools of political understanding and not the goal of political inquiry. Moreover, to the extent that usage of these tools is also based on subjective decisions, greater tolerance must be offered to those researchers who prefer to gather "qualitative" data that is not easily subjected to quantification and computer techniques. A third warning concerns the nature of collected data. Many behavioral studies were based on relatively contemporary data because those data were the most sophisticated and most accessible. Nevertheless, the reliability of these data is questionable because they do not provide a picture of changes over time. Post-behavioralists warn that research based on contemporary (or cross-sectional) data must also take into account any possible trends that do not appear in the data. They hope that researchers will gather data over time (or times-series data) to increase sensitivity to historical changes. If they can do so, they will have a stronger basis for claiming the *general* validity of their results.

The fifth revision more directly relates political understanding to the testing process. On the one hand, researchers should generate theories and hypotheses that can be tested against readily accessible data. During the 1950s and 1960s, this was manifest in the volumes of voters' studies for which statistics were easily available. On the other hand, are we to neglect studies of questions where data are unavailable or even nonexistent? Do we neglect studying campaign financing because candidates do not wish to reveal their funding sources? Do we ignore questions about nonvoters for lack of data? This was very often the case during the behavioral period. Then the argument was that nothing supportable could be said in such studies because few tests could be performed; whatever was said was little more than supposition or speculation. Post-behavioralists disagree. They say that, in these cases, researchers should develop theories and hypotheses that make sense according to the things we do know. To every extent possible, they should generate hypotheses that are theoretically testible, develop conceptual frameworks that can be useful for considering alternative interpretations, and then act the part of investigative reporters searching out the facts. They hope that there will be two results. First, that subjective studies such as interviews with a few candidates or nonvoters will suggest areas for inquiry where data do exist. Second, that publication of such suggestive research may help build public pressure to make some of the data more accessible. For example, in recent years, many candidates running for public office must make records of their campaign finances a part of the public record. Having done subjective background work, political analysts can now analyze these data more effectively.

Together these fourth and fifth revisions add up not only to a continuing demand for rigorous testing but also to a recognition that the tests themselves should not determine the course of political studies. Scientific methods should serve the goal but not determine the direction of political understanding. When scientific methods cannot be employed fully, we employ them partially; when they cannot be applied partially, we try to apply reasoned understanding rather than fantasy, speculation or poetry. This, of course, is the case in the natural sciences as well. When a plague strikes and the cure is unknown or unavailable, natural scientists suggest remedies based on reasoned possibilities; rarely do they sit by and idly watch people die. Albert Camus' novel *The Plague* graphically illustrates this.

POLITICAL SCIENCE I Post-behavioralism today seems to justify a methodological pluralism that allows people with very different preconceptions to employ the same scientific method to the best of their ability. Some political analysts are so convinced of this that they view the 1970s and 1980s as an era of intellectual "detente" among the various approaches in the discipline. I disagree. I will suggest why post-behavioralism is likely to be adopted as the preferred method by advocates of the Logic of Political Realism but not by advocates of the Logic of Political Opportunities. I will suggest that the links between political realists' preconceptions and post-behavioralist methodology are strong enough to warrant the label; Political Science I.

Despite its five major and important revisions of behavioralism, post-behavioralism reproduces the controversial preconceptions associated with the Logic of Political Realism. Both behavioralism and post-behavioralism tend to focus the researcher's vision on individual behavior and conflict, rather than on less observable and less testable social ties and modes of cooperation. Both methods tend to assume the subjective realitivism of political values, albeit in slightly different ways. Whereas behavioralists often refused to admit to value biases, modern post-behavioralists do admit to them and then justify their tolerance of a plurality of open value biases. This viewpoint, however, is simply another way of affirming that intellectual justice is fairness (i.e., everyone should have the chance to express their own values). That values can have a social or nonsubjective basis is not considered. Moreover, research aimed at enhancing humane values essentially begs the question of which particular values are humane. In practice, this means that most post-behavioral research assumes the values inherent in Justice as Fairness without giving due consideration to the possibility of Justice as Goodness or the nature of the good society. From this perspective, post-behavioral analysis of American politics is likely to reconfirm the essential pluralism of America when compared to other societies that take Justice as Goodness as their primary value orientation.

Most importantly, both behavioralists and post-behavioralists are still mainly concerned with studying what presently exists in the political world. Despite recent claims to value and method tolerance, they look at present politics to uncover the laws that define and limit human behavior. They look at developing tests that can be done within the contraints of the present. They still wish to dissociate themselves from "unscientific" speculation and concern with broad historical trends or future possibilities. Therefore, they reproduce not only the preconceptions inherent in the constitutive models of the Logic of Political Realism, but the general attitude of that logic. Although there are clearly exceptions, I believe it is fair to state that adherents of the Logic of Political Realism will find in post-behavioralism a sensible and scientific method that reconfirms most of their basic preconceptions.

This basic linkage between political realism and post-behavioralism may be labeled Political Science I. Here is the diagram.

POLITICAL SCIENCE I

Methods: Post-Behavioralism
                                      ↑
Preconceptions: Logic of Political Realism (Politics as Conflict-Resolution, Justice as Fairness, American Pluralism, and Cross-National Comparison)

Because post-behavioralists have revised, not revolutionized, earlier behavioralism that was already consistent with political realism, this later continuity between method and preconceptions should not be surprising.

Is it probable that post-behavioralism will also be attractive to people whose preconceptions cluster around the Logic of Political Opportunities? I suggest not. Critics of both behavioralism and post-behavioralism often argue that these methods tend to support the American political system today and those who benefit by that system, regardless of the good intentions of researchers or the particular uses of the research. Like the natural scientific method from which they evolved, behavioral and post-behavioral methods continue to assume that people behave in patterned and predictable ways, much like atomic particles. Yet, this assumption forces one to focus on limits rather than on opportunities for change.

First, the methodological focus on behavior itself neglects the possible meanings people attached to that behavior. A Chicano activist may participate in elections or pressure groups because he sees no other effective alternative at present, not because he believes American politics allow for fair pluralistic competition. If we do not focus on the underlying reasons of his behavior or the lack of effective alternatives, then we are prone to consider America a thriving pluralistic society when it may not be so. In brief, the focus on behavior tends to affirm American pluralism by ignoring diverse motives, intentions, and circumstances. At the very most, we can expect behavioralists and post-behavioralists to describe the ways in which people today act in patterns; but we cannot expect them to analyze the motives, intentions, and circumstances that explain the meaning of that behavior or the possibilities for altering that behavior.

Second, and related to the first, behavioralism and post-behavioralism are predicated upon discovering and testing patterns of behavior that exist today. To the extent that one is a political realist who basically supports the status quo, this information is quite useful. Knowing patterns of present behavior provides one with the information necessary for developing a more peaceful, fair, and pluralistic society through minor reforms. The reforms are necessarily minor because the assumption inherent in the methods is that people do not change in any basic ways. If they are competitive today, they will be competitive tomorrow; at most we can rearrange institutions to alter slightly the nature of that competition.

However, advocates of the Logic of Political Opportunities do not find such knowledge very useful. They are less interested in rearranging types of competition and more interested in nurturing new human relationships that are cooperative. The details of present behavior patterns do not provide them with an understanding of how these patterns came to be established or how they can be changed to conform with the good society or egalitarianism. From their perspective, a sensitivity to historical and cultural changes reveals that people are not like atoms; people can and have changed their behavioral patterns either to achieve new goals or to adjust to new circumstances. Behavioral and post-behavioral methods are simply not *adequate* for the purposes of these analysts; these methods do not provide the kinds of information useful to people interested in expanding the opportunities for new human relationships.

Third, the two methods are themselves bound to a particular historical and cultural milieu. One reason these methods have been even relatively successful for generating and testing patterned political behavior is that they are applied to modern bureaucratic societies. In America today, our behavior is so patterned and predictable because most of us are bureaucrats in one capacity or another. In school, we are either rewarded for conforming to our teachers' expectations or punished for disregarding them. So too in the workplace and politics. We are either rewarded for being "responsible" according to our superiors' norms or penalized for being "irresponsible"according to the same norms. Bureaucratic reward and penalty structures generally assure that our behavior will be patterned and predictable. Political realists generally accept this bureaucratic structure and then inquire into its intricacies. But people interested in expanding political opportunities generally question the bureaucratic structure, consider how it evolved, and then suggest how we might go about changing it and the patterns it rewards. This requires a different methodological approach.

SUMMARY In this chapter, I have traced the reasons why focusing on behavior seemed to be superior to traditional consideration of official documents and norms, how Logical Positivists provided an analysis that justified the adaptation of natural science methods to political studies; the behavioral method which resulted and flourished among political scientists; and the criticisms upon which modern post-behavioralism developed. Moreover, I have argued that there are good reasons why people with preconceptions consistent with the Logic of Political Realism would adopt post-behavioral methodology. This constituted the basis for Political Science I.

I concluded by suggesting that there are good reasons why people with preconceptions consistent with the Logic of Political Opportunities would not adopt post-behavioral methods. If this is the case, then what methods do they see as superior for their purposes? This is the subject matter of the next chapter and the foundation for Political Science II.

SELECTED REFERENCES Easton, David. "The New Revolution in Political Science." *The American Political Science Review* 63 (1969): 1051-1061.

Eulau, Heinz and March, James G., eds. *Political Science*. Englewood Cliffs, N.J.: Prentice-Hall, 1969.

Fowler, Robert Booth. *Believing Skeptics.* Westport, Conn.: Greenwood Press, 1978.

Graham, George J. and Carey, George W., eds. *The Post-Behavioral Era.* New York: David McKay, 1972.

Hempel, Carl G. *Aspects of Scientific Explanation.* New York: The Free Press, 1965.

Hoover, Kenneth R. *The Elements of Social Scientific Thinking.* New York: St. Martin's Press, 1976.

Nagel, Ernest. *The Structure of Science.* New York: Harcourt, Brace and World, 1961.

Polsby, Nelson, Dentler, Robert A. and Smith, Paul A., eds. *Politics and Social Life.* Boston: Houghton Mifflin, 1963.

Rudner, Richard S. *Philosophy of Social Science.* Englewood Cliffs, N.J.: Prentice-Hall, 1966.

Spraegens, Thomas A. *The Dilemma of Contemporary Political Theory: Toward a Postbehavioral Science of Politics.* New York: Dunellen, 1973.

Wolin, Sheldon. "Political Theory as a Vocation" *The American Political Science Review* 63 (1969): 1062-1082.

7

THE INTERPRETIVE
APPROACH:
POLITICAL SCIENCE II

Unlike post-behavioralism, the interpretive approach to the study of politics is not a cohesive set of perspectives and methods. Rather it is the common basis of several modes of political study developed during varying periods. Nevertheless, I believe that this common basis is significant and consistent enough to distinguish the interpretive approach from post-behavioralism.

In this chapter, I will trace the scientific logic of this common basis and consider a number of variations on it. Included is a discussion of "phenomenology" which is the philosophy at the foundations of the interpretive approach, interpretive methods of doing political analysis, criticisms of these methods, and a brief discussion of Marxist methodology as the major international alternative to post-behavioralism and as a methodology which today incorporates other interpretive methods. This chapter is primarily an introduction to alternatives to post-behavioralism.

I will conclude this chapter by suggesting that adherents to the Logic of Political Opportunities have good reasons for adopting the interpretive approach as a more sensible and scientific method for studying politics than post-behavioralism is. It is more adequate to their purposes. Again, this particular link between alternative preconceptions and alternative methods constitutes what I call Political Science II.

PHENOMENOLOGY: MULTIPLE REALITIES

At the same historical moment when Logical Positivists were laying the foundation for what ultimately became post-behavioralism, other philosophers were developing a contrary system of thought. Known as Phenomenologists, they suggested that language and understanding were less a function of things in the world and more a function of people's interpretations of those things. The following story highlights the importance of interpretation for political understanding. It is an analysis of the multiple possibilities for understanding, and a general exploration of the steps or methods of political analysis. This will set the stage for exploring the criticisms of phenomenology and the basis for interpretive variations.

Courtroom Interpretations

A man named Simon is arrested for breaking and entering into the home of a noted Hollywood starlet. As the prosecutor builds his case, the "facts" lead him to believe the following: Simon methodically planned to disarm the electronic security system, steal a number of priceless art objects in the house, and escape in his van parked outside. The prosecutor plans to call witnesses who will testify to Simon's knowledge of electronics, to Simon's history of criminal activity, to his ownership of a van that a neighbor noticed parked outside the starlet's home, and to the priceless statuette police discovered in Simon's van. From the prosecutor's perspective, the case is clearcut. Simon is a common criminal who is **170** responsible for his actions and deserves imprisonment.

In his discussion with his attorney, Simon relates his own perceptions of the night in question. He drove his van to the starlet's home at her invitation. When he rang the bell at the gate, a voice over the intercom told him that the electronic mechanism was out of order; if he just jiggled the mechanism a bit, the gate would open. It did. Simon spent the next hour with the starlet only to discover she was a real bore. When he got up to leave, she became hysterical at his rejection. She pleaded that he stay, but he refused. When he left the house, she followed him with the statuette in hand. She wielded the statuette as a weapon. Simon grabbed her arm on the downswing, removed the object from her hand, got into the van, and drove away. He does not remember how the statuette got into the van, but surmises that he must have unconsciously placed it in the van when he left. Later that night, the police arrested him at home; only then had he realized that he had taken the statuette whose worth had never crossed his mind. Ultimately, Simon sees himself as a victim of both the starlet and circumstances.

Simon's own attorney, knowing Simon's background, does not believe his story. She knows that he came from a broken home, a ghetto childhood, and a street gang culture. Simon had gotten involved with drugs and a number of petty crimes as a youth. He had spent some time in boys' reformatories where he most likely picked up his breaking and entering skills. In her mind, Simon is a victim of society and an ineffective penal system. She suggests to Simon that he plead guilty, claim mitigating circumstances, and thus get off with a relatively light sentence.

Simon gets extremely upset on hearing her recommendation. He starts screaming that she is no different from the prosecutor. All she is interested in is getting the case over with and collecting her fee from the state. Simon is so upset that his attorney feels that she had better leave immediately lest he get violent. Simon is obviously unstable; perhaps he is not even mentally competent to stand trial, she thinks. On her own initiative, with some support from the prosecutor and the court, she gets Simon to submit to a psychiatric examination.

After several interviews, the court-appointed psychiatrist concludes that Simon is a schizophrenic neurotic with paranoid tendencies that become manifest in the presence of women. As a child, Simon resented the domination of his mother: he rebels against her by projecting his resentment on other women, be it the Hollywood starlet or his own defense attorney. Simon is no longer able to distinguish between his friends and enemies and is incompetent to stand trial.

Simon gets increasingly resentful of all these people interested in "helping" him but not in believing him. In despair, he calls on his old family minister. The minister comes to the jail and listens to Simon's story. The minister then counsels him to consider if he has yet made peace with God. Simon should accept the help those around him offer, because they are experts. But more important, he should learn not to fight against the forces in the world but to consider them trials of his own moral worth on his earthly pilgrimage. Simon finds this advice of little use in his present situation. For him, the important point is that he is innocent.

Perceiving "Facts"

This story illustrates a number of significant points which are often ignored in post-behavioral analyses. The first point is that our perceptions of "facts" are contingent on our preconceptions. Did Simon breach the electronic security system or did he merely jiggle the mechanism as told? The prosecutor and the defense attorney both knew that Simon has the electronic knowledge to breach the system as well as a history of criminal activity. In their minds, Simon may be a "criminal-type" who must not be considered as a trustworthy reporter of facts; but they have no reason to disbelieve the starlet's story that she has never met Simon and certainly did not invite him to jiggle the mechanism. From the psychiatrist's perspective, having classified Simon as a schizophrenic neurotic with paranoid tendencies, it is quite conceivable that Simon actually *believes* he did not commit a crime. This may be Simon's psyche playing tricks on his mind as a defense mechanism. Or from the minister's perspective, it is unimportant if Simon actually broke and entered, or merely jiggled; what counts is his relation to God. Nevertheless Simon remembers meeting the starlet, being invited to her home, and being asked to jiggle the mechanism. But with everyone around him denying this, he may also begin to wonder if his mind was not playing tricks or if his memory has not been distorted in time. If Simon has preconceived self-doubts, he may revise his original perceptions of the "facts" in light of the pressures of other people.

Philosophers known as Phenomenologists suggest that we forego our attachment to objective "facts" and be more concerned with perceived "phenomena." All observations depend on the instruments of observation. People use their five senses, their emotional predispositions and their cognitive structures as primary instruments for observing the world. But sometimes our senses fool us; sometimes our emotions shape our perceptions; sometimes our cognitive structures filter out aspects of reality. Moreover, all our instruments of observation are limited in one sense or another. Like judges in athletic competition, we are judges of the world: we might be positioned at one angle so that we do not see the same event as someone positioned at a slightly different angle. To make matters worse, we often must rely on indirect observation. Things written in books, in documents, in statistical files, or even in memory open up new avenues of human distortion of the "facts." By pointing out that "facts" are really phenomena subject to distortion by people, Phenomenologists alert us to the subjective aspect of even the most "certain" knowledge.

The second point is that even if we can arrive at an intersubjective agreement about the phenomena involved, we still must interpret the meaning of the phenomena. In our story, although everyone agreed that Simon entered the starlet's home, no one really agreed on why he entered the home. The prosecutor interpreted his acts as part of a planned robbery attempt; Simon saw them as a response to an invitation; his attorney viewed them as a manifestation of his impoverished childhood; the psychiatrist saw them as projections of his childhood resentment against his mother; and the minister saw them as a result of Simon's inability to be at peace with his maker. Had we brought in fifty more experts from various fields, we would quite likely have gotten close to fifty other interpretations on the meaning of Simon's actions.

According to Phenomenologists, how investigators interpret the meaning of particular actions tells us as much about the investigators as the actions themselves. Some investigators assume that people determine their own motives, choose related intentions, and act consistently with both. This is the basic assumption of human free will and responsibility. Other investigators believe that people's actions are determined by their psychological predispositions: early childhood experiences, particularly family experiences, result in personalities more prone to engage in some actions than are others. This is a variety of psychological determinism. Still others believe that people's actions are determined by economic pressures, cultural pressures, or other environmental stimuli. Phenomenologists argue that the meaning of people's actions lies in all these factors and more. To engage in one mode of interpretation to the exclusion of others is to narrow unjustly the realm of possible meanings.

Even if we can finally agree, to some extent, on Simon's actions and on the motives and intentions that inform his actions, we must also interpret the realm of action, that is, the opportunities and constraints on actions at any particular moment. For example, we might want to say that Simon had the opportunity to breach the security system because he received an education in breaking and entering at reform school. Or we might want to suggest that Simon was constrained from receiving an invitation from the starlet because he moved in lower class circles and she moved in upper class circles. And like the child who continually asks "Why?" we might want to ask, "Why do reforms schools become breeding grounds for greater criminal sophistication?" or "Why do class divisions exist?" Obviously, we can pose an infinite number of questions and develop an unlimited set of interpretations to explain how situational factors affected Simon's actions.

Together, these three points imply that there can be no one "true" explanation for any single action nor can there be one general explanation or general law encompassing a series of actions. Unlike post-behavioralists, Phenomenologists believe that all perception and understanding is limited by the analyst's particular viewpoint. The analyst may stress preconceptions, only to ignore motives, intentions, and situational factors. Or the analyst may focus on psychological motives to the exclusion of sociological factors. And even if the analyst is brilliant at synthesizing all of these factors into a logical, consistent explanation, there is always the possibility of different but equally logical, consistent explanations. As individuals and scholars, each of us brings unique sets of preconceptions, motives and intentions, and situational factors to understand better our worlds; consequently each of us develops different perceptions and explanations of events in our worlds. To the extent that this phenomenological perspective is warranted, we each see separate realities; or collectively, we live among multiple realities.

Phenomenological Methodology

Phenomenologists begin with the assumption that though some people may *behave* similarly, they do not *act* similarly. For example, two individuals may have voted for Democrat Fred Harris for president in the 1972 primaries. Their physical behavior was identical. The first individual, however, might have had a number of preconceptions, motives and intentions that led her to believe that Fred Harris was the ideal candidate. The second individual may have disliked Harris but figured, given the political situation in 1972, that Harris' candidacy would improve the chances of Richard Nixon in the final election. Therefore, although the two individuals behaved the same, the meanings of either their behavior or actions were significantly different. Phenomenologists are not really interested in generating and testing broad hypotheses; they believe understanding is a matter of reconstructing the complexities that explain particular actions or events.

1. Empathy. Step one should be an attempt to become sensitive to the various preconceptions, motives, intentions, and situational opportunities and constraints of the involved actors. Were we to study the actions of a group of Asian policy makers, we may want to sensitize ourselves to their preconceptual worlds: How do they categorize the world? What things do they take for granted? Were we to study the action of dissidents at home, we may try to become aware of their motives and intentions: Are they spoiled youth rebelling against their parents? Are they idealistic citizens hoping to create a better world? Are they some combination of both? Are some of them more one than the other? And we cannot forget to consider how our actors view their choices within their own realm of action. Were we to study the voting practices of some individuals, we may want to ask: Do they believe voting is an effective form of participation? Do they vote because they see no other practical opportunity for participation? Is their voting merely ritualistic exercise? The main idea of sensitizing oneself in all these ways is to become aware of how our actors perceive and experience the actions we study. It may be appropriate to label this first step in research: *empathy*.

There are any number of ways of developing empathetic understanding. We might study the writings and words of the actors. We might study secondary interpretations of the actors. Or we could try to live with the actors for a time or talk to those who have. More abstractly, we could study their history and culture and try to imagine ourselves in their situation. None of these methods is foolproof. The middle class scholar who lives among the poor to better empathize with them can never fully put himself in the position of actually experiencing poverty as they do. At the very least, he knows he can leave at any moment whereas the poor see little chance of exit. Nevertheless, it seems fair to say that a scholar who has lived among the poor has somewhat of a better chance of understanding what it means to be poor, than one who has only read about poverty.

Empathy is only a first and a limited step. Not only is empathy never more than partial, empathy may add new distortions. For example, empathy can lead me to believe that poor people are more or less resigned to their poverty. But poor people themselves might not recognize their own resentment boiling under the surface. One might interpret the culture of poverty as having a number of mechanisms for displacing frustration and aggression in ways which do not challenge poverty. Or one might interpret apparent resignation as a manifestation of the balance of power: if poor people rebel, they will get massacred by the forces of the status quo. Empathy is one step in understanding; theory is a second one.

2. Theoretical Interpretation. Almost unavoidably, actors are unaware of many of their own basic preconceptions, motives, intentions, and circumstances. We have all met individuals who claim to be unbiased but are not; who express one motive for acting when another is obvious to us, who express the best intentions in the world but rationalize hideous acts, who claim total freedom for their own decisions but are under immense social pressures. Indeed, many of us are experts at deceiving ourselves as well as others.

In order to interpret empathetic understanding, we need some criteria for sorting out which factors are significant or insignificant, which factors are conceivable or inconceivable, or which factors seem to be self-deceptive. There are no objective, universal criteria for doing this. To some extent, all researchers will employ their own personal criteria, which are a product of the researchers' perspectives on reality. Thus, the psychoanalyst who can empathize with the frustrations of political terrorists may, nevertheless, interpret "aggression" in terms of "neurotic fixations." He is likely to emphasize that unconscious motivation is more significant than the terrorists' intentions are. In another sense, the anthropologist may locate the terrorists' "violent tendencies" in the terrorists' particular "cultural milieu." To some extent, all researchers will fit their empathetic notions into their own preconceived categories with which the actors may or may not agree.

If the researcher necessarily places his own mark on analysis, he has two responsibilities. One is to avow openly his own criteria of significance. Phenomenologists often call this self-reflexiveness which allows those reading and using the research the option of questioning the analyst's criteria or the application of the criteria. A second responsibility is to systematize these criteria to ensure that they are logically related and consistently applied. This is the realm of phenomenological theory.

Phenomenological theory consists of building abstract, logically consistent models which attach significance to diverse aspects of behavior. Theories of socialization and acculturation tend to emphasize the significance of human preconceptions; theories of psychology focus heavily on unconscious or conditioned motives; theories of philosophy or ethics stress intentions; theories of economics tend to assume the significance of situational factors. According to Phenomenologists, none of these abstract theories is necessarily right or wrong; they are either useful or not in providing the analyst with a systematic set of categories and ideas for interpreting actions. Indeed, each theory offers a different angle of observation, which may help us understand another version of reality.

This second step is extemely delicate. The role of theory is not to develop general laws which apply to all people at all times. Rather, theory is mainly a statement of significance and a guide to selecting factors relevant to explanation. Phenomenological understanding concerns particular people acting in particular circumstances. To go beyond particularity is to distort drastically the meaning of action. Theory pulls one towards generality and the wise analyst will simultaneously take advantage of this pull and yet resist it.

3. Imaginative Reconstruction. Empathy provides a basis for understanding particular actions; theory provides a systematic perspective for general understanding. The real challenge of phenomenological research is to synthesize the particular and the general to reconstruct actions in ways which highlight their meaning. Phenomenologists offer no firm rules for accomplishing this; it is an imaginative and creative process. Nevertheless, they do supply a number of general guidelines.

First, a reconstruction is a retelling of an action or set of actions from a specified angle with an emphasis on the logical relations between aspects of action. Consider this question: Why did Kathy participate in a civil rights demonstration? Having already taken steps one and two, we might decide to look at Kathy's actions from the perspective of her religious background. We then reconstruct the series of actions that led to her participation in light of that background. A Quaker family and education sensitized her to the values of equality and humaneness. In college, she joined the American Friends Service Committee which reinforced and rewarded her childhood preconceptions. When this group was aroused by a particularly poignant racial issue, it decided to organize a civil rights demonstration. As a member of the group, it was only natural that

Kathy participate in the group's activities. Hence, she participated in the demonstration. We have reconstructed her actions from a specified angle — her religious background, and we have logically interrelated a series of actions — joining the group, participating in group activities, participating in the demonstration. Of course, we could have reconstructed her actions in numerous other ways, perhaps by looking at her participation in light of her economic background or in light of the state of racism in her particular locality.

Second, such reconstructions should be as comprehensive as possible. They should include some interpretation of how preconceptions, motives, intentions, and situational factors blend to produce the actions being investigated. This comprehensiveness can be achieved in several ways. A common way is for the researcher to reconstruct events with one aspect of action as primary and then use this aspect to explain secondary factors. In Kathy's case, we may focus mainly on her childhood preconceptions and then explain her motives, intentions and understanding of the situation in light of those preconceptions — e.g., her religious upbringing sensitized her to the smallest manifestation of racism in her situation. A less common but equally valid way of achieving comprehensiveness is to look at the same actions from many perspectives, within one study. One section could be on the cultural background of the actors, a second section could interpret the actors' actions on the basis of their avowed ideologies, and perhaps a third could reconstruct their actions in terms of the economic constraints in their realm of action. As we do in a cubist painting, we could get many views of the same action in a single work. Thus, we could reconstruct Kathy's actions on the basis of her religious preconceptions and we could then reconstruct her actions on the basis of the structured opportunities and constraints of college life. This way, we at least tap two of our multiple realities.

A final guideline is that the researcher should maintain an experimental disposition when reconstructing actions. Imagination plays a large role here. Many of the great thinkers of the modern era have opened people's eyes to new realities and have suggested new ways to perceive common actions. Georg Hegel suggested we look at the world from the perspective of the superrationality of history; Karl Marx suggested we look from the perspective of class-conflict; Sigmund Freud suggested the perspective of the unconscious and childhood sexuality; Max Weber suggested the perspective of bureaucratization. There are literally no limits to the possibilities for reconstruction: every new one will conceivably provide us with a panorama of a new slice of multiple realities. Moreover, by understanding new slices of these realities we might open up new vistas for human action, expanding people's opportunities and choices in the future. Or conversely, they might help us understand how to avoid a constriction of future choices. George Orwell's novel, *Nineteen Eighty-Four* was his imaginative reconstruction of the possible dangers which might emerge from industrial society. Orwell's hope was to project present trends into the future so that we might know what kind of future we might avoid.

4. Testing Reconstructions. There is no ultimate test or set of tests for confirming either the validity or the falsity of imaginative reconstructions of actions. Preconceptions and motives cannot be observed; they can only be inferred from an actor's background, reports, and others' analysis of background and reports in light of actions. No sure test demonstrates that an actor necessarily recognizes or follows his own intentions. And of course, which particular situational factors have the greatest effect on anyone's actions is more a subject of speculation than of rigorous testing. Nevertheless, the lack of specified tests does not necessarily imply that all reconstructions are equally valid or invalid. Again, a few general guidelines indicate why this is so.

Drawing from the reconstruction process itself, we can suggest that specification of the angle of vision, rigorous logic in relating aspects of action, maximal comprehensiveness, and an experimental disposition should inform good interpretations. In relation to this, we might consider if the reconstruction makes sense to the actors being studied; this is done to get a sense of the empathetic understanding that informs the work. We might consider whether the reconstruction makes sense from the perspective of one or of several theories; this is done to get a sense of the theoretical understanding that informs the work. None of these considerations will validate or falsify an interpretation. Rather, they measure if the interpretation can be communicated meaningfully to others who are interested in understanding multiple realities. This "making sense to others" is the philosophical notion of "warranty."

Sometimes, of course, a particular interpretation is not warranted in the eyes of others. But this is no less true in the natural than in the human sciences. Some considered Galileo's ideas on light and his telescope to be inventions of the Devil; some today consider Marx's ideas on class struggle to be naive. But this is only to say that some people look at reality through a different set of lenses from which Galileo's or Marx's ideas make no sense. Were one to switch lenses, their ideas might make perfect sense.

It is more important if a reconstruction can logically account for a host of actions that may appear to contradict the interpretation. Drawing on our example of Kathy, a critic may condemn our religious reconstruction by pointing out that Kathy had cut all ties to Quaker religion before entering college, joining the American Friends, and participating in the civil rights demonstration. The critic might further suggest that we could better reconstruct Kathy's actions by focusing on ideological factors current among her fellow students. Our faith in our own reconstruction will be seriously challenged if we cannot account for her anomalous renunciation of faith. At this point, we may suggest that her renunciation, within the loose context of Quakerism, constitutes more a disapproval of particular Quaker institutions and less a turning away from religious faith; in joining the American Friends, she finds an acceptable Quaker institution which reinforces her religious faith. And we would present some evidence that this was actually the case. If this explanation of the anomaly does not seem warranted to us, we may find a new one, revise our interpretation, qualify it, or discard it. The point here is that a good reconstruction is one which manifests a willingness and an ability to confront the critics in a systematic, logical way.

A final guideline relates to our own purposes as investigators. Reconstruction is a time-consuming and sometimes painful, expensive process. As researchers, we usually engage in the process with either implicit or explicit goals in mind. We might want to see how a common event appears in the eyes of others or we might want to impress our colleagues with our breadth or depth of knowledge. In a personal sense then, the adequacy of our reconstructions is tested by how well they help us fulfill our goals. But to see how well they help us fulfill our goals, we must reconstruct our own actions in order to interpret them. We cannot escape this vicious circle of interpretation; learning about others is to learn about ourselves and learning about ourselves forces us to learn about others. Perhaps, some speculate, it is the necessity and the ability to reconstruct which is what makes people unique in nature.

Ultimately, the test of a good interpretation is not a set of criteria but time and experience. On the one hand, an interpretation that makes sense to people over time becomes integrated into people's preconceptions and is then adopted as "common sense." On the other hand, an interpretation which helps people achieve their practical goals in life is one that is likely to be taken seriously for some time. No interpretation is either true or false, but some interpretations are considered useful for the purpose of informing human actions.

PHENOMENOLOGICAL METHODOLOGY: THE CRITIQUES

Among the various interpretive methods of political study, the phenomenological approach is perhaps among the least popular. To behavioralists and post-behavioralists, it is unscientific. Nevertheless, the reason I have spent so much effort in presenting the phenomenological approach is that it informs the logic of other interpretive methodologies. As we shall see, advocates of other interpretive approaches generally accept the philosophical basis of phenomenology but criticize it for being too narrow and therefore not very useful. If behavioralists and post-behavioralists are critics from without, supporters of other interpretive methods are critics from within.

Critics from Without
On the whole, behavioralists and post-behavioralists consider phenomenological reconstructions to lie in the realm of science fiction rather than of science. They are the appropriate goals for poets, novelists, and even journalists, but they certainly have no place in the laboratory of political behavior. Presenting just a few reasons will be adequate for understanding the main thrust of this critique.

First, Phenomenologists employ terms which are too vague and certainly too wide-ranging. By their very nature, preconceptions and motives, which cannot be pictured clearly in words, are distorted when described in words. Interpretors are free to create any image of these factors without providing any means for determining the accuracy of their images. How can we know, for example, that Kathy actually was motivated by "religious feelings?" We can certainly ask, but on what basis can we interpret her response? And Phenomenologists give researchers license to reject her response. Perhaps, they may say, her motivation is more unconscious and she herself does not recognize it. But this is license to speculate and fantasize.

Moreover, Phenomenologists tell us that we may look at any set of events from innumerable angles. As political scientists, then, they grant license to dabble in other specialities ranging from biology to economics. Because none of us can possibly be trained in all these fields, they justify intellectual dilitantism rather than serious scholarship based on specialization. We should be humble enough, as political scientists, to stick to our own specialty.

The second related reason is that Phenomenologists justify speculation on matters that simply cannot be observed by the human senses or by instruments which magnify the human senses. The "meaning" of behavior is always a question of speculation. At best, we can observe various patterns of behavior. For example, how can we possibly know if 100 years ago, Southern blacks developed preconceptions that led them to be submissive to dominant white groups? Or, how can we know if their submissiveness was a product of a rational evaluation of the racial balance of coercion? We can only guess at these factors. However, through systematic observation, we can clearly define submission, see if it existed in behavior, and consider if it was associated with other observable factors. We might hypothesize, for instance, that Southern blacks tended to be more submissive to whites than Northern blacks were, according to specific indicators. To do more would be to go beyond the boundaries of scientific inquiry.

Most important of all, Phenomenologists provide no rigorous standards for testing their reconstructions or interpretations against actual experience. Nonobservable behavior cannot be tested according to scientific norms. And phenomenological interpretations can rarely be falsified by any kind of evidence. Assume that the Phenomenologist suggests that several enacted bills tend to benefit the ruling elites. But, we counter, the third bill provides large welfare benefits for the masses. Instead of either rejecting or revising the interpretation, the Phenomenologist suggests that the welfare bill "really" was a way in which elites hoped to buy off dissent, promote acquiescence, and provide a political atmosphere in which elite interests would be maximized. All of science, however, is based on the ability to confirm or disconfirm ideas on the basis of data; but if no data necessarily confirm or disconfirm ideas, then we are back to the realm of science fiction.

These three criticisms suggest that phenomenology is not a scientific approach. What, then, is phenomenology from the critic's perspective? Though some behavioralists and post-behavioralists do not say this, it is clear by their critiques that they view this interpretive methodology as a licence to engage in ideology under the guise of science. Anyone who is free to use vague concepts, dabble in all fields, speculate about meanings, and neglect testing, all in the name of science, has a powerful tool for promoting his own ideology. If we want drastic changes, we simply empathize, theorize, reconstruct, and interpret in ways that support our personal goals; then we call it science in the hope that the scientific label will help us persuade others. But, according to the critics, science and ideology should be mutually exclusive: facts should be separate from values, general laws should be distinct from personalistic interests.

This is a rather harsh indictment of the phenomenological approach, which is only slightly tempered by post-behavioralists today. Post-behavioralists are sensitive to the ways in which values creep into scientific studies, to the need to generate imaginative theories and hypotheses which are not culturally bound, to the problems inherent in scientific testing, and to the relevance of scientific studies to society. Post-behavioralists sometimes consider phenomenological interpretations "suggestive" or more technically "heuristic." Phenomenologists can alert "real" political scientists to their value biases, to the conventional decisions made in the research process, to the several possibilities of interpreting data, and even to the ways in which findings can be applied to humanistic ends. Of course, a good novelist could do the same. Ultimately though, Phenomenologists are not scientists because they do not develop general hypotheses about observable behavior that can be tested according to the scientific norms of modern society.

Critics from Within Advocates of other interpretive methods will generally side with phenomenologists when confronted by the above criticisms. They believe that many of the problems with behavioralism have been reproduced in post-behavioralism. Both mainstream methodologies tend to distort experience, ignore the conventionality of scientific decisions, and, in the hands of American political scientists, justify the present inegalitarian constellation of political power. Technical definitions, sophisticated hardware, and even the new desire for relevance are all limited to narrow perceptions of American politics and America's role in the world as benign. Politically, incremental reforms are the morality of these political scientists.

Rather than going into the countercritique at length, let us see how these sometime allies of the Phenomenologists distinguish themselves from the Phenomenologists. First, they argue that the Phenomenologist does not advance our knowledge very far because he treats all actions as unique; actions are products of unique preconceptions, motives, and intentions of actors as well as unique configurations of special situations. Consequently, the collective sum of phenemenological knowledge is a set of interpretations of many unrelated actions. The logic of phenomenology is to produce fragmented knowledge.

The critics from within suggest that this need not be the case. Although any two individuals may have different preconceptions, motives, and intentions, there may be good reasons for treating them similarly. If they are members of the same subculture, influenced by the same factors, the likelihood is that their preconceptions, motives, and intentions will be more similar than they are different. To the extent that this reasoning is appropriate, we can generalize our interpretations to explain the collective actions of the entire subculture. Or, although any two individuals may react differently to the demands of poverty during any single historical period, it may be that situational constraints will affect them more similarly than it will differently. Again, we could now justify general interpretations of the actions of this historical group of impoverished people. These more general interpretations will allow us to consider cultural and historical trends affecting collective actions over time. And consideration of these trends will give us some leeway in projecting present understandings into the future.

Second, these critics suggest that the existence of multiple realities is more a future possibility than a prevailing norm. One perspective here is that people sharing a common human psychology and a common human language tend to perceive either the same reality or closely allied realities. According to Freud, people's perceptions are necessarily linked to their common need to live with neuroses; according to the later Wittgenstein, people's perceptions are loosely linked to their shared languages. Advocates of these views are likely to suggest that psychological and linguistic constraints are more significant than are other ones; thus, a good interpretation will emerge from these considerations. Another perspective is almost the opposite; people's similar perceptions tend to be a product of their similar social circumstances. According to Max Weber, the bureaucratization of society and politics in the twentieth century may be one of the most significant factors in interpreting twentieth century actions in industrial societies. According to Karl Marx, how people reproduce their own lives in the economic system is the most significant determinant of psychology, language, and even bureaucracy. Others might suggest the greater significance of nationalism, racial relations, or sexual relations.

Those who accept interpretive analysis but criticize the Phenomenologists argue that some angles of perceptions are clearly more important than others are. But, as one can see from the above paragraph, they rarely agree among themselves which angles are most significant; they rarely agree if political actions are better explained in terms of national interests, technological needs, or economic relations. Thus while behavioralists and then post-behavioralists have been relatively unified for the past quarter century, advocates of interpretive methods of politics have often been at each other's throats. And when Phenomenologists suggest that they are all equally justified in perceiving politics differently because there are multiple worlds of perceptions, these critics from within turn back upon the Phenomenologists as well as upon each other.

Why such "viciousness" among intellectuals who share a general interpretive perspective? I can suggest two probable reasons. One is that it is not unusual for members of a minority, in this case an intellectual and methodological minority, to spend more time fighting one another than fighting the mainstream. Everyone wants to unify to replace the behavioralists and post-behavioralists, or at least limit them to one corner of the discipline, but everyone wants unity on their own particular terms. Another reason may be even more directly political. As we stated early in this book, how one approaches political understanding often defines what one can consider appropriate political action. Behavioralists and post-behavioralists tend to agree on procedural values and the limits of political action. Interpretive political analysts, however, tend to focus on substantive political values (i.e., the "good" society) but often disagree on the nature of those values. Some believe the good society is a religious hierarchy and defend the significance of religion in explaining political actions; others believe the good society is an economically egalitarian community and, in explaining politics, defend the significance of economic struggle. This is not to say that they are any more or any less ideological than are behavioralists and post-behavioralists. Rather, it is to reinforce the point that the analysts' preconceptions will at least partially shape their understanding of particular methodologies.

MARXIST METHODOLOGY TODAY

In this section, I will look at modern Marxist methodology as an example of the alternatives offered by the critics from within and as an indication of a very recent trend. That is, despite the fact that Marxists have criticized Phenomenologists' methodology as not very useful and overly fragmented, they have increasingly accepted the importance of both uniqueness and multiple realities.

Classical
Marxism

The thoughts of Karl Marx and his followers prior to World War I is obviously subject to a number of interpretations. Here, I only hope to present the bare outlines of their views on political analysis with the foreknowledge that all I write could be treated as overly simplistic. My hope here is to catch the spirit of early Marxist methodology.

Early Marxists began their analyses with the assumption that the most significant angle of perceiving reality is the economic. How people produce, relate to one another in production processes, and enhance their production capacity is so significant an aspect of human life that it tends to shape other human relations. For example, once people produce on stationary farmlands, they must create some kind of militia to protect this production capacity from invasion by others. Or, once people find it useful to produce cooperatively, they must create a sophisticated language that facilitates communication and the ability to coordinate different aspects of production. Or, if people find it necessary to work in factories, they will develop a psychology that allows them to respond to time clocks, superiors' orders and monthly paychecks. The ultimate assumption here is that one's relations and modes of production tend to shape most other aspects of one's social and political life. While there may be individual exceptions, people will generally act in accordance with this assumption.

Much of early Marxist analysis was aimed at reconstructing how it had happened that, by the nineteenth century, more and more people were forced to sell their labor for wages (wage-laborers or the proletariat class) while a few owned the major tools of production and thereby reaped large profits (employers or the capitalist class). This was not just a scholarly interest; it was also a political interest. Marxist analysts hoped that by answering this question they would be able to show the processes by which the proletariat class could overthrow the capitalist class and establish an egalitarian society.

Two aspects of their reconstruction concern us here. First, in tracing several thousand years of economic history, they located the source of changes in contradictions. By the nineteenth century, one of the major contradictions of capitalism was, they believed, that it forced workers to live under extremely impoverished conditions at the very moment it expanded production to the edge of abundance. Since workers had an interest in seeing that they produced this abundance as a class while capitalists expropriated it in the form of profits, workers would also see their interest as a class in overthrowing the expropriators. This is one of the things Marxists mean when they say capitalism produces the seeds of its own destruction.

Second, however, overthrowing the capitalist class would not be an easy task. Using economic lenses, Marxists reconstructed several thousand years of political history. They suggested that the need for government arose once producers generated surpluses and a few people succeeded in expropriating those surpluses. Government

historically developed as an instrument of the dominant (or expropriating) economic class for insuring its ability to continue ex-
propriation and to control the threat of dissatisfied producers. In
other words, government developed as an instrument of coercion to
control the lower classes. This had not changed in the nineteenth
century when government had taken on pseudodemocratic forms.
Thus, for the proletariat to overthrow the capitalist class, they would
also have to overthrow their governors and take hold of government
for their own purposes.

On the basis of these and other more complex interpretations,
the early Marxists projected a number of present trends into the
future. One, the proletariat would organize as a cohesive class able to
overthrow both the capitalist class and its political instruments; two,
freed from class domination, the proletariat would begin the transition to an egalitarian, socialist community. More technical economic
projections were also made. Prior to World War I, it appeared that
many of these projections were becoming historical realities.
Throughout the capitalist world, workers had organized radical trade
unions and political parties avowedly hoping to overthrow capitalists. In many cases, the threat of these workers' movements led to a
suspension of democratic rights and procedures, reinforcing the
Marxists' point that the state was an instrument of the dominant
class. Moreover, immediately after World War I, the first successful
socialist revolution took place in Russia and then Lenin proclaimed
the beginning of the transition to socialism, equality, and community.

At the very moment, however, when these Marxist projections
seemed validated, they were questioned even by the Marxists themselves. In no capitalist country did the proletariat organize as a
cohesive class; many of the proletariat unions and parties were more
interested in winning a larger slice of the capitalist pie than in
overthrowing capitalists. And of course the Bolshevik Revolution
took place in a nation that could only be called capitalist with great
difficulty. Moreover, it was only a very few years later that the
Bolshevik Revolution seemed to turn "sour;" rather than a move
toward an egalitarian society, the Russian people were increasingly
dominated first by the Communist Party and then by Stalin. Did these
events necessarily falsify Marxist interpretations as some critics
claim? Or were they mere anomalies that could be eliminated by
further explanation? Those unsympathetic to Marxist goals claimed
falsification; they claimed that the interpretation was unscientific
and laden with values, and that it should finally be tossed back into
the intellectual dustbin of history. I have suggested earlier in this
chapter, however, that no event will necessarily falsify an interpretation. Either that event can be treated as an anomaly (as most Marxists
perceived at the time) or it can be seen as an indication of the limited
utility of the interpretation (as modern Marxists tend to perceive
today).

Methodological Anomalies

From a Marxist perspective, there was one overwhelming question which needed to be answered in the early years of the twentieth century: Why had the proletariat not united in order to pose a serious threat to capitalist rule? This anomaly called for a serious application of Marxist methodology. There were two major results.

Some Marxists decided to reinvestigate the economic contradictions of capitalism: they argued that the nature of those contradictions had changed since the nineteenth century. What was new? Lenin answered in a booklet called *Imperialism*. By exploiting labor and resources in overseas colonies, capitalists were able to ease temporarily crises at home. Although Western laborers' wages did rise somewhat, laborers in other lands paid the costs. The result was that laborers in capitalist countries tended to limit their economic demands to bread and butter issues and to support incremental welfare reforms to appease those worse off. This explained the lack of revolutionary impulse among workers. This did not contradict Marxists' earlier interpretation, but it meant that the timetable would be put off until workers in both capitalist and peripheral nations realized that they had a common international interest in overthrowing the international capitalist class. After all, Marx did say, "Workers of the *world*, unite!"

Another reinterpretation focused less on economic contradictions and more on the way workers were systematically forced into passivity. In the 1920s, Antonio Gramsci suggested that the analyst's economic lenses must be tempered by a concern for politics, ideology, and culture. Although economic contradictions create the conditions that make a proletariat revolution objectively possible, it is the realm of human preconceptions, motives, and intentions that explains if workers take advantage of those conditions. Building on some of Lenin's work, Gramsci developed the notion of "hegemony;" an interpretive device for suggesting that capitalists employ the means of intellectual production to control the perceptions of workers. If politicians, teachers, priests, and intellectuals continually promote the belief that individual hard work and procedural reforms are the best way for a worker to enhance his economic position, the worker will less likely perceive the possibility of revolution. At this stage, he will be torn between his objective economic interest (based on class.contradictions) and his common sense (based on his ideas). Gramsci suggested the need for a communist party to counter capitalists' hegemonic ideas by building the basis for a socialist culture, ideology, and politics prior to the revolution. Then workers would have both the opportunity and the will to overthrow capitalists.

For our purposes, these reinterpretations of Marxism demonstrate several sides to the interpretive methods of political analysis, be they Marxist or not. One is that it is always possible to explain anomalies within the context of a given interpretive methodology;

Marxism is not unique. Thus, a patient may say to his Freudian psychoanalyst, "This therapy is not helping me at all." The psychoanalyst can readily explain this anomaly by responding, "You are merely projecting your internal fears on me. That is an important step forward!" Ultimately, the strength of the explanation of the anomaly is not its truth or its falsity but its utility. Some Marxists believed that there were so many anomalies from this perspective that they would find it more useful to look at the world differently; others found the explanations of the anomaly reasonable and maintained their allegiance to Marxist methods. Similarly, under conditions like our psychiatric example, some patients will find it useful to continue therapy and others will storm out. Moreover, these reinterpretations suggest a large degree of flexibility in interpretive political science. On the whole, Lenin's "imperialism" explanation tended to maintain that economic conditions determined political actions. But Gramsci's analysis altered this somewhat; economic conditions may create an atmosphere in which political actions will determine future economic relations. Gramsci was among the first of many Marxists who later began to consider political lenses, religious lenses, ideological lenses, and other lenses nearly or even equally significant to economic ones. It was during the Stalinist era and its aftermath that Marxists began to discover the Phenomenologists' multiple realities and to incorporate it into their methodology.

Modern Marxist Methology

Two major anomalies shook the methodological world of Marxists in the 1930s. First, the advent of Stalinism seemed to indicate that the overthrow of capitalism did not automatically result in an egalitarian, socialist society. One could no longer assume that socialization of the means of production determined the establishment of the good society. In particular, Marxists became sensitive to the need to investigate the role of bureaucratization. Second, the growth of Fascism in major industrial nations indicated to some that, to some extent, political forces could exert more influence over economic development than many Marxists had believed possible. This anomaly was strengthened after World War II when it became clear in developing nations that political decision making had a large effect on nations' economic futures. A third anomaly should be mentioned, even though its long term effect on Marxist methodologies is still unclear. During the last quarter of this century, a number of national liberation movements have indicated that Marxist methodology must be adapted to the different cultural environments in different ways. African traditions and relations differ from Asian or European ones; and Marxist methodology must reflect these differences.

As these anomalies began to add up, Marxist scholars entered into an international debate on revisions in classical Marxist methodology. Some scholars maintained an adherence to the unique signifi-

cance of the economic aspects of life as the prime determinants of
social and political relations. Others suggested that this economic
angle of perception must be augmented by other angles: bureaucracy, politics, mass psychology, and culture, to name a few. And some
scholars went so far to suggest that Marxists must become
phenomenologists; never ignoring the economic interpretations but
never relying on them without tapping other reconstructions of
people's multiple realities. This debate continues today.

Precisely because more and more contemporary Marxists believe that it is a significant intellectual endeavor to take politics
seriously, more and more political scientists have tested Marxist
methods to understand how politics affects economic questions,
social questions, and a host of others. No longer looking at politics as
a mere reflection of economic relations, Marxist political analysts
have published interesting works on the role of the state in organizing dominant classes, promoting acquiescence among subordinate
classes, serving as an arena of class conflict and also as an instrument
of the capitalist class. But even in the conventional latter case, the
role of the state can no longer be assumed. Because there are
contending Marxist analyses, advocates of the instrumental view
must provide evidence showing how the state has become an instrument, is used as an instrument, and reproduces itself as an instrument of the dominant class. Ultimately, various Marxist interpretations of the state rise and fall according to how well they make sense
to their audiences.

In America, Marxist scholars have been especially interested in
complementing traditional economic perspectives with historical
interpretations of racial and sexual divisions in the last two or three
hundred years. Why? The answer here applies to all the interpretive
methods of political analysis. During the 1960s and 1970s, Marxists
realized that they needed the political support of minorities and
feminists. They could not win this political support by telling minorities that their problems would automatically be solved by socialism,
nor could they win feminist support this way because their own
organizations often practiced sexist policies. Thus, for political expe-
diency, American Marxists synthesized classical and interpretive
methodological approaches with at least two more interpretive angles aimed at tapping our multiple realities.

**POLITICAL
SCIENCE II** People whose political preconceptions are consistent with the Logic
of Political Opportunities are likely to have good reasons for adopting
one of the interpretive methods as more sensible and useful than
post-behavioralism is. This link between a particular set of preconceptions and a particular methodological approach is the foundation
of what I call Political Science II. Or diagrammatically:

POLITICAL SCIENCE II

Methods: Interpretive Approach

Preconceptions: Logic of Political Opportunities (Politics as Communi-
                                               ty-Building, Justice as Goodness, American Elitism, and
                                               Cross-Cultural Comparison)

In this section, I will provide the basis for this argument and then
give some consideration to the "scientific" basis of Political Science
II.

First, the notion of multiple realities implies extended political
opportunities. Each of us lives in the present, tends to view the
present from socially acceptable perspectives and ultimately considers our own views relatively natural. This is only to say that we
adapt to our circumstances. Post-behavioral analysis is eminently
suitable for helping us to understand how we might adapt more fully
and more happily. Nevertheless, at least some people do not wish to
adapt but wish to change their circumstances; they believe that
maximal human happiness cannot be achieved within the bounds of
their present political and social systems. The notion of multiple
realities implies that we can view our present circumstances from a
new angle, derive new insight into it, and possibly become more
sensitive to its problems and potentials for change.

Consider the person who has grown up with television, watched
commercials all his life, considered them insults to his intelligence,
but who sees no real alternative to them. Were that person to look at
himself from either the perspective of a peasant in a nonindustrial
society or the perspective of a possible future society, he might be
able to see how his situation came about and how he might help
change it rather than adapt to it. Present consumer advocates sometimes interpret the growth of the advertising industry as the corporations' need to create steady demand through psychological pressure. To the extent that our person accepts this interpretation, he
might challenge the corporations' right to dominate the airways by
engaging in appropriate political actions. Furthermore, he might
search for alternative means of informing consumers of available
products without such psychological manipulation. Or he might
consider what kind of political system would support consumers
searching for such alternatives. The assumption behind multiple
realities is that we can always step out of our present set of
preconceptions to get a new perspective on constraints and
opportunities.

Moreover, the idea of multiple realities tends to justify extending our notion of politics and appropriate realms of political action.
On the one hand, analysts are justified in looking at politics from
economic, anthropological, sociological, and many other angles. On
the other hand, analysts are justified in using their political lenses to

explore how decisions constrain or expand people's options in nongovernmental arenas of life. This broadening of the political realm engenders a broadening of the realm of appropriate political action to all aspects of community life. Thus, political action may now include both changing the government and the social structure. Here, we find a consistency with the definition of Politics as Community-Building (discussed in Chapter 2).

Second, for people having a moral standard of Justice as Goodness (discussed in Chapter 3), the interpretive methodologies offer some advantages. One advantage is that they can engage in analysis from a perspective suitable to the kind of community they desire. As specified earlier, enthusiasts of a theocracy can reconstruct political actions in ways which focus on religious causes and effects; advocates of egalitarian socialist communities can take economic categories as the basis of their political focus. This allows them to understand politics in ways useful to fulfilling their moral goals. Another advantage is that the less phenomenological methodologies generally assume a social basis for community. A cultural approach assumes people share some important norms; an economic approach assumes people in some sectors share crucial economic interests. These assumptions, often justified by philosophical and historical arguments, then become the basis for arguing that shared affections, norms, and interests are the potential basis for establishing the desired community. Interpretations focusing on preconceptions, motives, intentions, and situational factors then reveal both the barriers and the paths to making the potential a reality. As specified earlier, however, because people disagree about the nature of the good society, they will often consider their standards of methodological significance superior to those that tap other realities.

Third, the interpretive approach is perfectly suited to analysis of elitism in American politics (discussed in Chapter 4). It allows researchers to consider preconceptions and motives as limits to the boundaries of that pluralism. It gives them some flexibility in interpreting the intentions of politicians who say one thing but do another. It provides some basis for relating political structures to other social structures that may influence political decisions in subtle ways. Some of the most interesting of the recent elite theories of American politics are imaginative reconstructions of the thought processes and motives of American elites that demonstrate how those elites can potentially benefit disproportionately from pluralistic processes. Rather than treating pluralism and elitism as opposites, some researchers have tried to demonstrate that the former is a major determinant of the latter.

Finally, the interpretive methods are especially suitable to scholars interested in comparing American politics to the politics of other nations in ways which do not necessarily favor the American political system, i.e., Cross-Cultural Comparison (discussed in Chapter 5). We may now imagine ourselves in the position of a peasant in a developing nation to understand why that peasant may act in revolutionary ways. Or we may put ourselves in the place of a Russian worker to see why he might prefer Russian communism to American capitalism. We may find his preferences are determined by propaganda, as we have always expected; but we may also find that the Soviet economic or political systems offer some advantages to him over his American counterparts. Either way, we have not prejudiced our study beforehand by imposing American categories and norms on foreign cultures. Thus, the interpretive methods of politics are more suitable than is post-behavioralism, in the eyes of those pursuing cross-cultural comparisons.

By combining these points, we see that the interpretive approach is quite consistent with the four models that constitute the Logic of Political Opportunities. It provides much greater leeway than does post-behavioralism for people whose preconceptions are at odds with mainstream American politics. This leeway consists of greater flexibility for understanding the bases of this dissatisfaction and for understanding the alternative political and social relations that may ease this dissatisfaction. The interpretive methodologies do not necessarily imply criticism of American politics; they are certainly flexible enough to allow researchers the room to conclude that little political change is possible—this has often been the case with Freudian interpretations. Nevertheless, they also allow researchers the room to conclude that significant changes in the American polity are desirable and possible—this has been the main message of American Marxists and other adherents of the Logic of Political Possibilities.

Behavioralists and post-behavioralists agree that their own methods are scientific. Up to this point, I have avoided presenting the arguments that the interpretive methodologies are also scientific from the perspective of their users. The reason is that advocates of the interpretive approach do not agree among themselves on this question.

Many Phenomenologists suggest that the study of political action can never be scientific in the same way that the study of natural behavior is today. Although they agree with post-behavioralists that science consists of the development of general, testable hypotheses, they disagree that these general, testable hypotheses can help us understand politics. They cannot.

Atomic particles and other natural phenomena *behave* according to laws. The job of the natural scientist is to discover those laws and to test them against natural behavior. But people are unique in the natural world. They do not behave; they *act*. Their actions have meaning in the sense that they result from everchanging combinations of preconceptions, motives, intentions, and situations. To the extent that we can establish patterns of behavior, we have not yet considered the multiple realities that inform that behavior. And the moment we discover those patterns, we may choose to behave differently, break patterns, or create new ones. Atomic behavior is lawful and predictable; human action is everchanging and creative. Thus, the best we can do as political analysts is to interpret human changes and creativity; the attempt to establish and test laws of political behavior will necessarily result in a distortion.

Two implications result from this argument. One is that the scientific method is an inappropriate tool for studying political actions. The second is that there simply cannot be a political *science*. University departments and organizations bearing this label should drop the word *science*; they should be renamed departments or organizations of politics or political studies. But even these labels are misnomers, since the study of politics now encompasses the study of all aspects of human activities.

Others disagree. They believe that their interpretive approaches are indeed scientific—more scientific than post-behavioralism and equally scientific to physics, though less developed than physics today. On the one hand, science denotes a field of inquiry open to all methods of enhancing human understanding. Post-behavioralists unjustly constrict political science to one major methodology without seriously considering the value of alternative approaches; the interpretive *sciences*, on the other hand, suggest the possibility of innumerable approaches, unfolding our understanding of multiple realities.

Although physicists have reached a modicum of agreement on some hypotheses and have developed sophisticated laboratory techniques, they are often within the realm of doing interpretive science. To the extent that physicists are people, their own analyses are shaped by their preconceptions, motives, intentions, and surroundings. These subjective elements often determine what they will study, how they will study, how they will interpret their results, and whom they will try to persuade. Furthermore, not all of physics is based on observations. No physicist has ever "observed" gravity or light waves. Rather gravity and light waves are imaginative reconstructions that account for a whole series of movements in the empirical world. Furthermore, even the surest knowledge of physicists is subject to reinterpretation just as in the interpretive sciences of politics. Newton's mechanical theories can be challenged by Einstein's relativistic theories; theories of light waves must withstand the challenge of theories of light particles. Indeed, some philosophers of science suggest that science does not progress in a linear fashion; but that scientists change their intellectual perspectives to discover new interpretations that are useful to them in their circumstances. To the extent that this viewpoint is warranted, both political and natural scientists pursue useful knowledge rather than pursue universal truths.

Finally, the interpretive approaches are scientific in the same sense as either post-behavioralism or physics are. The major test of good scientific analysis, in all cases, is specification of preconceptions, rigorous logic, comprehensiveness, openness of experimentalism, willingness to meet criticisms and accountability for anomalies, and ultimately usefulness in accomplishing human goals. By this test, science is not a particular method, but it is, more aptly, a disposition for research which is consistent with numerous methodologies.

SUMMARY In this chapter, I have considered the importance of interpretation, the Phenomenologists' methods for doing political analysis, critiques of those methods by opponents and sympathizers, and one example of the evolution of an important interpretive approach, Marxism. Moreover, I have argued that there are good reasons why adherents of the Logic of Political Opportunities (and its constituent models) are likely to adopt a method from the interpretive approach rather than from post-behavioralism. This link constitutes the basis of Political Science II.

I concluded by suggesting that at least some adherents of the interpretive approach believe that no science of human action is possible. The implication is that the natural sciences have little to offer to political analysts. Nevertheless, some adherents of the interpretive approach believe that science is not a matter of a particular method; but that it is a disposition for studying any phenomena. From this perspective, a wide variety of methods are conceivably "scientific."

If you agree with this last point, you must then concede the possibility that there is not necessarily *one* political science but at least *two* political sciences. For some people this may be unsettling. After all, they may think, there is only one physics, one chemistry, one astronomy, etc. Nevertheless, in the next chapter, I will argue that the situation of acknowledging two political sciences is little different from the situation in most natural sciences where alternatives in thinking and analysis also coexist.

SELECTED REFERENCES Agger, Ben. *Western Marxism*. Santa Monica, Calif.: Goodyear Publishers, 1979.

Berger, Peter and Luckmann, Thomas. *The Social Construction of Reality*. Garden City, New York: Doubleday, 1966.

Edelman, Murray. *Politics as Symbolic Action*. Chicago: Markham, 1971.

Freund, Julien. *The Sociology of Max Weber*. New York: Vintage, 1969.

Gramsci, Antonio. *Selections from the Prison Notebooks*. Edited by Q. Hoare and G.N. Smith. New York: International Publishers, 1971.

Jung, Hwa Yol, ed. *Existential Phenomenology and Political Theory: A Reader*. Chicago: Regnery, 1972.

Louch, A.R. *Explanation and Human Action*. Berkeley: University of California Press, 1966.

Natanson, Maurice, ed. *Philosophy of the Social Sciences*. New York: Random House, 1963.

Winch, Peter. *The Idea of a Social Science*. London: Routledge and Kegan Paul, 1958.

Wolin, Sheldon. *Politics and Vision*. Boston: Little, Brown and Co., 1960.

THE "SCIENTIFIC"
STUDY OF POLITICS

CHAPTER EIGHT Picture a short man with dishevelled grey hair who neglects the charms of society. He is locked away in his laboratory, a sunken concrete structure on a dirt road, miles from town. He symbolizes the separation of science and society. He discovers new truths. Is the world ready for this?

This culturally nurtured picture of the man of science is certainly at odds with what students see in their classrooms and in the media. Actual political scientists are often men in three piece suits or women in stylish clothes. They have modern offices, air-conditioned computer space, homes in town, or in nearby suburbs connected by super highways. They are under pressure to publish books and articles for tenure or to advance professionally. Their writings, which may or may not have much to do with truths, are published whether the world is ready or not. After all, what could a political scientist publish that would have much effect on the world? Henry Kissinger is dancing in a Washington, D.C. disco.

Given our cultural understanding of science, it should not be surprising that many students are skeptical of the "scientific" nature of political study. The incongruity between the image of the scientist and the political scientist's actual appearance is reinforced in many ways. Scientific textbooks provide laws of nature, a history of solved problems, a specific method for finding further solutions, and appendices listing correct answers to practice problems in each chapter. On the contrary, many political science textbooks only speculate on laws of human nature, outline many problems without suggesting true solutions, provide tentative methods for solving such problems, and virtually never list correct answers in the appendices. In the classroom, real scientists minimize their speaking time to maximize education by experimentation; the proof is in the pudding. Political scientists talk and talk with few effective demonstrations of their political knowledge. In the newspapers, important scientific advances are published and discussed regularly. Although the political scientist does occasionally make headlines; those headlines will more likely refer to his or her politics and not political studies. Finally, students in the sciences take objective exams to reproduce correct methods and answers; in political science courses, essay or subjective tests seem to be the norm. Thus are the incongruities between the scientist and the political scientist enlarged.

So far, this book has not focused on this incongruity, although I have added several reasons for suspecting that this incongruity is quite real. One reason is that I have argued that there are at least two political sciences. To be more accurate, I should add that I can also conceive of several more political sciences constituted by different combinations of preconceptions and methods. I have overtly stated that I find no reason for believing that one political
science is more scientific than the other is. But perhaps this implies

one is not more scientific than the other because neither are very scientific at all. Both distort reality rather than reveal its fixed foundations.

A second reason is that I have said that both political sciences tend to have their own ideological flavorings. Those who tend to support the status quo or incremental reforms will find Political Science I more to their liking; those critical of the present are likely to adopt some variant of Political Science II. Perhaps then, both distort reality because those who employ them have an ideological interest in presenting reality in a way that will help them achieve their particular values. From this, it is easy to take the next step and conclude that both political sciences are forms of propaganda rather than variant modes of scientific understanding.

To say that the political sciences are actually "unscientific" is to make a comparison between them and the natural sciences. The above reasoning only makes sense when we consider the natural sciences "unitary" and "nonideological". And of course, most of us do.

Most of us believe that the scientist searches out truths based on sophisticated testing. Regardless of whether the scientist is an Alaskan Aleut or an African Ibo, she can agree that the only logical solution to two plus two is four. There is only one true answer to scientific problems. Furthermore, most of us believe that science is not flavored by ideologies. A New Zealand revolutionary and a Lapland reactionary can agree that masses always attract one another, according to a fixed mathematical formula. Science cancels out value differences among people interested in searching for noncontradictory truths. At its best, science delivers correct answers to problems. Unlike political science, it does not deliver several, contradictory interpretations or ideological speculations. Of course, there have been scientific quacks who reproduce such ideological interpretations but they are the exceptions.

In the following sections of this chapter, I will suggest that this common view of the natural sciences is a major distortion of the actual practices of natural scientists. Like political scientists, the work of natural scientists is not unitary but is constituted by diverse interpretations and speculations. Like political scientists, the work of natural scientists is informed by the political and ideological milieu in which scientists develop their own preconceptions. I hope to show that our two political sciences are not less but perhaps are more "scientific" than the natural sciences.

NATURAL SCIENTIFIC KNOWLEDGE

Natural scientists and political scientists share an interest in understanding the relations among phenomena in the world. For both, understanding includes processes of perceiving the empirical world, explaining the relationships among things perceived, and testing explanations against real world events. Each process requires some degree of interpretation and speculation.

Natural scientists are systematic perceivers of the world. They spend a good deal of time simply recording and organizing their observations. Ultimately, they must rely on the accuracy of their five senses and their psyches in recording and organizing. Sophisticated instruments like microscopes, telescopes, or computers do not diminish this reliance on human senses and psyches; instruments are merely extensions of human sensibilities.

How accurate are scientists as observers of the world? To answer this, we must be sensitive to several possibilities. We know that our senses occasionally deceive us. The mirage of a desert oasis is only one of many examples. Furthermore, we know that our minds can process our observations in ways which also cause distortions. Three witnesses to the same crime regularly provide three different and contradictory descriptions. Looking through a microscope or telescope or organizing data in computer banks does not eliminate distorted observations; scientists, as fallible people, must ultimately record observations and program computers.

I can think of three possible answers to the question of accuracy of scientific observation. One, is that under normal circumstances, scientists will perceive what is "really" happening in the world. This means that usually one scientist perceives a table occupying a particular space and another scientist perceives the same thing. The only difficulties arise in abnormal circumstances when some scientists have not had their eyes checked or when they are under such great mental or physical stress that their observations are distorted. Here we have the assumption of *objective* scientific observation.

A second possibility is that we all observe the world differently. People's five senses do not operate exactly the same. Is there any reason to believe that 20-20 vision provides a more accurate picture than 10-300 vision? Moreover, people's psyches operate quite differently. One person will see an inkblot image and describe a spider; another will describe a bird. The idea that people project their own images onto the world, rather than simply record the images of the world, has been a common theme in fiction and philosophy for centuries. To the extent that we take this possibility seriously, we support the assumption of *subjective* observation.

The third possibility is a variant of the first two. Perhaps people with similar cultural backgrounds that emphasize the development of particular senses and psychological perspectives do indeed perceive the same things. People with different cultural backgrounds, different development of the senses and different psychologies will agree that they perceive things differently from the first group. We know, for example, that sighted people tend to agree on observations and blind people tend to agree on observations, but the observations of the two groups are distinctly dissimilar. We also know, according to common folklore anyway, that where we perceive "snow," certain Eskimo groups perceive innumerable varities of snow. When groups systematically observe the same phenomena differently, we speak of *intersubjective* observation.

No scientific method exists for discovering which of these three possibilities best describes reality. Even when several thousand people look at the same phenomena and record the same description, important questions remain: Do they all mean the same thing by the language or symbols that they use in recording data? Would observors from other times, other social groups, or other cultures perceive the same things? Are there external pressures which compel people to record what they are expected to record, rather than what they actually perceive? Such questions can only be answered in one of two ways. We can engage in an interpretive analysis of the preconceptions, motives, intentions, and situations of scientific observors. Or, we can merely assume that one possibility is more likely than another is and get on with the work of science.

Most natural scientists take the latter route. They assume that scientists have the same natural senses and, when using the same sorts of equipment, scientists will record the same objective reality; only as exceptions will they project their subjective inner realities on the empirical world. This is not a scientifically based assumption. It is a speculation or an interpretation based on the reconstruction of evidence. In this sense, there is no pure science; speculations and interpretation play as necessary a role in the pure sciences as they do in the political sciences. And we should be aware of the fact that counterspeculations and counterinterpretations do exist among natural scientists.

Beyond being perceptive observers, natural scientists attempt to explain the relationships among the things they have observed. Historically, much natural scientific explanation has consisted of the positing of regularities among observed phenomena. The most familiar among these explanations may be the law of gravity that suggests that masses attract one another in a regular and predictable way summarized in a mathematical formula. Nevertheless, the positing of regularities rests on another nonscientific assumption based on speculation and interpretation. And as we shall see, some natural scientists adopt contradictory assumptions.

Are there really patterned relationships among phenomena in the natural world? At least two possibilities exist here. The first is that there are indeed patterned relationships (laws of nature) which predate human existence and which will likely postdate human existence as well. The role of the scientist is to discover and test these natural laws as the basis for explanation. If this is true, we might ask why there are laws of nature. Why, for example, do masses attract one another in a regular way? Newton himself pondered this question. His answer was ultimately speculative but meaningful within the context of his own society: God had created the laws of nature.

While this may or may not be true (according to the skeptical wisdom of our own time), no scientist has been able to demonstrate this according to scientific norms. Here, physics and metaphysical philosophy merge.

The other possibility is that there are no regular or patterned relationships in the world. Rather than behaving according to static laws, nature and human nature are continually evolving and changing. Thus, when Heraclitus stepped into a flowing river for the second time, he was stepping into a new or changed river. Many scientists find this possibility nonsensical. They ask, "If the world is really changing, how is it possible that we have already discovered so many regularities?" One answer is that these "regularities" are basically creations of the human mind. If we randomly tossed out several numbers, with enough time and energy, we could probably create a formula that suggests a regular pattern among these numbers. But this formula would not mean that the numbers are naturally ordered; it would mean that we have created an order by logic and imagination. So too with the natural world; all our scientific laws are projections of our minds. This is simply a complex case of the common notion of self-fulfilling prophecies.

Another answer is that there might be temporary regularities in the world. The law of gravity might hold true until the next ice age when the relations between masses may alter dramatically. Scientists are able to observe and explain only a short moment in the eons of time; conceivably our own time is little more than an aberation in billions of years of universal history. From this perspective, it can be suggested that scientific explanations should focus more seriously on natural changes rather than on regularities.

Again, scientists have no scientific method for testing whether the world is or is not based on such regularities, on randomness, or on changes. Rather, they conventionally adopt the assumption of regularity based on their own speculations and interpretations. Thus, the possibility of scientific explanation is itself based on nonscientific reasoning.

Whether or not scientists adopt the assumption of either natural regularity or changes, a great many of their explanations are based on either regularity or change in nonobservable phenomena. Is the phenomenon of light better explained as waves or as particles, neither of which any scientist has ever observed? Is an atom better characterized by electrons circling the nucleus along predictable paths or by electrons circling the nucleus within a given range of random paths? Because we cannot trace or observe the relative movements of specific electrons to answer this question, should we toss out the question? Or should we, as scientists have done, continue to reconstruct the structure of the atom in ways we find useful?

Furthermore, much scientific explanation is based on fantasies as creative as those spun in scientific fiction stories. No scientist has ever observed a frictionless plane. No scientist has ever seen the conservation of energy and matter. No scientist has ever witnessed the expansion of the universe. And certainly no scientist has watched prehistorical dinosaurs or a flaming ball of gas shooting off from the sun to become the planet Earth. These are all imaginary reconstructions that have been consistently considered useful bases of explanations among natural scientists. Thus, the natural sciences are not based on observation alone. Throughout their history, scientists' imagination and creativity have played a significant role. If this is true, have we any "scientific" reason for barring imagination and creativity from the political sciences?

Finally, understanding in both the natural and political worlds requires testing explanations against events in the world. Yet, the possibility of testing explanations is fraught with questions requiring nonscientific answers. Some of these questions I have raised in earlier chapters; some I now raise for the first time.

Does any test really validate or invalidate an explanation? We can never be certain that operational processes really reproduce the meanings of nominal words. We can never be fully certain that extenuating factors or circumstances, even in a controlled laboratory experiment, do not affect our tests. And much natural scientific testing takes place outside controlled laboratories. We can always find some room for discretion in interpreting test results. Ultimately, the whole testing process itself rests on a great deal of faith.

We should also consider the fact that the validation or invalidation of some scientific explanations require no tests in the conventional sense; some explanations either make or do not make sense according to past data. Consider the plight of Charles Darwin. He had no way of testing whether his theories of evolution were valid or not. The basic constraint was that evolution is a slow process occurring over millions of years while Darwin's own lifetime and those of his associates spanned only a few decades. Darwin's theories became serious scientific ideas because they seemed to be sensible reconstructions of current knowledge about life forms. The sensibility of his theories to others, and not evidence from laboratory tests, was what allowed them to survive the counterreconstructions of religious fundamentalists.

Some scientists suggest that the ultimate test of all scientific explanation is its prediction value. Do predictions deduced from scientific explanations come true or not? If so, they are good explanations. If not, they are poor explanations. Unfortunately, this neat criterion has two basic problems. The first is that much scientific explanation has no obvious prediction value. Darwin's theories help us understand the evolution of species but they provide little basis for predicting future trends in evolution. A second problem is that we may be able to predict things quite accurately without any idea of why our predictions come true. For example, some early civilizations were quite sophisticated in predicting eclipses even though they had no idea that eclipses are related to the relative juxtaposition of the earth, moon, and sun. Similarly, professors can predict rather accurately how many students will show up in class by statistical processes alone, even though they may have no idea of why the predicted number of students do or do not appear. We may want to use prediction as one test of explanations, but to go beyond this is to make science something very different from what it already is.

Which tests confirm or disconfirm explanations? Scientists have no scientific answers. Laboratory tests, logical reconstructions, or prediction value are merely a few of the many possibilities. At one time or another, scientists use several modes of testing. Ultimately, the choice of tests may be a product of abstract philosophical thinking or of politics, i.e., of which mode of testing is most likely to persuade one's colleagues. The possibility of a pure science again eludes us.

The nonscientific assumptions underlying scientific understanding have been debated for thousands of years. Assumptions of constancy versus change, mathematical versus material or mechanistic models, the focus on experience versus symbolic formalism, complexity versus simplicity, reductionism versus holism, or discontinuity versus continuity are only a few of the controversies that have divided natural scientists over the years. Science has never been and probably never will be unitary. Scientific "truths" are always arguable, contingent on particular scientists' assumptions about description, explanation, and testing.

It is becoming more common today for natural scientists to suggest that scientific understanding is often a matter of the preconceptions scientists bring to their studies. Noted physicist John Archibald Wheeler recently said,

What is so hard is to give up thinking of nature as a machine that goes on independent of the observer. What we conceive of as reality is a few iron posts of observation with papier-mache constructions between them that is but the elaborate work of our imagination.
(*Newsweek*, March 12, 1979, pp. 61-62)

Presently there are several schools of natural scientists who claim the prestigious mantle of science. There is reason to believe that several schools can simultaneously merit that claim. That there are also at least two schools of political science, two political sciences, is not significantly different. Diversity of perspectives and imagination are characteristic of all sciences—be they natural or political.

NATURAL SCIENTIFIC IDEOLOGY Some people characterize scientific study by its openness. Observations, explanations, and tests should be published in detail; so that they can be opposed by counterobservations, counterexplanations and countertests. Ultimately, scientific studies demonstrate their worth by surviving or even flourishing in the open marketplace of scientific dialogue.

Perhaps our two political sciences are unscientific because their ideological flavoring forecloses openness. Advocates of Political Science I generally interpret data in ways consistent with the status quo; advocates of Political Science II usually reconstruct events in ways consistent with basic criticism of the status quo. Both publish their studies, but neither takes the counterinterpretations very seriously. They both speak mainly among themselves. Implicity then, the ideological nature of our political sciences forecloses the existence of a real marketplace of ideas.

Although this may be the case among political scientists, there is no reason to believe it is any less the case among natural scientists. They too have their ideologies that limit the openness of dialogue and the openness of exchange in the marketplace of ideas. The only major difference is that natural scientists' ideology is more subtle and inconspicuous. Let me attempt to make their ideology somewhat more conspicuous.

For the past three hundred years, natural scientists have promoted two ideas which have become the basic constituents of many modern cultures. One idea is that natural scientists can and have developed solutions to problems which have plagued humankind since the beginning of time. The notion here is that scientific progress is equivalent to human progress. A second idea is that natural scientists can and have increased the storehouse of human knowledge. We know more about our world today than we did yesterday. Together, these ideas constitute the prevailing view that the possibilities for human and scientific progress are virtually unlimited.

As a group, scientists have benefited immensely from the cultural permeation of these ideas. They have gained personal wealth, vast research facilities, high social status, and even political power. Who could justifiably doubt that they merit these benefits? After all, they have put their special expertise to use in the name of humankind and truth. In the past, few expressed such a doubt while most simply considered it ridiculous. Nevertheless, doubt is growing today, perhaps for good reasons.

Have the natural sciences increased people's ability to solve basic problems? Without hesitation, we may answer yes. Natural scientific research and application have helped us eliminate major diseases, increase agricultural output, maximize industrial production, and stimulate dramatic growth in people's standards of living. They have helped us develop sophisticated transportation and communication networks that allow people access to new experiences during single lifetimes. And not in the least, the natural sciences have helped us expand beyond earth's land mass by opening access to the ocean depths and to outer space. Natural scientific solutions to human problems and the benefits people have derived are of incalculable worth.

However, equally incalculable may be the price people have had to pay for scientific advances. The elimination of major diseases has left some parts of the world overpopulated. Maximization of agricultural and industrial output has caused resource depletion, environmental degradation, and energy shortages. Moreover, this economic maximization has primarily benefited Western peoples while increasing other people's dependency and harsh life conditions. Our sophisticated transportation and communications systems, when considered in light of advanced military technology, now provide the ability to destroy the human race many times over. And it is as not yet clear if ocean and space exploration will demand a tremendous human price.

Consequently, while the natural sciences have solved basic problems, they have made possible new and potentially catastrophic problems. Because the benefits and costs of science are incalculable, we can only interpret the relative weighting. Has scientific progress engendered human progress or will humans ultimately suffer from scientific advancement? Let us look at several possible answers.

One we may label the *realistic* approach. Scientific advances simultaneously solve basic problems and engender new ones. But the record of scientists in solving the new ones is generally quite good. For example, although scientific advances have improved people's ability to produce food, overpopulation has resulted because starvation was once the main control on population growth. Scientists, however, have developed sophisticated contraceptive devices and relatively safe sterilization or abortion procedures, which allows people to limit population growth voluntarily. Indeed, in the 1970s some nations fear underpopulation problems. Or, we might focus on energy sources as another example. Scientists developed energy sources that allowed great advancement in civilization, but now those energy sources are scarce. How have scientists responded? Today they are seeking and succeeding in finding new and efficient sources of energy by drawing on nuclear technology and solar technology. Realistically, we live in complex societies in which problems will continually arise to threaten societies; but, going backward would be catastrophic when moving forward has historically resulted in new solutions and a better standard of living for most people. On the whole, the benefits of science outweigh the costs of science.

This realistic approach has been seriously challenged in recent years. Scientists have indeed solved problems and engendered new ones, but solutions to many of the newest and most dangerous seem to be nowhere in sight. In fact, these problems may be getting more serious. Despite major efforts to solve the pollution problems that affect people's health, people in major cities all over the world live in progressively unhealthy atmospheres. And in 1979, it became clear that the scientists' "safe" energy alternative of nuclear power plants was questionable; a major radiation leak in one plant in America alerted people to the very real possibilities of a meltdown and a nuclear explosion, as well as to the continuing problem of "normal" radiation emissions or the disposal of nuclear wastes. Increasingly, groups of people have suggested that many scientific advances are too dangerous; they have outstripped people's ability to control their harmful effects.

A second approach may be labeled the "purist" view. According to this view, the scientists' job is merely to advance human understanding of their world. Scientists, however, cannot, do not, and should not exert ultimate control over their advancements. That is the job of citizens and their government. Thus, Galileo invented a telescope, which added to our knowledge of optics and of the universe. But Galileo cannot be held responsible for the fact that one of the first uses of his telescope was by sea captains interested in winning military advantages over enemies. On the whole, the problems of the modern world cannot be laid on the doorstep of modern science. If there are problems, it is because others have used and abused scientific knowledge. A corollary to this view is that, as citizens, scientists should work for the benign use of their discoveries.

Like the first view, this one has encountered serious criticism during the past decade. It may have been the case in the nineteenth century that scientists were objective seekers of knowledge hidden away in their private laboratories or observatories. And it may have been the case that they then defined their own problems, developed their own methods, followed the thread of knowledge wherever it led, and only then published results. But this is definitely not the case today. Scientific research is now inextricably tied to particular interests in society.

Without going into great detail, let us trace the career of a "typical" scientist. He is educated and sponsored by funds drawn from private industries and government sources. He later gets a job in which his research laboratory, computer time, and other necessary paraphenalia are paid for by private or government grants. He will present and publish scientific papers at meetings or in journals that are subsidized by private industries or governmental sources. He will be judged by his colleagues, whose prestige and successes are partial products of their achievements and of their ability to nurture good relations with private or governmental agencies. Ultimately, he may rise to the top of his profession and judge others according to the same standards by which he was judged.

What are the implications of such a career pattern? One is that our "typical" scientist is unlikely to follow the thread of knowledge wherever it may lead. He will research problems for which funding is available. He will shape his research to ensure his future ability to win further funding. And he will present his research so that his elder colleagues will consider it serious, useful work. Consequently, our "typical" modern scientist will do work that primarily benefits private industry or pursure those interests that dominate government agencies. This means that his work will not simply be the pure pursuit of knowledge but the pursuit of knowledge beneficial to particular groups.

Another implication is that our "typical" scientist will develop self-interests consistent with supporting the present industrial and political structures. They are his scientific lifelines. As a citizen then, he will very likely add his voice or even his expertise in favor of the political status quo. Obviously there are exceptions, but today's scientific establishment is structured to produce compliant scientists who solve and support problems defined by particular interests but not by other, potentially more general, interests. According to the critics, the natural scientists' complicity in the status quo makes them at least partially responsible for the problems existing today.

Currently, there are at least two other views that suggest that the human costs of science either outweigh or equal the benefits. One view, taken to extremes, is this: If scientific advances cause more human problems than they solve, people may be better off without the wonders of science. Critics with this view often advocate "back to nature" life styles consisting of simplicity, rural life, natural foods, craftsmanship, and humanistic social relations. We would be much better off at Walden Pond than in mechanized, computerized, dirty, bureaucratized, congested cities. Others with this view advocate a less dramatic withdrawal from scientific life. Where possible, they suggest, have natural childbirths, eat natural foods, avoid automobiles, and simplify your life. Total withdrawal from scientific society is not practical today, but let us be examples to others for avoiding the major pitfalls of scientific "advancements," they advise.

Another point of view is that the progress of science has been relatively anarchistic. During some periods, the benefits of scientific advances outweighed the costs; during other times, the costs outweighed the benefits. Were this to continue, two conclusions might be warranted. First, the idea that scientific progress is human progress would always be a partial myth. Second, scientific advances might continue to be extraordinarily beneficial to some groups while being inhumanly damaging to other groups. New advances in fertilizers or steel processing might continue to benefit agricultural and industrial corporations, but workers and community people would pay the price of living with unhealthy work conditions and unhealthy neighborhood conditions. The alternative is to restructure the scientific establishment. Because natural scientific studies have such immense effects on workers' and communities' lives, workers and communities should have a much greater say over the nature of scientific education, over the funding of scientific research, and over the uses of scientific achievements. Unless the scientific establishment is made more democratic, these critics believe that science will not necessarily benefit humankind but will be potentially damaging to most people.

Which perspective on the relationship between scientific achievement and human progress is correct? This is a political question. Some people believe that the benefits derived from nuclear power plants far outweigh the potential risks; others argue that the risks outweigh the benefits. While I cannot provide a "correct" answer, it is worthwhile pointing out where scientists generally stand on this question. On the whole, natural scientists take the "realistic" or the "purist" approach. This should not be surprising. Both approaches justify the continuation of scientists reaping wealth, research resources, social prestige, and political power as they have in the past. More interesting is the fact that both approaches are consistent with Political Science I. The "realistic" approach suggests that incremental changes will be adequate for confronting major problems. This approach is consistent with The Logic of Political Realism. The "purist" approach implies that scientific study and political values are basically distinct though scientists, as citizens, have some responsibility to see that their research is used for humane purposes. This is the same argument which constituted the basis of the post-behavioral revolution. Together, these approaches constitute the mainstream ideology of natural scientific disciplines today. As Political Science I does, they tend to justify the present structure of government and society, and only then do they suggest possibilities for reform.

Nevertheless, at least a minority of natural scientists believe that scientific progress does not necessarily engender human progress. Their approaches to this issue are consistent with Political Science II. In congruence with the Logic of Political Opportunities, they suggest that scientific research and public values are inextricably interwined and that some means of making the scientific establishment democratic and bringing it under public scrutiny should be considered. Moreover, they argue that more scientific research should be done from a greater multiplicity of perspectives, including perspectives that help create the technology necessary for a more democratic and egalitarian society. This, of course, is a major basis of the interpretive methods of political science. Like advocates of Political Science II, these scientists tend to suggest a radical restructuring of scientific research and society as a whole.

In these ways, the natural sciences reproduce the ideological divisions current in the political sciences. Like political scientists, natural scientists mature with specific preconceptions which, at least partially, shape the kind of research they find justified and the kind of polity and society which will allow them to carry on such research. Although the ideological divisions among natural scientists are not as conspicuous as those among political scientists, we have good reasons for believing that the research of both is somewhat shaped by these ideologies. If this is the case, then we cannot condemn political scientists for being "unscientific" due to ideological influences unless we also condemn natural scientists for the same reason. But to condemn both is to condemn everything we have ever called science.

A second component of the notion of scientific progress is that natural scientists have progressively added to the storehouse of human knowledge. Each year, we understand our natural world a little better. And even if it is unclear whether scientific advancement is more beneficial or more costly to humans today, at least natural scientists can claim that progressive knowledge may potentially increase the ratio of benefits over costs. Perhaps our two political sciences are not really deserving of the label "science" until they demonstrate that they too have added to the human storehouse of progressive political knowledge. Even some political scientists suggest that Plato and Aristotle knew as much about politics 2,000 years ago as we know today.

Until the 1960s, most natural scientists and most people took for granted the idea that the natural sciences have progressively increased our knowledge of the world. For most people, the proof was in the scientific pudding; people used to fantasize about navigating the ocean floors or flying through the air, but we can and regularly do both. From this perspective, the idea that scientific knowledge had not progressed seemed absurd.

Nevertheless, during the past few decades, some scientists began to suggest that the proof was not in the pudding. Although we can do more than we could before, it is unclear that we know more than earlier civilizations knew. And in some cases, we may know less than earlier civilizations did.

Consider the traditional Chinese practice of acupuncture. Based on a philosophy of life forces little understood by Western people, the placement of needles in particular areas of the body serves a number of medical purposes. One of these is anesthesia. Western physicians and medical researchers have witnessed serious operations where acupuncture served as the exclusive means of anesthesia; and they have talked to patients during these operations and watched them literally get up from the operating table and walk away. As sophisticated as Western medical technology is, physicians and researchers cannot explain why acupuncture is relatively more effective than some of their own techniques are. Chinese acupuncture, the traditional uses of herbs, or a number of unexplained engineering feats of past civilizations are indications that modern scientists may have lost a good deal of past knowledge over time and space.

Another reason for reserving judgment on the progress of scientific knowledge is that we have become more sensitive to the relativity of that knowledge. Newton provided one set of mechanistic lenses for perceiving and understanding the natural world. Older "teleological" or "anthropomorphic" spectacles occasionally reappear in the annals of modern science to provide new insights (or to reconstruct old insights). And now Einstein's scientific relativism provides another set of lenses based on different notions of time and space. And these lenses may suggest that scientists will never find a master key or a master law for explaining natural phenomena. Is one set of lenses superior to another or is each set simply different? Do they focus our vision on one aspect of reality only to distort our vision of other aspects?

In the early 1960s, Thomas Kuhn published his book *The Structure of Scientific Revolutions*. The book almost immediately became the central focus of controversies that continue today. Kuhn's basic thesis was that scientific progress is an extremely limited notion. On the one hand, the history of science is the history of different "paradigms" or lenses through which scientists view the world. In one era, Newtonian lenses prevail; in another era, Einsteinian lenses prevail. No paradigm is superior to another; it only reveals a different vision of reality. In this sense, there is no progress in the growth of scientific knowledge; rather scientific revolutions are mainly changes in scientists' perspectives and not increases in their knowledge.

On the other hand, Kuhn's argument did not imply that the concept of scientific progress was useless: he suggested that the concept was relative. Once scientists adopted a Newtonian paradigm, for example, they then spent the next few centuries deducing and testing hypotheses, focusing their lenses on different aspects of the natural world, and trying to explain apparent anomalies. Although we cannot say that the Newtonian paradigm is better or worse than other paradigms are, we can say that our knowledge of it increases as scientists apply and revise it. Kuhn considered this "normal science"; the basis of scientific education and everyday research. Nevertheless, scientists often forget that they are working within the constraints of a single, relativistic paradigm; moreover they develop a self-interest in promoting their paradigm as the only way to research the world. Thus, they will preach the idea of scientific progress without realizing that it is never absolute but always relative to particular paradigms.

The immediate storm that followed Kuhn's book indicated, at the very least, that scholars within the natural and social scientific community took his theses seriously. Kuhn's theses seemed to capture the growing feeling that scientific progress is not a matter of the continual accumulation of "truths"; and Kuhn's reconstruction of the history of the natural sciences convinced many people that we may not know more about our world today than people in past civilizations once knew. We may be better manipulators of the world, but we are not necessarily more knowledgeable.

Scholars who agreed with Kuhn were troubled by one aspect of his reconstruction: Why do scientists change paradigms and adopt new lenses if this does not increase their understanding of the world? Kuhn suggested that this is partially a matter of scientific norms and partially a matter of scientific politics. First, scientists are faced with a number of anomalies that they cannot explain without shedding their old preconceptions and adopting a new paradigm. They are unlikely to do this unless a new paradigm is available. Second, because so many scientists have a stake in the old paradigm, they will resist efforts at developing new paradigms. Consequently, changes in scientific paradigms are relatively rare. Nevertheless, when anomalies become especially pressing and when younger members of the scientific professions begin to coalesce around an alternative set of lenses, it becomes a matter of time before the old preconceptions give way to the new.

Friendly critics punched a number of holes in Kuhn's explanation. Why is it that some anomalies become so serious that scientists are willing to look for alternative paradigms? We have already seen that virtually any anomaly can be interpreted in such a way that it no longer poses a problem. If predictions based on Newtonian gravity fail, we simply hypothesize the existence of a hidden or unknown mass; we do not throw out the Newtonian paradigm. Furthermore, why must there be one old guard protecting one paradigm who are replaced by one new guard defending one new paradigm? There are good reasons for believing that several sets of preconceptions or lenses can exist simultaneously.

Why then do scientists shift their lenses, adopt new or different perspectives, develop new problems, and offer new reconstructions of data? One possibility, which Kuhn ignores, is that outside forces pressure the scientific establishment to go in one or another direction. Since the beginning of the twentieth century, pressures by social groups, large economic interests, and political elites have played a major role in shaping the preconceptions of scientists, in defining serious problems, and in supporting research. When does an anomaly become serious? Perhaps when powerful social groups believe it is serious enough to invest a great deal of resources in finding solutions. And to some extent, these groups desire solutions that will be beneficial to them first and to the scientific establishment only second. Under these circumstances, research scientists have the incentive to develop new perspectives and the power to overcome the hesitancy of their colleagues. It may not be mere coincidence that the Newtonian paradigm became widespread with the growth of capitalist systems while the Einsteinian paradigm spread in an epoch when governments were forced to intervene in the capitalist economies. To the extent that Newtonian perspectives helped solve problems specific to the early capitalist era, its adherents may have been consistently rewarded. To the extent that Newtonian perspectives did not help solve the anomalies of late capitalist or early socialist societies, new perpectives like Einstein's may have been increasingly rewarded.

To the extent that this reconstruction is persuasive, we may say that natural scientists do not *clearly* or *necessarily* increase the storehouse of human knowledge. To some extent, they provide a number of different perspectives that rise and fall according to the needs of the powerful in society. This is not to imply that natural scientists are the political tools of elites. After all, dissident social groups have usually exerted enough pressures to have some scientists adopt lenses that solve the problems they consider serious. One should always approach the common notion of scientific progress cautiously. When one does, it becomes apparent, once again, that natural and political scientists are not significantly different. Neither may provide increased knowledge; but both potentially provide systematic, logical, and even persuasive modes of perceiving and, at least tentatively, understanding the world from a variety of angles.

WHERE NATURAL SCIENTISTS DARE NOT TREAD

In one important sense the natural and the political sciences are equally scientific. Both demand a rigor that is absent from most person-in-the-street opinions. Maximal clarity, systematic logic, accounting for data, and willingness to face anomalies presented in counterarguments are pervasive indicators of the scientific nature of a study. In both the natural and the political sciences, a variety of preconceptions and methods can and do inform studies; in both, ideologies play a more or less subtle role. Because all scientists are human, all scientists are influenced by the diversities and preferences which form an inescapable part of the human condition. And the precise nature of those diversities and preferences are partly shaped by the particular polities and societies in which humans live.

Nevertheless, the different subject matters of the respective sciences do make a significant difference. Natural scientific studies generally concern the behavior of natural phenomena. They trace *how* atomic particles react to one another, *how* chemicals combine under specified conditions to produce predictable reactions, *how* various masses affect the movement of other masses, and so forth. Over several thousand years of study, natural scientists have become quite sophisticated in using these tracings to predict future behavior of natural phenomena. This sophistication is one of the reasons why people outside the natural sciences have come to believe in the natural sciences. If we can predict how chemicals react under specified conditions, then we can artificially create those specified conditions to engender predictable results which we, or particular groups, find useful.

Natural scientists have mainly been limited to asking such "how" questions. Within the scientific community, "why" questions are usually deemed inappropriate. *Why* atomic particles react as they do, *why* chemicals react in predictable ways or *why* masses affect one another as they do ultimately is the same as asking, "Why is the world the way it is?" On the whole, scientists' answer to this question has been and continues to be based on religious faith. Newton's centuries old answer of "God produced the universe that way" has its modern analogue in Einstein's statement that "God does not play dice with the universe." Like parents faced with their children's interminable "why" questions, scientists ultimately resort to some sort of first cause, uncaused cause or unmoved mover to explain how the whole thing got started the way it did.

Natural scientists have no choice in this case. Given views of the nature which have persisted for centuries, natural scientists cannot imagine the following kinds of answers: Atoms react as they do because they have preconceptions which make such actions appear sensible to them. Chemicals react as they do because such reactions fulfill their emotional needs or because they have intentionally agreed to do so. Masses attract one another because their other options in their circumstances are too painful. These kinds of answers are unimaginable because they require an assumption that most people are unwilling to make: natural phenomena have an unconscious, subconscious, or conscious control over their behavior. Such categories are generally reserved for human beings; and in fact, they distinguish the human species from other species. Of course, there are a few gray areas such as animal psychology or physiological psychology of people where these distinctions between natural and human behavior blur.

Political scientists do have broader options than natural scientists do. On the one hand, they can and have asked innumerable "how" questions concerning people's political behavior. The behavioral and post-behavioral methods provide them, if only tentatively so, with a means of generating and testing patterns of people's behavior in the political realm. Political scientists have not been nearly as successful as natural scientists have been in answering these questions in ways that allow them to predict outcomes accurately. There are two primary reasons for this. First, political scientists have been trying to develop their prediction powers systematically for less than three decades; natural scientists have been doing this for more than three centuries. Conceivably, time will reconcile this difference. Second, political scientists' subject matter may simply be more variable than natural scientists' subject matter is. People have mixed and changing preconceptions, motives, intentions, histories, and cultures that are difficult to cut through in order to establish patterns of behavior; the behavior of natural phenomena may be less complex and more easily recognizable simply because these human attributes are lacking. Nevertheless, it is at least theoretically conceivable that political scientists may one day develop laws and hypotheses as certain (relatively speaking) as those of their naturalist colleagues.

On the other hand, political scientists can, have, and virtually always do ask "why" questions without immediately having answers based on faith. People not only behave, they act out of unconscious, subconscious, or conscious reasons within changing circumstances. *Why* were groups willing to engage in revolutionary activities? *Why* are societies conflictual or harmonious? *Why* do people hold particular political values? These are all questions which can be answered without immediately invoking a deity or, a first cause. Although political scientists may not agree on the answers to these "why" questions to the same degree that natural scientists agree on answers to their "how" questions, political scientists do provide us with a rich library of interpretations that help us sort out political actions in an intelligible way. Even disagreement adds a new dimension to our understanding—a dimension lacking in most natural sciences.

Here, we arrive at a final irony. The modern political sciences may be more "scientific" than the natural sciences are. Political Science I may ultimately develop a capacity to describe, explain, and predict nearly as well as the natural sciences do. Political Science II has already developed a capacity to interpret political actions in ways presently inaccessible to natural scientists. Newton spent a good part of his life trying to understand how apples fell from trees; political scientists can potentially understand how and why people pluck apples from trees. And, of course, the trees are trees of knowledge.

SUMMARY This chapter was a consideration of if two political "sciences" can conceivably coexist. I began by suggesting that our general standard of "science" is taken from the natural sciences that are often perceived as unitary and nonideological. Were this standard warranted, it would cast considerable doubt on the scientific nature of our two political sciences; I have argued that both political sciences are not unitary but are ideologically informed. I then suggested, however, that neither the natural nor the political sciences are either unitary or nonideological.

In two senses, the natural sciences are not unitary. First, many of the decisions underlying natural scientific study are based on conventions, interpretations, and speculations. Second, these conventions, interpretations, and speculations are subjected to alternative viewpoints among natural scientists. Consequently, the history of science reveals that there are, and always have been, several alternative schools of scientific reasoning and study. To the extent that our two political sciences are alternative schools of reasoning and study as well, they are not significantly different. Thus, to argue that the political sciences are not "scientific" because they are not unitary would imply that the natural sciences are not "scientific" for the same reason. This would eliminate "science" as an intelligible concept.

Moreover, the natural sciences are informed by ideological preferences, though in ways more subtle than the political sciences are. At the hub of natural scientific ideology is the belief that scientific progress is human progress. Included are the ideas that natural scientists have developed solutions to pressing human problems and that they have increased the storehouse of human knowledge. I have suggested that there are good reasons for believing that the benefits of scientific advancements are conceivably outweighed by the costs and that the growth of scientific knowledge is more problematic than we would normally think. Nevertheless, most scientists maintain and promote a belief in progress that, not coincidentally, justifies their self-interest in controlling important resources. Implicitly, these scientific realists reproduce the ideological bent of Political Science I. Alternatively, some natural scientists believe that the scientific establishment should be made more democratic to ensure that scientific progress will benefit society as a whole. These scientists reproduce the ideologically bent of Political Science II.

Having argued that the natural and the political sciences offer alternative perspectives and ideologies, I concluded by suggesting the possibility that the political sciences may be more "scientific." Whereas the natural sciences are adept at explaining "how" phenomena relate to one another, they cannot help us understand "why" phenomena relate to one another as they do. Conceivably, the political sciences can answer both "how" and "why" questions. This means that the *potential* scope of political explanation is much broader than that of natural scientific studies.

SELECTED REFERENCES

Becker, Carl. *The Heavenly City of the Eighteenth Century Philosophers.* New Haven, Conn. Yale University Press, 1932.

Hartz, Louis. *The Liberal Tradition in America.* New York: Harcourt, Brace and World, 1955.

Holton, Gerald. *Thematic Origins of Scientific Thought: Kepler to Einstein.* Cambridge, Mass.: Harvard University Press, 1973.

Janik, Allan and Toulmin, Stephen. *Wittgenstein's Vienna.* New York: Simon and Schuster, 1973.

Kaplan, Abraham. *The Conduct of Inquiry.* San Francisco: Chandler Publishing Company, 1964.

Kuhn, Thomas. *The Structure of Scientific Revolutions.* Chicago: Phoenix Books, 1964.

Lakatos, Imre and Musgrave, Alan, eds. *Criticism and the Growth of Knowledge.* Cambridge: Cambridge University Press, 1970.

Pennock, J. Roland and Chapman, John W., eds. *Participation in Politics.* New York: Lieber-Atherton, 1975.

Popper, Karl. *The Logic of Scientific Discovery.* New York: Basic Books, 1959.

9

POLITICAL ADEQUATION:
SUMMARY AND CONCLUSION

CHAPTER NINE This book began with the statement, "There are at least two political sciences." I have argued that American political analysts have two primary approaches to the study of politics: Political Science I and Political Science II. Despite the diversity and ideological implications of these political sciences, they are equally scientific. Nevertheless, each is likely to be used by different groups of political analysts. Political Science I is most apt to be adopted by analysts who support basic American political structures and who desire incremental changes, at most; Political Science II is more likely to be used by analysts who are critical of American political structures and desire major changes. In brief, the two political sciences are adequate for different political purposes.

In this final chapter, I will summarize my basic arguments, suggest several qualifications, and further develop the idea of political adequation. My intent is to provide the reader with a clear standard for judging this and other political studies.

RECAPITULATION Part One of this book was intended to be an exploration of the alternative preconceptions and the controversies that inform modern political studies. I hoped to show that two logical sets of preconceptions about politics underlie the major controversies in modern political thinking.

Chapter 2 considered the question, "What is politics?" I suggested that although there is no correct answer to this question, two specifiable answers do exist among modern political analysts. These two answers were reconstructed in terms of two models: Politics as Conflict-Resolution and Politics as Community-Building. The former model assumes the significance and value of individualism, competition, and peaceful means for resolving potentially violent conflicts. The latter model assumes the significance and value of social interdependence, cooperation, and communitarian relationships. In the First Transition, I asked why an analyst would prefer adopting one model rather than adopting another, since both models simultaneously clarify and distort the political world. I suggested that assumed significance and value in Politics as Conflict-Resolution is consistent with the values in Justice as Fairness; and assumed significance and value in Politics as Community-Building is consistent with the values in Justice as Goodness. This consistency between a model of politics and a model of values means that particular understandings of politics will be more useful to people who hold particular values.

Chapter 3 developed more fully the two models of political values. Justice as Fairness gives priority to political processes that give no one an especial advantage in competition for wealth, power, and status. An implication is that if the processes or competition are deemed fair, then the results, whatever they may be, must also be considered just. This avoids the philosophical and moral problem of predetermining moral ends in politics; this is a question which each individual must answer for himself. The values involved in Justice as Fairness are usually associated with the political ideology of liberalism, though I specified that this is not always the case. Justice as Goodness is an alternative model of values that gives first priority to results rather than to processes. Its central concern is to justify a vision of the good society based on preferred social relationships, egalitarian political and social structures, and a non-alienated community. It is based on the assumption that, under appropriate circumstances, most individuals will agree to these goals. The processes for achieving these goals are usually treated as secondary. Justice as Goodness is a set of values most often associated with the political ideology of socialism today; however, I again qualified this association.

In the Second Transition, I considered why a person might adopt one set of value priorities rather than adopt the alternative set. My analysis was that there are good reasons why one would adopt the model of values most consistent with one's understanding of society. For Americans and American political analysts, this meant the following: Those who believe that the American polity is generally pluralistic will affirm Justice as Fairness; those who believe that the American polity is highly elitist will most likely adopt Justice as Goodness.

Chapter 4 developed the foundations of the two alternative understandings of American politics and society. The American Pluralism Theory emphasizes the importance of individual and group competition. In its latest variant, it argues that government may have to aid the least competitive groups and regulate the most powerful groups to assure fair competition. This model of American politics is logically related to Justice as Fairness and to Politics as Conflict-Resolution. The American Elitist Theory stresses the significance of inequalities of wealth and political power in America. Originally, it viewed the American government as a tool of upper class interests. More recent variations consider the possibility that upper class domination is less a matter of such instrumentality and more a matter of structured relations between the upper class power elite and government or, of unfair competition in the political marketplace. This critical view of American government is logically related to Justice as Goodness and to Politics as Community-Building.

The Third Transition considered why a person might prefer either the pluralist model or the elitist model of American politics. I argued here that one's comparative referent may be a determining factor. If the analyst believes that other nation-states are more authoritarian or elitist than America is, he is likely to believe that America is a relatively pluralist polity. If he believes that alternative culture perspectives should be taken seriously, he is likely to be more sensitive to degrees of American elitism. How one compares American politics with the politics of other nations affects how one views American politics.

In Chapter 5, I reconstructed two models of how analysts compare American politics with politics elsewhere. Cross-National Comparison consists of generating broad hypotheses testable across many nation-states. Its ultimate goal is to develop social scientific laws that can help us understand the similarities and differences among many political systems. In use, this model of comparison often leads to an affirmation of America's relative pluralism. Cross-Cultural Comparison is the major alternative model. It usually consists of historical and cultural interpretations that pinpoint similarities and differences among specific polities at specific times. It sensitizes the analyst to his own preconceptions and to the alternative preconceptions of people in other nations. In use, this means that the analyst has greater flexibility in applying others' preconceptions to American politics and in finding American politics highly elitist.

The Final Transition was an attempt to summarize the logical connections among the various models of political thinking and to discuss the essence of those connections. Here, I argued that Politics as Conflict-Resolution, Justice as Fairness, American Pluralism, and Cross-National Comparison tend to be consistent with one another. These models share a basic assumption: The realistic possibilities for progressive political change in America are extremely limited. Using the label, The Logic of Political Realism, I inferred that this is a viewpoint that would make sense and be acceptable to people who feel they benefit from the present American political system.

Alternatively, I argued that Politics as Community-Building, Justice as Goodness, American Elitism, and Cross-Culture Comparison are models consistent with one another. They share this basic assumption: The ultimate opportunities for progressive political change in America are virtually unlimited. I labeled this The Logic of Political Opportunities. This logic is especially likely to seem sensible and acceptable to Americans who feel that they, or those they are concerned with, are not reaping adequate benefits in the context of the present American political system. I concluded the Final Transition by raising the possibility that "scientific" analysis might help us decide which of these two preconceptual logics is more valid.

Part Two was a consideration of the scientific nature of political analysis. My basic argument was that "science" does not offer any pat answers to the question of which logic is most valid; rather it reinforces the distinctions among the alternative political preconceptions. On the basis of these reinforced distinctions, I argued that there are two relatively distinct political sciences today.

Chapter 6 was a brief consideration of the philosophical basis and historical development of Post-Behavioralism. I looked at the shift of political analysis from documents and norms to political behavior. The focus on political behavior, along with the arguments of the Logic Positivists, provided the basis for adapting the natural scientific method to the study of politics. This adaptation was known as behavioralism. Behavioralism was criticized for claiming objectivity when it, in fact, reproduced the notions of significance and value inherent in the Logic of Political Realism. Post-behavioralism is the modern response to these criticisms. I suggested, however, that post-behavioralist science still assumes the inherent validity of the Logic of Political Realism. Consequently, it cannot provide an external standard of "science" for judging the relative validity of the Logic of Political Realism. This internal linkage between realist preconceptions and post-behavioral methods constituted the basis of Political Science I.

Chapter 7 considered an alternative approach to the scientific study of politics; the Interpretive Approach. Here, I developed the counterlogic of Phenomenologists and of their methods for studying politics. Their concern with perception, multiple realities, and imaginative reconstructions was criticized by post-behavioralists but formed the basis for other interpretive methods of political analysis. As an example, I presented the basic development of Marxist methods. Although not all advocates of the Interpretive Approach believe that they are engaging in the "scientific" study of politics or that the "scientific" study of politics is possible, many do. The latter simply have a notion of science that is broader than the post-behavioralists would allow. I concluded by suggesting that a logical linkage exists between the Logic of Political Opportunities and the Interpretive Approach to scientific study. Again this linkage means that the Interpretive Approach cannot provide an external standard of "science" for judging the relative validity of our preconceptual logics. Rather, the internal linkage between change-oriented preconceptions and interpretive methods constitutes the basis of an alternative political science, Political Science II.

Chapter 8 considered the conceivability of two coexisting political sciences informed by ideological orientations. In this chapter, I considered the possibility that neither Political Science I nor Political Science II is really "scientific" according to the norms of the natural sciences. I argued that our general view of the natural sciences as unitary and as nonideological misrepresents the practices of actual natural scientists. They too have alternative approaches to their studies and they too do research informed by ideological norms. Consequently, the coexistence of our two political sciences is no more problematic than the coexistence of competing schools in the natural sciences is. I concluded by offering what some might consider an outrageous proposal: The political sciences may even be more "scientific" than the natural sciences are. The former can ask "how" and "why" questions about politics while the latter simply ask "how" with little opportunity for asking "why"—because people act for reasons but natural phenomena, like atomic particles, simply behave.

On the basis of this argument, I believe it is warranted to conclude that there are indeed at least two political sciences today. Both are formally employed by professional political scientists and informally reproduced by people in their daily perceptions and opinions.

SOME QUALIFICATIONS In this section, I will anticipate some criticisms of my "two political sciences" thesis for two reasons. First, to the extent that the criticisms are justified, the thesis must be qualified. Second, because this book is a political study of the study of politics, all of the preceding arguments in earlier chapters apply. This book is not written by someone who considers himself above the two political sciences; rather it is written by an adherent of Political Science II.

I anticipate four major criticism of this book. Most of these have already surfaced in prepublication reviews. These criticisms ultimately suggest that the two political sciences thesis does not adequately represent modern American political science. And to some extent, all of the criticisms are valid.

The first criticism is that the book never really takes a stand on which of the two political sciences is more sensible or scientific. Should I not have compared the two political sciences, point by point, to determine which provides the greatest clarification and the least distortion of political reality? This criticism may be restated: The author has not *resolved the conflict* between the two political sciences.

A second criticism is that the book is overly simplistic. A few basic controversies and a few methods have been considered, but these do not tap either the intricacy or the range of alternatives used by political scientists today. A rephrasing of this criticism might read: The author has been *unfair* in not presenting the *plurality* of arguments and methods in modern political science.

Third, I neglect to make appropriate references to major political analysts and political studies; the most important producers and products in modern political science. After all, how can one analyze political science without investigating the landmark contributions of "greats" like Harold Lasswell, David Truman, David Easton, and so forth? Again, this criticism may be restated: The author neglects to consider the *observable behavior* of important political scientists.

I anticipate that these three criticisms will be preludes to a fourth, more serious one. I have written an extremely biased book. On the one hand, a close reading of each chapter reveals that I prefer the models and methods of Political Science II. On the other hand, this book is itself organized as a speculative interpretation or reconstruction of political science. In other words: The author does not present an adequate account of modern political science because he does not present an *objective* account of political science.

Each of these criticisms is justified in a very specific sense: they are significant if one is an adherent of Political Science I. They are less significant or even trivial from the perspective of one who adheres to Political Science II. Let us see why.

First, I do not attempt to reconcile the conflict between the two political sciences; I have, however, attempted to clarify the nature of the conflict. On the one hand, unlike advocates of Political Science I, I personally do not define politics or political studies in terms of conflict-resolution. I use a much broader concept of politics akin to community-building. On the other hand, trying to solve the conflict between the two political sciences serves no particular purpose for me. Unlike advocates of Political Science I, I am not interested in promoting peace among conflicting viewpoints. Nevertheless, I am interested in clarifying conflict in order to understand present barriers to a more community-oriented study of politics.

Second, I certainly have been unfair in not representing the plurality of approaches in political science today. I might have been more sensitive to theories of political psychology and socialization or to modes of analysis like systems theory, structural functionalism, and political development. To the extent that I have omitted consideration of these and others, I have not presented a detailed analysis of the entire scope of modern political science. This is obviously important to advocates of Political Science I who view fairness and pluralism in American life as valuable. Nevertheless, although I too value fairness and pluralism, my first priority is to promote intellectual egalitarianism by overcoming intellectual elitism in America today. I have reconstructed what I see as the basic contours of modern American political science because I believe Political Science I and its advocates have dominated the discipline and subordinated Political Science II and its users. My goal has been to promote equal legitimacy for Political Science II.

Third, I have indeed neglected political science's "greats" and their landmark studies. This is certainly an important omission from the perspective of anyone who sees behavior as the primary focus of understanding. My own view, however, is that this behavior must be understood in terms of the preconceptions, motive and intentions, and circumstances of political analysts. I hope that this will sensitize me and readers to the multiple possibilities of doing political studies. In the recent past, I believe Political Science II has been a possibility all too often ignored. Finally, this book is certainly not an objective study of the study of politics today. I do not believe an objective study is possible. Although this is no problem for advocates of Political Science II, it directly contradicts the goals of Political Science I.

In other words, each of these anticipated criticisms is justified from the perspective of Political Science I. Consequently, adherents of this perspective are likely to find my reconstruction of political science inadequate. Moreover, since Political Science II consists of a number of interpretive methods of analysis, from a multiplicity of viewpoints, many of its adherents will find studies from different viewpoints adequate to their own purposes. My major goal here has been to reveal another slice of the reality of political studies. Knowing this, the reader should recognize that one can reconstruct modern political science so that differences are reconciled or so that Political Sciences III, IV, V, etc. are also developed.

POLITICAL ADEQUATION Why does anyone prefer one political science over the alternative? In this concluding section, I will develop a notion of "political adequation" that begins to answer this question and that potentially serves as a standard for judging the value of political studies.

In 1969, John G. Gunnell investigated the foundations of political studies and wrote:

It is obvious that what one person or community may accept as intelligibility will be rejected by another and that what will constitute scientific understanding in one historical period may be viewed as inadequate at a later time.*

Gunnell's argument, which I consider to fall within the scope of Political Science II, was criticized by A. James Gregor, who I consider an advocate of Political Science I. Gregor's basic response was "Gunnell is confused."** Gunnell's counterresponse was to say that Gregor engaged in "precisely the kind of ritualism that I wish to question." He went on to label parts of Gregor's argument as "pompous nonsense."*** Although the spirited nature of this Gunnell-Gregor debate has diminished considerably since 1969, the divisions in political studies represented there continue today in somewhat altered modes. Why do particular political analysts commit themselves to one political science or the other, and then think, if not say outright, that the alternative is "confused" or "nonsense?"

Let me offer a notion of "political adequation" to suggest an answer to this question. Political adequation is the idea that particular modes of political thought and analysis are adopted because they are (1) consistent with one's political preconceptions and (2) useful in terms of one's perceived political interests. In other words, one political science or the other is adopted because it makes sense and

---

*John G. Gunnell, "Deduction, Explanation and Social Scientific Inquiry" in *The American Political Science Review* 63 (December 1969), p. 1245.

**A. James Gregor, "Gunnell on 'Deductivism', the 'Logic' of Science and Scientific Explanation: A Riposte" in *The American Political Science Review* 63 (December 1969), p. 1257.

***John G. Gunnell, "Science and the Philosophy of Science: A Rejoinder to ... Gregor" in *The American Political Science Review* 63 (December 1969), p. 1261.

helps particular people to understand better how to achieve their own political goals. The basic assumption underlying political adequation is that political knowing and doing are interrelated. Below I will explore the meaning and implications of this idea.

Recall Judith and Marco from Chapter 1. Judith developed her inchoate political preconceptions and modes of understanding in Beverly Hills, amidst those Americans who have benefited most from the American polity and social structure. Under these circumstances, she was likely to develop a political personality characterized by the notions of significance and value in Political Science I. Moreover, she was apt to receive many cues on the general goodness of America in comparison with other nations. Finally, she was probably taught that her own political interests lie in affirming the present political and social systems or some minor variations in them. In short, who Judith is and what she desires in politics increases the chances that Political Science I will seem sensible to her and adequate in terms of her perceived political interests.

Marco, having grown up amidst poverty and racism in East Los Angeles, was more likely to develop a political personality characterized by the preconceptions of Political Science II. He was probably cued throughout his childhood to believe that what some call the "general good" in America is really an excuse to dominate poor people and minorities. Given his mixed cultural heritage, he was apt to develop a sensitivity to alternative ways of thinking about politics. Finally, he probably matured into an adult who saw his political interests in criticizing American political and social structures in the hope that progressive change could be accomplished. Who Marco is and what he hopes for in politics suggests that Political Science II thought and analysis will seem more sensible and adequate to his politics.

Furthermore, both Judith and Marco would have good reasons for considering the other's thought and analysis as "confused" or as "nonsense." On the one hand, because their preconceptions are so different, they will assume different things and have difficulty understanding the sense of opposing viewpoints. On the other hand, since their personalities are intertwined with their viewpoints, they might consider the offer of an alternative as a covert attack on themselves. In all likelihood, Judith would perceive Marco as an irrational malcontent; Marco would consider Judith a confused rationalizer of the status quo. Under these circumstances, it is no wonder that intercommunication is so very problematic.

Another possibility exists here which should not be neglected. Conceivably, Judith could emerge from her Beverly Hills environment, criticize that environment, and join a radical feminist movement; by pluck or by luck, Marco might leave East Los Angeles, escape poverty and racism, and come to see America as the land of golden opportunuity. Particular individuals can and do alter their circumstances within the present system. They perceive new political interests and adopt unexpected modes of political thought and analysis. Nevertheless, I suspect that such individuals are more the exception than they are the average.

Of course, most Americans and American political scientists do not come from Beverly Hills' luxury or East Los Angeles' poverty. Their own circumstances are somewhere in between these extremes. Consequently, most Americans have good reason to be ambivalent about their own preconceptions and modes of analysis. From one perspective, they have a political interest in defending the present political and social systems lest new alternatives push them into weaker, poorer positions. From another perspective, they have a political interest in exploring new alternatives that potentially could increase their socio-political status. How do Americans resolve this ambivalence?

In many cases, they take their cues from political leaders. When leaders assure people that the "welfare state" is looking out for their welfare, that more jobs are opening up daily, or that each can succeed on their own merit, citizens "generally" accept this for lack of significant counterevidence. The implication is that Americans "generally" affirm the need to protect traditional political and social structures, and to adopt the preconceptions and methods of analysis of Political Science I. In part, this explains why the American political system has been so stable for so long.

Leaders' assurances, however, are not very convincing when people experience politics and society in contrary ways. When people feel grave economic insecurities, see their real wages dropping, find home buying out of reach, experience soaring medical costs and energy shortages, they become somewhat skeptical of the political system that claims to look out for their welfare. When citizens hear politicians and corporate officials asking for their trust, they are unlikely to give it if they are daily innundated with stories about political and corporate corruption. In these circumstances, Americans are more likely to resolve their ambivalence in ways more critical of present institutions. They are more likely to search for new answers, for new political alternatives and even for new ways of relating to one another. If this occurs, they may find the political thought and analysis of Political Science II more adequate to their purposes.

I believe the 1970s was a decade in which more and more Americans found it difficult to resolve their ambivalence in favor of established institutions. It was a decade during which the political alienation of Americans was matched only by their increasing distrust of American political and social institutions.

Unless this alienation is diminished and trust is restored, we can expect more of us to support the search for alternatives. The political thinking and analysis of Political Science II is presently the major aid in this search. It is politically adequate for helping us understand the opportunities ahead.

My conclusion then is that how we think and study politics is a matter of integrating our backgrounds and present circumstances in light of our daily political experiences. How each of us synthesizes thought and practice ultimately determines how we approach the study of politics. For some of us, Political Science I will present an adequate approach; for others, Political Science II will seem preferable. As our thoughts and practices change over time, we can expect the two political sciences to be replaced by others more adequate to our new perceptions and new political interests.

Political adequation can serve as a standard to help us in this synthetic process. It alerts us to the idea that abstract thought and analysis about politics are themselves aspects of politics. When you read studies akin to Political Science I, you should be alert to the notions of value and significance that make these studies partial viewpoints, ideologically informed; similarly when you read Political Science II studies, you should remember their political biases. Which studies make most sense to you and seem most scientific is probably a good indicator of your own political commitments.

CONCLUSION Both political sciences, if done well according to their own standards, are equally sensible and scientific. If one is interested in "understanding for understanding's sake," one cannot go wrong choosing either system of political thought and analysis. I have learned from both. And I admire political thinkers in both political sciences who bring their own brands of logic and testing to their political studies. Understanding, even for its own sake, is a challenging path.

Most of us, however, cannot afford the luxury of pursuing political knowledge for its own sake. Unless that pursuit were significant to us, we might better spend our scarce time, energy, and resources in other activities. Most of us are in positions where politics is significant to us and understanding politics is a very practical endeavor. Those of us who feel personally or indirectly deprived by the present political system have a practical interest in understanding how to change that system. And given the fact that there are discontented people, those of us who feel benefited by the political system have an interest in understanding it, so we can better protect it. In addition, whether we wish to change or to defend the political system, many of us have political views that are basic parts of our personalities. Thus, understanding politics is one way of understanding ourselves.

To the extent that we do find politics significant, the ways in which we find politics significant will affect our studies and our actions. Consequently, I feel it is important to judge political studies, not only in terms of the knowledge they develop, but also in light of the ways they narrow or expand intellectual and political opportunities. Needless to say, this is a reconstruction of my own preconceptions.

As a political analyst and a political participant, I am interested in expanding intellectual and political opportunities aimed at facilitating egalitarian changes. This book has been written in the hope that, as we enter the 1980s, we recognize that alternative ways of understanding politics and acting in politics already exist. If we do resolve our current ambivalence in critical ways, we might search out those alternatives as a means to more adequate political knowledge.

†